ALSO BY KENNETH SEWELL

Red Star Rogue: The Untold Story of a Soviet Submarine's Nuclear Strike Attempt on the U.S. (with Clint Richmond)

ALL HANDS DOWN

The True Story of the Soviet Attack
on the USS Scorpion

Kenneth Sewell
and
Jerome Preisler

Simon & Schuster
NEW YORK LONDON TORONTO SYDNEY

SIMON & SCHUSTER
1230 Avenue of the Americas
New York, NY 10020

Designed by Paul Dippolito

Manufactured in the United States of America

ISBN-13: 978-0-7432-9798-1

For the families left waiting in the storm.

CONTENTS

ALL
HANDS
DOWN

PROLOGUE: ABYSS

ITS BALLAST TANKS FULL, HEAVY WITH FOUR SETS OF
iron descent weights, the deepwater submergence vehicle *Alvin*
drops toward the ocean floor. The cramped, chill titanium sphere
of its control room is darkened, or mostly so. There is a faint glow
from its instrument panels, and a greenish cast to the pale cocoon
of light outside the observation ports. Several small lights, used by
the crew to take notes or operate cameras and tape recorders, have
been turned off. When you are going to look out into the dark, you
keep the sphere's interior as dim as possible.

Almost insectile in its contours, *Alvin* floats down and down
like a firefly through a moonless, starless nocturnal sky.

On the surface, where the craft commenced its journey, the day
is still young. For those aboard the *Alvin* the transition from daylight to total darkness was rapid and dramatic. The submersible
began its descent bathed in the pale orange morning sunlight that
penetrates the first few meters of the ocean surface. Water absorbs
one hundred times more red light than blue, and as *Alvin* slipped

below the waves, everything outside would have taken on an increasingly bluish tint.

To the human eye, white objects appear blue underwater, and red objects fade to gray.

About six minutes into the dive, the sun's rays would have ceased to filter through the water altogether, leaving *Alvin* in darkness except for the glow of a thallium/iodide metal vapor light several feet above the main view port.

The T/I emits an intense beam in the green spectrum. That is the wavelength to which the eye is most sensitive, making it very efficient as a driving light. Fifteen feet in front of the submersible the pool of illumination is quite bright. Further ahead it begins to weaken and transitions to a murky twilight.

The pilot's habit is to switch on *Alvin*'s T/I fairly early in his dive. Without it, he would not be able to see anything outside, and he likes to judge his rate of descent by the movement of what is known as marine snow. This suspended detritus is mostly organic and is composed of anything from the fecal matter of aquatic life forms to bits and pieces of dead sea creatures broken down by the relentless motion of the water and biological forces. The particulate is gradually—almost imperceptibly—traveling downward to the bottom sediment, but for the purposes of measuring relative velocity with the naked eye, it can be regarded as stationary.

Looking out while the driving light is on, the pilot can see marine snow seemingly drifting *upward* in the water column, and experience has taught him how fast that movement should appear when he's descending at the proper rate. If the upward drift of the particles looks very slow, something is wrong with his ballast and he isn't descending at the speed he should be—a steady rate of thirty meters, or slightly over a hundred feet, per minute.

For the pilot, this visual estimate of downward movement provides a comfort factor, and so far everything looks to be working fine. There are no problems.

Like aircraft pilots in flight over surface terrain, those who have sat at the controls of deepwater submersibles use the term "altitude" when referring to their distance above the seabed, which in this case is about 10,300 feet beneath the surface. Descending at its steady rate of thirty meters, or slightly over a hundred feet, per minute, *Alvin* reaches a depth of 6,000 feet below the surface—or an *altitude* of 4,300 feet, by the reckoning of its pilot and co-pilot—about an hour into the dive.

This is deep in what marinologists call the abyssal zone, an ocean depth where the sun does not penetrate, and hasn't since the dawn of time. The temperature is near freezing. No gravitational currents stir the water, no storm surges are felt. Here, beyond the influence of tide and weather, it is an everlasting midnight, as still as the furthest reaches of outer space.

Because photosynthesis cannot occur here, the region lacks any form of plant life and supports just a few unique species of marine animals. There are giant squid, sixteen-inch-long tubeworms, deep-sea clams that measure a foot across, and other biological wonders adapted to the lightlessness and immense pressure bearing upon them—which may be up to six hundred times greater than the atmospheric pressure on the earth's surface. Exposed to these conditions, a human body would be crushed, the ribcage collapsing around the lungs, blood vessels bursting, the soft organs turning to pulp.

A nuclear submarine reaches its depth limit at between 1,500 and 3,000 feet underwater, depending on its design. When that maximum limit is exceeded, its metal hull yields to the surrounding pressure and implodes.

Alvin, in stark contrast, is at home in the abyss. Its crew compartment's spherical hull allows for the uniform distribution of ocean pressure in what is known as an isostatic manner. In principle, the hull works much like a simple arch. Its curvature resolves the forces working against it into compressive stresses—or stresses that steel and titanium, the high-strength materials used in deep-submersible pressure hulls, are able to resist.

There are some drawbacks to this design. Manufacturing spherical shapes to the demanding tolerances required for deep-diving ocean exploration is expensive. The sphere also lacks the sleek hydrodynamic shape that would allow *Alvin* to move quickly through the water, and its curved interior walls do not easily accommodate the rectangular housings that encase critical instruments needed for the submersible's operation. These surfaces are, moreover, uncomfortable for its occupants—for most people sitting against curved walls results in achy backs and shoulders. But speed isn't a requirement for *Alvin,* and the relatively short duration of its mission is well within the limits of the crew's endurance.

As the submersible continues going down at its unvarying rate, the crew experiences a smooth, stable trip to the bottom. *Alvin's* external weight stacks and attached scientific equipment have been distributed to balance the craft's center of gravity, and the result is a perfectly even trim. There is no list. There is no pitch. If you are *Alvin's* pilot, you're thinking that things are going well. So far.

The creation of the Woods Hole Oceanographic Institution, or WHOI, in Cape Cod, Massachusetts, *Alvin* is small, lightweight, and easy to assemble, disassemble, maintain, and fix. It is therefore easily deployed to remote waters. *Alvin's* missions range from marine biological or geological surveys to the extraordinary covert mission on which it is now engaged—one that the military intelligence officers topside have kept secret from the civilian research contingent on R/V *Atlantis II,* its mother ship. Mostly French and American scientists, they do not even realize they have traveled over a thousand miles southeast of where they are supposed to be searching for the sunken ocean liner RMS *Titanic.* But any concern about secrecy has been left behind on the surface.

For the pilot, what matters now is the mission and maintaining his focus. Below the surface, he worries less about men than nature, the millions of pounds of seawater relentlessly searching for a single flaw in the hull or piping. And he survives by being consistent and following procedures.

When everything works, it doesn't take the pilot long to complete his checklists and commence the dive. Depending on the mission, the trip to the bottom might take anywhere from thirty minutes to several hours. He tries not to let it run too late into the day.

Typically, he should be finished with his underwater tasks and working his way back up no later than four o'clock in the afternoon. By then, the observers will be stiff, cramped, and perhaps feeling the effects of mild hypothermia. Despite the watch caps, sweaters, sweatshirts, long johns, and wool socks they pile on throughout the descent, it is cold inside *Alvin*. And the deeper it goes, the colder it gets. The titanium walls are uninsulated and wet from condensation, and the observers avoid leaning against them.

But in an odd way everyone is glad to accept the clamminess. Dry air pulls moisture off people's skin, cooling their bodies. Humid air evaporates less moisture and makes people feel warmer. As the moist breath of the crew condenses on the walls and runs down into the compartment's bilge area, it keeps the relative humidity within the sphere up at around 50 percent. This practical exploitation of human biological functions helps mitigate the bone-chilling cold of the abyss.

Alvin's pilot and co-pilot are mindful of their passengers' comfort, but safety remains their primary consideration, which is why they want to be back up before sundown. Upon resurfacing the submersible still has to meet its tender, hook up with the A-frame hoist on her stern, and be lifted aboard. When you are operating in the middle of the ocean a lot can go wrong. Conditions are apt to change quickly, and unexpected factors like stormy weather, equipment failure, or a sick passenger on *Alvin* can create a life-threatening situation. The darkness of night greatly enhances the dangers. It is just a matter of good sense to follow a consistent routine, and part of that means carrying out *Alvin*'s recovery in daylight.

Right around when it drops below the 4,300-foot altitude mark, *Alvin*'s pilot turns on his Fathometer. A device used to measure the depth and contours of the ocean floor, it transmits regular active sonar pulses, or pings, and receives their echoes off the bottom. The Fathometer's readings should be consistent with the pilot's information about the region's bathymetric and topographic features. He has studied his charts before the dive, and a significant discrepancy could mean *Alvin* is off course, or even that the charts are in error—it happens; the ocean's bottom is still a largely unexplored frontier, so he is making periodic comparisons. On rare instances during typical scientific dives, he will use the pinger mode of his underwater telephone to range to the surface and locate his position in the vertical descent column beneath the mother ship.

Today's dive, however, is anything but typical. There is a need for very precise navigation because of *Alvin*'s unique target, and that means using some elaborate instrumentation.

The system developed for tracking and guiding *Alvin*'s position is called ACNAV, or acoustic navigation. It relies on underwater beacons called transponders that receive and transmit electronic signals at preset frequencies. Each of Woods Hole's transponders has an outer case that looks like two yellow hardhats welded together. Before *Alvin* embarked on its dive, a technician on the mother ship's deck would have dropped between three and four of these weighted radio beacons to set points around the underwater target area on cables that will enable their later retrieval. Submersible navigation has a large number of complicated variables, but the basic idea is that the transponders create an acoustic grid on the ocean floor that can very accurately lead *Alvin*'s pilot to his target, and at the same time allow the mother ship to keep tabs on where underwater the vehicle is headed.

And so, the pilot is watching his Fathometer and checking the transponder readings, and in some cases is making corrections to his position. Out the corner of his eye, he also monitors the compartment's life support systems, bleeding in oxygen and watching CO_2 levels to maintain their proper concentrations in the breathing atmosphere. There are always small things like that to occupy him, but it gets dull after a while, and he generally finds reviewing the dive profile with the observers a welcome distraction. It relieves his monotony and sets them at ease—especially when his passenger is unaccustomed to deepwater submergence.

After all the dives he's done, his words tend to follow a similar pattern from one to the next. Well, he will tell them, we should get to the bottom soon. We'll probably be at this or that distance, and such and such a direction from where we're supposed to go. I'll drive over, and be available, and you can tell me step by step what you want me to do.

On today's mission, the pilot would have received most of his instructions in the predive briefing. The Navy intelligence operative he's chaperoned into the depths has a highly specific objective that is unique even to his experience.

His name is Bob Ballard. He is a self-styled undersea explorer whose public persona hides a double life no less mysterious than his surroundings, or the project he's veiled with the cover story of his search for the *Titanic*.

After a drop of almost two miles and ninety minutes, *Alvin* is finally approaching touchdown on the seafloor. The pilot's boredom with the prolonged descent is gone—this is where things sometimes get tricky, and kind of thrilling for him.

It is critical to see the bottom, and as he approaches within thirty-five feet of the ocean floor he strains to catch a view of the topography. If you haven't visited a particular area before, you need to know whether you have a flat, silty bottom or whether it's going to be rough. There have been dives that brought the submersible to terrible spots. Places like an area near the Galápagos that the scientists wryly named the Garden of Eden, where the rugged volcanic terrain was pockmarked with fields of conical structures known as hydrothermal vents. Some of the chimneys stood thirty feet tall and released shimmering white water—comparable to heat devils in the desert—that read hundreds of degrees centigrade, making them hot enough to melt the PVC plastic on *Alvin's* temperature probes.

These would become known to researchers as white smokers. The hottest vents, dubbed black smokers, spouted superheated water at such a great velocity that the dissolved minerals they released, precipitating in the cold ocean, roiled exactly like plumes of black smoke rising off an oil fire.

More common sights are jagged rocks, ledges, and outcrops. While hardly as spectacular as the black or white smokers, they can present serious hazards unless the pilot is alert and cautious. And then there is *Alvin's* present target—no natural wonder, but something man-made, full of cables, pipes, and projecting sheets of metal that can reach out to snare the small craft and prevent it from returning to the surface.

To know what he's lowering into, the pilot must stop and scan the bottom before going down any farther.

From his stool behind his forward viewport—there are two others, portside and starboard—he inspects the undersea landscape. He has the two rotating vertical lift propellers pointing up on either side of the submersible, and is ready to use them to kill his downward velocity should any dangerous environmental features come into sight. One problem for him is that his depth perception is somewhat reduced—it has been described as about a two-and-a-half-dimensional field of view.

To compensate for the visual distortion, *Alvin's* crews have fastened a circular sample basket to the nose of the submersible. The basket is four feet in diameter, and when the pilot wants to determine the height or width of something up ahead, he does a bit of mental manipulation, comparing it to the dimensions of the basket out front. It is an imperfect technique to say the least, but anyone who drives a submersible develops a knack for improvisation.

What the pilot finds below him now is mostly sediment. It is a geologically ancient area, with a thick carpet of material that has settled over the bottom during countless centuries to create a soft, regular terrain.

The conditions are as good as the pilot could hope for, and he prepares to release the descent weights in sequence. They are 208 pounds each and are attached to *Alvin*'s outer hull with magnetically operated latch mechanisms. The first is dropped to slow the vehicle's dive and allow for any last-minute maneuvering before touchdown. The second weight is dropped closer to the bottom to stop the descent, and give the pilot a chance to trim ballast should that become necessary.

One at a time, he drops his weights. Slowly, gently, *Alvin* continues toward the seabed, its lift props rotated downward to keep it at a hover.

Disturbed by the vehicle's propellers, the bottom sediment stirs up into the water and mixes with the marine snow in a churning cloud. But as *Alvin*'s horizontal thrusters propel the vehicle toward its predetermined coordinates, its driving light lances through the spectral haze to disclose pieces of metallic debris below—one, another, and then several more. Many are quite small, but some would be too large to carry aboard the submersible. Strewn about the ocean floor, they form a widespread, silt-covered trail. *Alvin* skims along over the debris trail on a southeasterly course. Now the contours of the bottom change, the horseshoe-shaped bulge of an eroded slope appearing up ahead. The submersible approaches the rise, crosses over its curved outer face, and then begins gliding above the sediment-filled caldera of a primeval, long-dead volcano.

The pilot and co-pilot, meanwhile, have turned on bright incandescent floodlights mounted high atop *Alvin*'s forebody, overriding the green glow of the more energy-efficient T/Is. The driving light rendered everything it struck in shades of gray to the vision; *Alvin*'s incandescents let the observers see what is outside in striking color.

The submersible's operators have also activated their exterior camera and video equipment to capture the images for subsequent analysis. Angled slightly down to illuminate the work area, two 35mm still cameras above the forward viewport snap away in the intense glow of strobes. At the same time, a low-light-level standard-scan television camera—again, oriented onto the work area—sends images to an interior monitor that are simultaneously viewed in real time and captured on videotape.

Inside *Alvin*'s crew compartment, a mood that is an odd mixture of anticipation and solemnity spreads through the exploratory team. The excitement of their imminent discovery is restrained by a sort of grim reverence, and perhaps a quiet, somber awareness of their own mortality.

Submariners have an old maxim that goes something like, "There are no atheists below a thousand feet." At greater than ten times that depth, *Alvin* is coming up on a potent reminder of why they say it.

The far slope of the crater below has disintegrated, perhaps having gradually crumbled away over the ages, or toppled in a sudden underwater avalanche when the sediment buildup atop it became unstable. There is no way for *Alvin*'s passengers to know, and at the moment their attention is otherwise occupied.

On the inside of the near slope, a ruined hull has come into view. It is broken in two, the segments resting in separate trenches and coated with silt and sludge—accumulations that haven't stirred in nearly twenty years, when the cloud of bottom matter billowed upward as the vessel impacted the slope, then went falling back to the bottom, coating the new objects with a light dusting.

As *Alvin*'s floodlight and camera-strobe flash on large segments of the sunken vessel, it maneuvers closer, moves the length of the ship on one side, then makes a second pass along the other.

From an open hatch in the forward section of the hull, a mooring line extends outward into the cold, motionless abyss. No man or group of men inside the vessel could have dislodged the hatch door. They would not have had a chance. The submarine went down too rapidly, and the pressure of the seawater outside would have been too overpowering for the hatch door to have been opened by anything but the massive pressure wave of compressed seawater that rushed through its interior compartments in a devastating, unstoppable surge.

The hull of the boat lies in two sections. Her bow faces north-northwest, and her aft section is at an eastward orientation. Lying on its side is the sail, a structure that houses a submarine's masts, periscope, and dive planes. It has separated from the hull, torn away by the force of its impact.

As *Alvin* travels aft, Ballard and company are met with a sight that is by equal measures awful and remarkable, laying out the sheer violence of the boat's destruction. Her main engine room has been pushed into the adjacent machinery compartment, their bulkheads ruptured. A collision of machinery from these sections ejected the propeller and its shaft, more evidence of the horrendous momentum that caused the vessel to collapse on itself like a spyglass.

Pointed at the wreck now, *Alvin*'s photographic and video equipment keeps working. But however useful it can be, Ballard knows this trip down is just a prelude, a trial run of sorts, mapping the submarine's grave for a far more ambitious return in the near future—one in which he intends to employ Woods Hole's newest technological marvel, the remotely operated vehicle Jason Jr., for the first time. Though it is still in its final stages of development, and untested in deepwater conditions, he is hoping the self-propelled robotic camera will be able to enter the boat and transmit never-before-seen images from within its torpedo room . . . images that may represent a history-making investigative breakthrough.

The nuclear attack submarine USS *Scorpion* (SSN-589) was among the pride of the Navy's fleet before it sank with all ninety-nine hands aboard in early spring of 1968. How that occurred remained an unsolved mystery for the United States Navy, and for the surviving families of the sailors who died with their sub. The time had come for the Navy to determine what had happened, to find conclusive answers.

Whether the government would ultimately keep its promise to reveal those answers is an altogether different story.

1. GORSHKOV'S GUN

"The flag of the Soviet Navy now proudly flies over the oceans of the world. Sooner or later, the U.S. will have to understand that it no longer has mastery of the seas."

—*Admiral of the Soviet Fleet Sergei Gorshkov, quoted in* Time *magazine, February 23, 1968*

I

CAPTAIN LLOYD BUCHER'S LEADING INTELLIGENCE men, Lieutenants Carl "Skip" Schumacher and Steve Harris, had identified the vessel from NATO military publications brought aboard ship before their deployment. An SO-1 variant of Soviet origin, it was designed for antisubmarine warfare. The Russians built these ships at their Zelenodolsk shipyard on the Crimean coast, and had exported several to the North Koreans and other Communist bloc nations.

It was the second vessel of its type that had shown itself to the USS *Pueblo* in the past thirty-six hours.

Late on January 21, 1968, Bucher had been informed of the first sighting over the sound-powered phone in his cabin, then rushed up to the flying bridge and brought his binoculars up to his eyes. Peering through the twilight, he'd spotted the dark form of the ship off to the starboard side of *Pueblo*'s bow, and estimated that it was just under six miles away. Schumacher had reported its distance at about eight miles when it appeared over the horizon, which meant it had gained over two miles on the Americans in a matter of moments.

Exhaling puffs of vapor into the frigid winter air, Bucher had stood in the gusts pleating the waters of the Tsushima Strait and done some hurried mental calculations. His best guess had been that the SO-1 was moving toward his vessel at approximately 25 knots. A good clip. With *Pueblo* pretty much at a stop, Bucher had figured it wouldn't be too long before the Soviet-made ship reached their position.

He hadn't been particularly concerned, though. At the time *Pueblo* had been drifting off Myang Do, north of the deepwater port of Wonsan, where it was suspected that the USSR had established a submarine base less than two hundred miles south of the Soviet Pacific Fleet's home port at Vladivostok, which was icebound for lengthy stretches of the year. The U.S. National Security Agency had wanted to monitor Russian naval traffic around these coastal cities and dispatched a pair of Auxiliary General Environmental Research/Signals Intelligence, or AGER SIGINT, vessels to the area. This was *Pueblo*'s maiden voyage; her sister ship, the USS *Banner*, had preceded her on operations months before.

In the ten days since *Pueblo* had left Sasebo, Japan, on January 11, 1968, her photographic intelligence people had made no visual observations of greater interest than Russian commercial freighters. But it was an entirely different story for the NSA communications technicians in her spook shack, formally designated the Special Operations Department (SOD) hut. On January 19, the communications technicians' monitoring equipment had snatched over thirty radar signals out of the air as *Pueblo* hovered off the craggy shoreline of Songjin, in North Korea's Hamyong Province on the Sea of Japan. They were particularly intrigued by a waveform emission identified with the Soviets' new Cross Slot long-range radar, a system meant to guide antiaircraft missiles to their targets. Because the Cross Slot transmitters were aimed skyward, and *Pueblo* was a small vessel with relatively low electronic intelligence (ELINT) masts, the communications technicians in the spook shack couldn't get a directional fix on their location without edging closer to shore—perhaps into waters North Korea claimed were within its territorial boundaries.

Meanwhile, Captain Bucher was hardly surprised by the presence of the SO-1 subchaser on January 21, taking it as evidence that the Soviets were conducting antisubmarine warfare exercises in the area—and confirmation that they did indeed have sub berths at Myang Do and Wonsan. In his eyes, the ship presented no threat. *Pueblo* was a quarter-century-old World War II military freighter that had been ostensibly refitted as an environmental research vessel. Yes, that was a transparent charade. Her two ELINT masts with their thicket of antennas clearly marked her as a spy ship. But in the complicated ballet of global espionage certain moves were tolerated on both sides of the Iron Curtain—they had to be, or a shooting war would be a foregone conclusion. *Pueblo* was in international waters. She had only two .50 caliber machine guns for weapons. Bucher hadn't expected trouble.

There atop the bridge in the dimness, he had done some additional silent reckoning. A skipper he'd served under back in his submariner days had taught him more than one seaman's rule of thumb, and Bucher had remembered them well. If his assessment was correct, the SO-1 would pass no closer to his ship than 1,500 yards—or slightly under a mile—if it stayed its course.

His field glasses held steady, Captain Bucher had kept watching the ship's approach. Beside him, Lieutenant Schumacher was looking through a pair of mounted 22-inch "Big Eyes" binocs. By now they had been joined on the bridge by Lieutenant Harris and Photographer's Mate First Class Lawrence Mack.

After a short while the SO-1 passed in the gloom like a racing shadow. Bucher had been right on all fronts. The ship's radar masts hadn't been rotating. There was no sign of anyone topside—not so much as a scattering of sailors on watch. Mack clicked away on his cameras, and his developed prints would later confirm its decks had been clear.

When the ship was gone, Bucher went below to the spook shack and sounded out the communications techs. He wanted to know whether their equipment had discerned any clue that the SO-1 had electronically probed them, or sent out radio bursts that might mean she'd notified others of *Pueblo*'s presence.

The techs reported no such intercepts. The SO-1 didn't seem to have noticed *Pueblo*. Or if it did, it hadn't identified her as an American vessel.

That had been the extent of the first encounter with a subchaser. The second occurred on January 23, under a cold, cheerless midday sun. Though Bucher hadn't started out feeling apprehensive, some incidents that had occurred between the two SO-1 sightings had put certain members of the crew on edge.

Shortly after noon on January 22, *Pueblo* was somewhere in the vicinity of Wonsan when a couple of trawlers came bearing toward it from straight ahead to the south. As they drew near, Bucher again found himself on the flying bridge with Mack, Schumacher, and a fourth man, Chief Warrant Officer Gene Lacy. It was Lacy who had alerted Bucher and, watching the vessels through the Big Eyes, agreed with the captain that they were Soviet-designed fishing boats with Korean ideograms on their bows. Bucher had noticed that they were uniform in their gray paint jobs and rigging, which was unusual for the motley North Korean fishing fleet. This made him privately wonder if they "might not be exactly what they appeared."

Soon the trawlers had pulled within several hundred yards of *Pueblo* and begun to circle her. The crowd of Korean fishermen on their decks gesticulated at the Americans, speaking excitedly to one another. Some had cameras and were taking pictures of the Yankee sailors as Mack repeatedly aimed his own telephoto lens at them. Captain Bucher noticed that many of his own hands had spilled onto the open weather decks for a look at the fishermen; he ordered those who weren't on watch duty to get back down below. *Pueblo* had more than double the crew of a hydrographic research vessel, and he'd intended to maintain the flimsy pretense that it was nothing more threatening than that. He also hadn't wanted some foolish verbal exchange between the crews to push the Koreans into a hostile act. The trawlers appeared unarmed, but he didn't want anyone aboard them getting upset enough to ram his ship.

Although nothing of that sort happened, there would be one or two more wrinkles to the incident before it was over. After the trawlers circled *Pueblo* once, they sailed off at a moderate speed, pulled near each other almost three miles to the northeast, and hove to. Then they reversed direction and again approached the *Pueblo*, coming within twenty-five yards as they steered another full circle around her, the fishermen on their decks still intently scrutinizing the Americans. Bucher had been apprehensive enough about a coordinated ramming of his ship that he'd ordered the engine room to stand ready to quit the scene at flank bell. But again the North Koreans did nothing more antagonistic than gawk. When the trawlers pulled away to the north for the second time, they kept going and did not reappear.

For the rest of that day, and on throughout the night, the communications techs broke radio silence and attempted to send a situation report with information about the run-in to a special National Security Agency/Naval Security Group receiving station in Kamiseya, Japan. Simple fishermen or not, it was clear the North Korean sailors would inform authorities about the American vessel with its odd-looking masts. If they hadn't already done that using ship-to-shore radio, they doubtless would talk when they returned to harbor.

But *Pueblo*'s communications techs were unable to get out their message. For some undetermined reason, their KW-7 Orestes cryptographic Teletype machine's transmissions did not seem to be reaching Kamiseya. Even attempts to patch them through via a major U.S. naval communications facility in Yokosuka failed. The spooks' thwarted, night-long attempts to establish a comlink left everyone in the SOD hut frazzled and exhausted.

That same night, with *Pueblo* idling off Wonsan, Quartermaster First Class Charles Law took note of several disquieting sights while on deck watch. At around nine o'clock he spotted the running lights of an estimated thirty to forty fishing boats leaving Wonsan harbor. Ninety minutes later, he saw another vessel coming from Wonsan—a merchantman. As it passed about a mile and a half away, Law studied it through his binoculars and discerned a Russian-made radar mast rising from its deck. As the night wore on, the spooks and other crewmen aboard *Pueblo* continued logging suspicious contacts—radar intercepts, aerial illumination flares, glimmering lights in the darkness. Chief Lacy grew nervous that the ship was under close scrutiny.

By all accounts, the morning of January 23 was uneventful.

After leaving his cabin sometime after seven o'clock, Bucher ordered *Pueblo* into a position closer to Wonsan, where her masts would be better able to sweep for radar and communications issuing from port. Everything onboard was routine. Breakfast was served. The watch changed. Laundry spun in the washing machine, and regular inspection and maintenance was done in the ship's interior spaces. Around nine-thirty, the communications technicians finally made contact with Kamiseya and transmitted their situation report (sitrep) of the night before, along with an update stating that the local interest in their ship seemed to have faded. There had been no further sign of Korean vessels. Captain Bucher would always insist his ship held steady in international waters, and perhaps he was correct—but the vagaries of wind and drift in a part of the sea dotted with islands and ragged peninsular juts would have made the territorial line *Pueblo* was straddling hair-thin, giving the militantly isolationist Koreans abundant leeway to dispute Bucher's claim.

Around twelve noon, Bucher and Lacy were at a table in the crowded wardroom, the two men having an easy chat as they dug into generous lunchtime portions of meatloaf, potatoes, and vegetables. Suddenly Quartermaster Law called from the bridge. A vessel had been spotted coming toward *Pueblo* from about eight miles to the south.

Undisturbed, Captain Bucher asked Law to notify him if the ship came within five miles of them, then got ready to start on a second helping of lunch. Possibly his tempered attitude was due to the relative innocuousness of the earlier encounters with the North Koreans. The *Banner*'s captain had mentioned being harassed by similar ships without any escalation of hostilities, and Bucher may have assumed this was more of the same.

If Bucher, in hindsight, ever reassessed his cool reaction to the news in view of the intercepts, flares, and shadowy vessels gliding from Wonsan the night before, he would keep such thoughts to himself. But nothing he could have done based on a more immediate level of concern would have changed what next transpired.

He had barely gotten a chance to lift his fork and knife to his seconds when Law called down again. The ship was at five miles and closing—it had crossed a lot of water in very little time. Law's best guess was that it was doing a rapid 40 knots.

Pushing up off his chair, Bucher abandoned Lacy and his newly refilled plate to head topside. From the pilothouse, he could see the vessel speeding straightaway toward *Pueblo*, its bow plowing up a V-shaped wave of foam. He figured he'd better get a closer look.

Out in the bitter cold of the flying bridge, Bucher took the Big Eyes and swung it toward the oncoming ship. She appeared to be a light cruiser flying a North Korean banner—a subchaser. He couldn't tell whether it was the same one that had glided past the other evening or yet another vessel of that class. But for the moment it hardly made a difference.

Bucher ordered Quartermaster Law to summon Schumacher, Harris, and Mack to the bridge. He also wanted the oceanographers up on deck in their nonregulation cold weather garb. They would make a show of lowering seawater receptacles over the side with winches—a sampling technique known as a Nansen cast. *Pueblo* was supposed to be a research vessel, and how better to preserve that appearance than by putting a team of scientists on exhibit?

As Bucher's orders were implemented, the vessel kept hauling toward *Pueblo* at something close to its maximum speed. His NATO identification guide in his hands, Harris slipped behind the Big Eyes and confirmed the skipper's on-the-spot determination. It was, in fact, an SO-1, he said. Then he rattled off its standard personnel complement and armaments: a crew of twenty-two, including three officers. Dual automatic cannon. Heavy machine guns. Depth charges. Other configurations were possible.

Bucher studied it through his binocs. The subchaser was at maybe a thousand yards and closing, its deck filled with uniformed hands, the operators of its dual-barreled 57mm autocannon training their weapon on the U.S. ship. They were at full battle stations.

Braced for the worst, Bucher relieved Chief Law of his watch duties and put Lacy, an experienced commissioned officer, in charge of the deck. He notified the engine room to stand by to pour on the steam. The binoculars pressed to his eyes, he continued to hope the Koreans' aggressive posture still would prove nothing more than a show.

But the SO-1 was circling *Pueblo* now, and getting nearer as it spun up a white ring of foam around her. Bucher saw a signal flag requesting his ship's nationality appear on its yardarm and had his signalman hoist an American flag in response. He ordered Schumacher to send out a message to Kamiseya that *Pueblo* was being challenged by a North Korean vessel, emphasizing that the communiqué be given midlevel priority. Before leaving Japan, he'd been given instructions not to provoke a conflict with the Koreans. He didn't want the situation escalating into an international incident, not before he was convinced it represented more than intimidation and bluster.

The evidence would rapidly pile up on him. He was rattling off further orders to the crew when Lacy shouted out that he saw three high-speed torpedo boats darting toward *Pueblo* in loose formation. Then the SO-1 raised another signal: *Heave to or I will fire.* The message left Bucher perplexed. "Heave to" was nautical language for bringing a vessel to a stop. And *Pueblo* wasn't going anywhere. What did the subchaser want?

Bucher hoisted an answering signal: *I am in international waters.*

The subchaser kept its flag on display as the PT boats buzzed closer.

Bucher knew his options had narrowed. The harassment of his ship had graduated to an outright threat. Still, there hadn't been any shots fired at her. With a demonstration of tremendous poise, he had the SOD hut send out an upgraded version of his original alert that would flash directly through to the naval high command and the White House. This would notify America's top military decision-makers that *Pueblo* was in grave jeopardy—but that the threat had not yet reached the threshold of an attack.

Bucher had scarcely ordered the heightened alert when two Soviet MiG fighter jets roared overhead, and another PT boat came skimming across the water in *Pueblo*'s direction. A heartbeat later, he saw a second subchaser appear in Yonghung Bay outside Wonsan Harbor. None to his surprise, it was also racing toward his ship.

As the first SO-1 hung slightly back to port now, the four tor-

pedo boats closed in on the Americans and began circling at about
fifty yards, their mounted machine guns pointed at her, the men
aboard them holding Russian SKS carbines. Bucher had the distinct impression that they were "soldiers or marines"—not sailors.

But the makeup of their crews was not among his principal
concerns. The *Pueblo* was surrounded by six hostile warships with
air support. Against that level of force superiority, Bucher knew
the two .50 calibers *Pueblo* had onboard were useless.

Bucher weighed the moves that were left to him. Even before
the PT boats had surrounded *Pueblo,* he had inquired about the
most gut-wrenching of all the contingencies a captain could pon-
der. It was he who bore ultimate accountability for the safety of the
ship and crew. Now he wanted to know: How long would it take
to scuttle? To send the *Pueblo* to the bottom?

A while, he was told. The men would need two hours to flood
the main engine room. And that alone wouldn't sink her. The auxiliary engine room's bulkhead also would have to be breached before she took on enough water to go down. Bucher didn't need to
be told that *Pueblo* would lose electric power—and the ability to
communicate with her fleet—in the meantime.

The captain would face one last test to his poise before events
spiraled out of control. As he was ordering a supplementary high-
priority message with updates about the MiG fighters, the additional warships, and their tightening squeeze on *Pueblo,* Bucher
saw one of the PT boats pull alongside the SO-1 at his stern, and
then counted a dozen armed men jumping down onto her deck.

They were, he realized, about to mount a boarding action.

Incredulous, Bucher ordered a withdrawal from the area and
the destruction of all classified material aboard the ship. With
luck, his belligerent company would decide to fall back within the
approximate bounds of sanity. But he refused to place any bets
given how far they had already strayed from it. And *Pueblo* would
not stand a chance if the Koreans chose to pursue her.

Bucher felt the shudder of her awakening engines. With the old ship at a standstill, she would need a few minutes to throttle up to full speed, but he preferred denying the Koreans the pleasure of thinking she had turned tail and run. The question, then, was how to buy some time. He gave it some quick thought, and then ordered a long series of signal flags raised in a cheeky farewell that he hoped would throw a little confusion at them:

Thank you for your consideration—am departing the area.

The SO-1 briefly lagged behind as *Pueblo* trudged forward in the water, her stacks belching dark chuffs of diesel smoke. But the PTs stayed with her, two of them sticking to her rear, the others crisscrossing in front of her bow to hinder her advance.

Then the subchaser sped up and was joined by the one Bucher had spotted coming out of Yonghung Bay. Bucher shouted for evasive maneuvers, but his heavy, sluggish vessel was repeatedly cut off and outflanked. The North Koreans were not about to let *Pueblo* take her leave.

As Captain Bucher would later recall, he was accompanied on the flying bridge by a CT3 (communications technician third class) named Stephen Robin and Signalman Wendell Leach when the North Koreans started their assault with a salvo from the subchaser's 57mm cannon. Charles Law—who Bucher thought climbed to the flying bridge after the fusillade—would say he was with the captain and the others at the time, and that a machine gun burst preceded the scream of cannon shells through the air. Their contradictory memories typify the differences in various accounts of what next transpired on *Pueblo,* and more generally illustrate the effect of combat on human perceptions.

People in life-threatening situations experience automatic physiological and psychological changes known as the alarm reaction. The heart rate increases. Glandular chemicals flood the bloodstream. The mind's awareness will tunnel in on what is most acutely necessary for survival, and filter out nonessential information. Most discrepancies of recall about the attack among certain members of *Pueblo*'s crew probably arose because of the speed of the events that overtook them and the subsequent pandemonium and trauma.

There is also no denying that the classified nature of *Pueblo*'s operational orders may have led to a deliberate blurring of other details. Bucher had been sworn to secrecy, as had the rest of the men aboard the ship. They would be legally and morally bound to their oaths even decades after the Cold War was over.

No matter if cannon shells or bullets initially struck the USS *Pueblo*, or whether Law was or wasn't on the flying bridge at the onset of the attack, they would agree that everyone on the bridge dove for cover as the windscreen disintegrated in a shower of plexiglass, and bits of metal and debris rained down from overhead, where the barrage struck the radar mast and one of her smokestacks. Bucher felt spears of shrapnel and plastic slash into his legs and buttocks, and commingled agony and embarrassment as a metal sliver "seared squarely" into his rectum. Blood flowed from Robin's neck, and Leach was wounded in the leg.

Down in the restricted space of the SOD hut, meanwhile, the CTs were sweatily trying to destroy everything in sight with fire axes and sledgehammers—documents, transmitters, photographic gear, whatever they could smash or burn. But the equipment had been built to withstand rough battle conditions. One crewman broke the handle of his fire axe when he slammed its head down on the KW-7 Orestes code box. He should not have been surprised when the case was only dented. The KW-7 used magnetic print heads to output entire lines of type at a time, and in a test of its design ruggedness was said to have been dropped fifteen feet without skipping a single letter. The physical blows to *Pueblo*'s unit would not have done more than superficial damage.

Outside *Pueblo*'s crypto spaces, the shelling and machine gun volleys persisted. The MiG warplanes returned for another pass, growling above her, firing a missile into the water ahead of her bow as though to leave no question of the vessel's fate if she did not submit. In a narrow, smoke-filled starboard passageway where an artillery shell had punched through the hull, two sailors struggled to hold wounded Fireman Duane Hodges upright and stop his bleeding. It was no easy task. The lower portion of his body was horribly mangled, his right leg connected to his torso by slender threads of flesh and muscle, his intestines protruding from a ragged gash in his abdomen. Others stumbled about in the choking haze, stunned and injured. Somebody called for a stretcher, put it in the middle of the floor, and lowered Hodges onto it. He would lie there on the cold steel floor of the passage for another half hour before expelling his final breath.

The time had again come for Captain Lloyd M. Bucher to grapple with one of the most painful decisions a skipper had to face. But it was evident his already limited choices had run out. *Pueblo* was boxed in and defenseless. He could comply with his attackers or more—perhaps all—of his men would perish.

About ten minutes after the North Koreans commenced firing on *Pueblo*, Bucher surrendered. *Pueblo* was brought to a dead stop in the water. A torpedo boat pulled astern and boarding ropes were thrown over her railing. North Korean soldiers in fur hats climbed onto *Pueblo*'s deck brandishing assault rifles. Two were officers.

Captain Bucher, beaten at gunpoint, would eventually be confined to the wardroom. *Pueblo*'s crew was gathered together and marched toward the fantail, where they were tied up and blindfolded with strips of torn bedsheets. In the moments before their blindfolds went on, a number of them glimpsed a massive destroyer hovering in the distance. Some guessed it was Russian. North Korea's naval fleet had nothing remotely on a scale with it.

Brought to Wonsan Harbor, the *Pueblo* was swarmed by Soviet technicians who were unaware U.S. spy satellites had the capability to photograph them. An unscheduled cargo flight would soon take off from the capital city of Pyonyang, its cabin loaded with almost eight hundred pounds of equipment and classified publications removed from the captured vessel. It would deliver at least one Orestes KW-7 unit and its operational manuals to the KGB in Moscow.

The crewmen of the USS *Pueblo* were not fortunate enough to leave North Korea as quickly as their plundered technology. They would suffer almost a year of incarceration and brutal torture before the administration of President Lyndon B. Johnson negotiated their release.

II

Several days after the *Pueblo* was seized, on February 2, 1968, Commander Francis Atwood Slattery of the Skipjack-class fast-attack submarine USS *Scorpion* received notice that his boat had been chosen to participate in NATO war games in the Mediterranean as a replacement for another Atlantic Fleet nuclear sub, the USS *Seawolf,* which had run aground off New England's coast while participating in top secret tracking tests. Commander Slattery had expected to visit the Med later that year, but now had less than two weeks to prepare for the early deployment.

A day after *Scorpion* got her orders, the Skate-class submarine USS *Swordfish* (SSN-579) sailed from Naval Station Pearl Harbor in Hawaii following overhaul, refueling, and refresher training for her crew. The sub was bound for the near vicinity of Vladivostok, in the Sea of Japan, where she was to perform a covert surveillance mission related to the worsening *Pueblo* hostage crisis.

In the predawn hours of February 24, the aging Soviet diesel-electric missile submarine K-129 (NATO designation Golf II) launched from Rybachiy Naval Base on the Kamchatka Peninsula under cover of darkness, navigated Avachinskaya Bay with her running lights off, and then slid beneath the waters of the North

Pacific. Over the next eleven days, her surreptitious journey would take her more than two thousand nautical miles into the waters off the Hawaiian Islands.

During this period, *Swordfish* had come near North Korea's Wonsan Harbor, where the *Pueblo*'s captors had put the ship at anchor after its seizure. While conducting nighttime signals intelligence (SIGINT) operations at periscope depth, the submarine struck a small chunk of ice that had broken loose from a glacier to drift undetected along the coast. The collision threw the standing officer of the deck off his feet, sheared off the submarine's electronic countermeasures (ECM) mast as well as a special operations mast, and bent back the attack periscope at a 45 degree angle.

The damage *Swordfish* sustained to her sail, periscope, and masts required that she leave her patrol box for repairs. She would head for the U.S. naval base at Japan's Yokosuka City to have them carried out.

Late on the night of March 7, the Soviet K-129 surfaced about 430 miles northwest of Pearl Harbor. Days earlier, the U.S. military's top secret underwater Sound Surveillance system, or SOSUS, had tracked the sub to her normal patrol box six to eight hundred miles to the northwest. Then she had slipped through the acoustic net.

The SOSUS hydrophones were designed to pick up noisy Russian-made diesels and nuclear ballistic submarines, but K-129's main engines had been cut, and she'd crept toward her mysterious destination on the power of a silent electric motor.

The men aboard the sub also had gotten some help finding the network's vulnerabilities. Where the detection ranges of hydrophonic arrays overlapped, it was very difficult to sneak past them. But there were other spots where oceanographic conditions or the sounds of commercial maritime traffic muffled the system's electronic ears. Aware of weaknesses in the network's coverage, K-129's crew would have attempted to penetrate them by keeping

the submarine's acoustic emissions below the detection threshold—and a mole in America's Atlantic Fleet headquarters had
been providing reams of SOSUS information to Soviet intelligence for months. How much or how little K-129 could exploit
the soft spots in the acoustic net is still unclear. But those in command of her would have tried—and at any rate, she was now exactly where they wanted her.

Close by was a point where the submerged Hawaiian Ridge
and a series of undersea outcrops called the Necker Ridge crossed
the Tropic of Cancer. On nautical charts, it was marked as a region
to be avoided because of the dense clusters of small, jagged islands
and atolls pocking the water's surface, or lurking hazardously just
below it. K-129 had ignored these warnings, and was on station to
perform her clandestine mission.

Minutes later, however, a sudden catastrophic event occurred
aboard the submarine. In orbit about two thousand miles above
the earth, a North American Air Defense reconnaissance satellite
picked up the distinct chemical heat signatures of burning Soviet
rocket fuel with its infrared sensors. At the same time, a naval station monitoring recordings from SOSUS hydrophones arrayed
along the Hawaiian Leeward Islands registered three unusual blips
corresponding to a series of powerful detonations aboard the sub.

The K-129 floundered on the surface for only minutes as
flames swept through her compartments, and her hull split at its
seams to let in the rushing sea. Then the sub took her doomed
crew into an uncontrolled three-mile dive to the ocean floor. Her
final resting place would be in thirteen thousand feet of water at
the coordinates 25° north latitude, 167° west longitude. Before the
explosions and flooding sent her to the depths, the submarine had
been in position to fire a SERB thermonuclear missile for a direct
hit on Pearl Harbor.

Over the next week, top officers in the Soviet Union's Pacific
Fleet headquarters grew worried about K-129's failure to transmit a

pair of regular situation reports. Unaware that she had abandoned her patrol area, they targeted that location for a massive search.

By March 17, a Soviet armada would be steaming across the Pacific to hunt for the vanished sub. That same day, KGB spies on regular lookout in the Japanese port city of Yokosuka reported the arrival of USS *Swordfish*.

In the gap between observation and conclusion an error that would lead to a vengeful act of war was committed.

Meanwhile, *Scorpion*'s exercises were smoothly underway in the Mediterranean.

III

The old man enjoyed relaxing in his handmade rocker, a glass of tea nearby. An avid reader, he'd lined the walls of his study with massive bookshelves. Stacks of books and papers cluttered the desk, tabletops, and floor, and in his quiet moments he would choose something to read from among them, bringing it out to the porch, and then spreading it open across his lap. As he squinted through his reading glasses at some thick old volume, he looked ordinary, no different from the other high-ranking government officials who fled the summer heat of Moscow for the cooler breezes of their country dachas. His retreat was in the village of Barvicha, an area popular with the capital's elite—the *crème de la Kremlin*, as the locals called them.

The witticism dripped with acid. In the eyes of the villagers, he was just another government bureaucrat enjoying the fruits of corruption. In this case, however, they were wrong. He was anything but ordinary, and he certainly was not corrupt.

The man often observed gently rocking in the shade of the wooden porch was Sergei Georgeyevich Gorshkov, the commander in chief of the Soviet Navy, one of just three officers ever bestowed with the title admiral of the fleet.

Gorshkov had a well-earned reputation as a tough, scrupulous administrator. Armed with a nearly perfect memory, he required absolute competence from his subordinates. His analytical mind demanded facts backed only by reliable data. The admiral refused to tolerate any attempt at speculative reasoning. A staff member who included unsubstantiated, inaccurate, or manipulated material in his reports was quickly transferred to a remote post, his career shattered.

From his father, Georgiy Mikhailovich, Gorshkov had learned obedience, discipline, respect for seniors, and absolute punctuality in his duties. But he was far from one-dimensional in his habits and interests. He enjoyed driving fast—not recklessly, but with calculated enthusiasm. He took advantage of his social status and the perks that accompanied rank. Several of his dachas were equipped with tennis courts, billiard tables, and saunas. He loved the sauna, often following a good sweat with a swim in a very cold ocean. His wife, Zinaida, was a classic Russian beauty and his perfect counterpart. He was withdrawn; she was outgoing. He preferred to read books and work on documents in solitude; she enjoyed attending parties and receiving guests. In all aspects, she perfectly filled the role of admiral's wife.

Some were surprised to learn that Gorshkov could be superstitious. He never conducted major business on Mondays. He dreaded anything associated with the number 13—especially Friday the 13th—and wore a safety pin on his vest or underwear as protection against the evil eye. But his fear of the spiteful handiwork of demons was balanced by his trust in the might of God. Like many Soviet citizens born before the October Revolution, his early schooling included religious doctrine. On long trips, or in his office over a cognac, he would astound his junior officers by telling Bible stories, an oddity for those raised in the religiously sterile world of Soviet Communism.

Gorshkov never used profanity when dressing down his subordinates. He didn't need to. He had his finger wag. Hurricanes, fires, flooding, were nothing compared to Gorshkov's gun, a forefinger he would point directly at the target of his displeasure with the thumb in a cocked position, like a boy playing soldier.

In the spring of 1961, Admiral Andrei Chabanenko, the commander of the Northern Fleet, would be reminded of the power Gorshkov wielded—and his willingness to sacrifice human life in its demonstration.

The incident that provoked Gorshkov's ire started out with a simple mishap. In the early morning hours of April 12, a seaman trainee was cleaning a panel in the ballistic missile submarine K-19 when he inadvertently pulled a fuse—part of a circuit that controlled the vessel's heavy diving planes. The ensuing loss of power threw the submarine into a steep dive. Unaware of what had caused the sudden descent, Captain First Rank Nikolai Zateyev issued a rapid-fire series of orders to blow all ballast tanks. Thirteen million pounds of submarine reared to the surface.

The big sub's ballast system contained enough air for one emergency blow at a depth of roughly a thousand feet. But though K-19 was much shallower when Zateyev ordered the blow, it had exhausted over half of her pressurized air reserve. Before she could go deep again, the air bottles would have to be refilled—and the captain had known that would take hours. Still, his annoyance aside, it would have to be done. After a short dive to clear the decks of debris, Zateyev surfaced and began the long process of replenishing his air tanks.

Just after nine o'clock, a command for a series of emergency maneuvers and a call to General Quarters rang out over the submarine's command speakers. Zateyev reached the bridge in time to see a dark periscope pass alongside his submarine perhaps three meters away, a thin stream of white water trailing from its base. An American spy submarine had been following K-19 and now—tired of the game—it was taking a few topside photos before departing the area. But the Americans had grossly misjudged their target's speed, and their sub's vulnerable broadside was about to come across K-19's hardened bow.

Only quick evasive action by the K-19 avoided a disastrous collision. Had her commander been slower to react, the American boat's hull would have cracked on impact like an eggshell striking the side of a metal skillet.

It is basic naval protocol for a superior officer to be held answerable for his men's actions—or reactions. Captain Zateyev had the responsibility of avoiding the American submarine. Likewise, the commander of the Northern Fleet, Admiral Chabanenko, was responsible for Zateyev's decisions. Four days after the incident, Chabanenko was summoned to Gorshkov's office. Admiral Gorshkov wanted a thorough account of the encounter with the American submarine—and the reason lay in his naval intelligence files. According to those reports, the submarine K-19 had encountered was the USS *Nautilus* (SSN-571). Famous for being the world's first nuclear submarine, it had been detected while operating in the area.

Gorshkov was disgusted with Zateyev and, by chain of accountability, his northern commander. The American submarine was a spy vessel, an invader in Soviet territorial waters, and spying was nothing less than an act of war that deserved an appropriate response. Destruction of the American sub, he insisted, would have been a major propaganda coup—which made the failure to do so a missed opportunity. *Nautilus* was the pride of the U.S. Navy, a symbol of capitalist scientific and technical superiority. Its sinking would have been a major blow to American prestige.

In Admiral Chabanenko's view, Zateyev had acted in accordance with international maritime law, Soviet Navy regulations, and common decency. Instigating a deadly collision was the conduct of pirates, not naval officers. Yes, Chabanenko would concede that liberties had been taken in recent years. Games of intimidation had occurred between Soviet vessels and ships flying the ensigns of NATO members. There had been accidents resulting in minor damage. But putting a dent in an enemy destroyer was one thing. Caving in the pressure hull of a submerged submarine was an immeasurably more serious matter, an act of seagoing murderers. But Chabanenko prudently kept his opinion private. He listened to the admiral's rebuke in decorous silence.

Eventually, the admiral's anger over the incident would cool. But that did not mean it had been altogether extinguished.

In his diplomatic relationships, Admiral Gorshkov was courteous, and at times even friendly, to men he considered to be spies. At his office suite in an enormous mansion on Moscow's Griboedov Street, he could be a pleasant host to naval attachés assigned to the U.S. embassy. But in private he dropped that facade. For Gorshkov, it was critical that the naval force he had built win the contest with its American rivals for dominance of the world's oceans. Someday, he believed, America's capitalist financial system would buckle under its own bloated weight. In the meantime, however, the USSR needed to ensure its survival. As the Cold War deepened, Gorshkov would become increasingly convinced that only a large, aggressive Red Navy capable of matching American seapower tit for tat—and delivering "punishing retaliatory blows" when necessary—could fend off U.S. imperialism.

But while the size of his navy would grow, the quality of its ships degraded. Quality required money; in Russia, that was scarce. And so, Gorshkov would make a deliberate choice to achieve oceangoing supremacy through numbers.

By 1968, however, the United States had maintained its economic advantage—and thus its military edge—far longer than the admiral had expected. American nuclear-armed carrier battle groups were a visible presence off the Soviet Union's territorial shores. Polaris ballistic missile submarines roamed its coastal waters unchallenged. Stealthy U.S. attack subs conducted espionage missions with impunity, sometimes coming within yards of Soviet ships and submarines as they sat tied to their piers.

America also had gained a defensive edge. The mainland United States was surrounded by a network of underwater hydrophones along its coasts, making it impossible for Soviet ballistic missile submarines to approach launching range without detection. Each day NATO's nuclear forces grew more powerful, their weapons systems more accurate, and submarine commanders more defiant of their Soviet counterparts. As the frequency and boldness of their aquatic jousts with Red Navy vessels increased, a consequent increase occurred in the incidence of collisions and near-misses between the two sides. This did not sit well with Gorshkov.

Then on March 8, the ballistic missile submarine K-129 vanished while on patrol in the Pacific Ocean, immediately leading many Russians to suspect an American submarine was responsible. Not long before her final contact with the Pacific Fleet, said her division commander, the vessel had signaled that U.S. air and naval antisubmarine units were tracking her.

On March 17, the USS *Swordfish* arrived at the U.S. Naval Ship Repair Facility at Yokosuka, her sail partially shrouded in canvas. Even as American eyewitnesses speculated wildly about what might have damaged her, Soviet spies reported the wounded submarine's entry into port to their superiors.

When these accounts reached him, the stubby Gorshkov was furious. Like most of his aides and advisors, he believed *Swordfish* responsible for sinking K-129. No matter whether it occurred by accident or design, this time the West would pay a price.

At the Red Navy's inner sanctum in Moscow, the admiral would show his wrathful side. Gorshkov's gun had once again appeared—loaded, cocked, and ready to fire.

2. OFF TO POKE THE BEAR

"Once again, *Scorpion* is off to poke the Russian bear with
a stick, just to see what happens, and that's what we get
paid to do!"

—*A former USS* Scorpion *crewman*

I

"HE COULD WALK ON HIS HANDS AS WELL AS HE DID
on his feet," said Joseph Perham of his younger cousin, Francis Atwood Slattery. "Try that, it ain't easy. I'm a natural athlete, and I
damn near broke my neck."

As a teenager in the late 1940s, Perham had found it both fascinating and amusing to watch Slattery circle their school gym up-
side down as if he had a built-in gyroscope, his legs high in the air,
his palms flat against the hardwood floor. Almost half a century
later the seventyish Perham, a noted Maine humorist and story-
teller, would still delight in the image of Frank showing off his
hand-walking ability in the gymnasium—but the passage of time
would impart a patina of reverence to the memory, shared as
something precious and irreplaceable, like a family heirloom long
ago entrusted to his safeguard. For Perham, Slattery's peculiar talent was a subtle window into his character, vital to any understanding of the special inner makeup that would lead him to

become, at age thirty-seven, the youngest officer ever to gain command of a state-of-the-art nuclear submarine.

One day at school, Perham recalled, he'd finally asked Frank why he didn't just try getting around the gym right-side-up for a change. Slattery had given him one of his familiar deadpan looks.

"Why should I?" he answered. "That would make me just like everybody else."

Frank Slattery needn't have been concerned about that. He was different and people knew it.

Dark-haired and handsome, Frank was a native of West Paris, a small rural village tucked away in the wooded hills of Oxford County, Maine. Back when Frank grew up in the 1940s, this community of about one thousand was still attached to the town of Paris, whose industries centered on the area's two major natural resources: feldspar and lumber. The quarried, processed stone went into the manufacture of fine china and ceramic goods. The wood was pulped or cut at the town's two largest lumber factories for use in a diverse variety of products. Penley's mill, where Frank Slattery's father, William, worked, specialized in clothespins, but it also turned out items like toothpicks, dowels, and bucket handles.

Though Frank enjoyed participating in sports and athletics—he belonged to the high school basketball team—it was in the classroom that he really excelled. In part that may have reflected the influence of his mother, Doris, an elementary school teacher. Good grades came easily to Frank. He had a curious, precise mind that always served him well at exam time. Friends and classmates envied how he learned his lessons without having to spend hours hunched over his textbooks. Somehow, he always figured out things before the rest of them.

Despite being physically slight, Frank is remembered today as a natural leader among the boys at school.

"Frank was always in control," said Joe Perham. "I think he was born old."

You could depend on Frank to handle responsibility. As a teenager, he would often stick around the house to keep a protective eye on his younger sister whenever boys from school would come visit her—not that he'd make himself an obvious nuisance. But his parents relied on him to be the man in charge while they were off at work, and Frank had a way of gently reminding his sister's potential suitors of certain respectful boundaries they weren't to overstep.

Frank Slattery showed equal diligence toward the jobs he would take on to put some extra spending money in his pocket. It was the same with his extracurricular activities at school. Slattery was elected senior class president, while Joe and Frank Perham held equivalent positions for the junior and sophomore classes. Slattery became editor-in-chief of *The Nautilus,* the school yearbook, in his graduating year—keeping a hands-on touch as one of its mimeograph operators. The yearbook's title notwithstanding, Paris was a landlocked town many miles west of the state's coastal sections.

By the end of Slattery's senior year in high school, his classmates had all learned that he'd made the grade at Annapolis. In the 1950 edition of *The Nautilus,* under a heading on its playful Senior Statistics page that reads "Greatest Necessities," his most pressing need is listed as a "Rowboat (With oars!)." Elsewhere in the yearbook, a versified encomium to West Paris High's graduating students says of him:

> *Francis is our smartest, and a Navy man is he,*
> *We'll remember him with fondness as he sails upon the sea.*

Possibly the clearest indication that Frank had not only pondered a naval career for some time, but also quietly mulled the dangerous uncertainties of service with the submarine fleet, is in a short story Slattery contributed to the yearbook titled "Undersea Drama":

The soft, oozy mud settled smoothly around his ankles as he plodded slowly across the ocean floor in his heavy lead shoes. Green water was surrounding him on all sides. It was hot and stuffy inside that rubber suit and he could feel his heart beating methodically and hear blood pound against his temples as the terrific pressure seemed to suppress him. That horrible push that was ever present on every square inch of his body trying to squeeze him like an accordion.

He was alone, the only living human in that vast wilderness of water. Deep down inside him he knew he wanted to turn back, he wanted to step back onto the comparative safety of the platform that had brought him to this infernal place where the weight of the whole ocean was upon him, but he could not turn back now. His life, his fortune—yes, his whole future depended on this trip into the depths.

His thoughts turned to his immediate dangers. That lifeline didn't look so good—My God! What was that—a drop of water on his shoulder?—his hair stood on end at the thought, he froze in his tracks. Then he saw it, a small trickle of water coming through a crack in the helmet. He emitted a scream which turned quickly to a gurgle as the helmet gave way leaving him enveloped by that slimy, green liquid.

With the weight of the ocean upon him he bent forward and sank out of sight beneath the mud.

II

In 1954, Frank Slattery graduated from the Naval Academy as a newly commissioned ensign and drew his first duty on the Fletcher-class destroyer USS *Daly*. By June of 1956 he'd completed submarine school in Groton, Connecticut, and gotten reassigned to the USS *Tunny* (SSG-282). With a storied combat history that went back to the early days of World War II, the

Tunny was part cutting-edge combat vessel, part artifact: a vintage Gato-class, diesel-powered fleet boat that had been converted to a guided missile submarine equipped to launch the nuclear-armed Regulus cruise missile. Limited to operational depths of around three hundred feet, the Gatos were what submariners called "thin skins"; a standard joke among the *Tunny's* crew was that she didn't need a depth gauge because they could always tell how deep she was by the number of leaks she sprang, and how fast the water was running in. They'd also wisecrack, a little edgily, about being jammed onto a rickety, claustrophobic old sub loaded to the gills with torpedoes, nuclear warheads, and JP-4 jet fuel for the Regulus missiles.

During Frank Slattery's eighteen months aboard the *Tunny*, his quick, dry wit made him a standout among a wardroom already considered a bunch of characters. When word arrived that junior officer John "Mac" Maclaren had been ordered onto the sub, the skipper told them he was hoping to finally get a straight man. Though Frank had never met Maclaren, he piped up and told the captain that their new arrival was reputed to be a real joker. As Maclaren stepped onto the boat for the first time, the executive officer walked over to him and said: "You must be Joker!" The handle stuck. For as long as he served on the *Tunny*, Maclaren was called Joker.

Maclaren would always chuckle over another incident involving Slattery, with whom he eventually grew close. It happened one day when the *Tunny* was pulling into Pier 10 at her homeport, the U.S. Naval Submarine Base in Pearl Harbor. Docking at Pier 10 was considered a piece of cake because the wind always blew in a favorable direction, making for an easy landing. The junior officers who'd man the conning tower often took advantage of this and came in at a fast clip. But Slattery, who had the conn, had approached the pier a little too quickly in the brisk tailwind and was late to order a backing bell. As a result, the *Tunny's* dive planes

raked across the wooden piles and sent splinters flying. The sub
stopped just before it would have sideswiped another vessel, and as
the irate skipper emerged on deck, he pointed toward the damaged
pilings and shavings of wood floating in the water.

"Frank, damn it, look at what you've done!" he growled.

Slattery, ever the cool customer, replied, "Yeah, it shows what
you can do if you really try."

In some ways, Frank Slattery's pointed wit was distinctively
made in Maine, where humor is honed to cut through the monotony of geographic isolation, the routine tedium of hard work and
chores, and the unrelenting oppressiveness of long, snowbound
winters. Frank's background also showed itself in an independence
that occasionally verged on contrariness, and a level composure
he'd maintain around anyone he hadn't known his entire life.

While stationed aboard the *Tunny*, Slattery participated in the
U.S. Navy's first strategic missile patrol off the shores of the Soviet
Union, a mission prompted by the escalating geopolitical tug-of-
war between the United States and the Soviets in the Middle East.
Between July and October 1958, President Dwight D. Eisenhower
deployed thousands of marine and infantry troops—and almost
the entire Sixth Fleet—to Lebanon to dash an insurgency resulting from tensions between the pro-Western Christian government
and Muslim rebels allied with the recently formed United Arab
Republic of Egypt and Syria. The Soviets, determined to establish
a foothold in the region, were supporting the UAR with arms,
money, and military advisors, and Eisenhower suspected they had
at least partially instigated the clash. Concerned about a Russian
countermove to the deployment Eisenhower was calling Operation Bluebat, the president's naval chiefs considered sending an
aircraft carrier out into Soviet-controlled waters as a deterrent. But
the *Tunny* was ultimately chosen for the mission instead, perhaps
because it was decided that the appearance of a surface warship
would be too provocative.

Leaving Pearl Harbor, the *Tunny* cruised to Adak, Alaska, to refuel, then went on to Yokosuka Naval Base in Japan for its final stop before sailing north into Russian waters.

At that time, Japan's constitution prohibited nuclear-armed vessels from entering its harbors, although it's believed a tacit understanding between high-level Japanese and U.S. officials gave American naval vessels permission to bring atomic weapons into port under the condition that they weren't offloaded. To reduce the chances of a public relations disaster, few Japanese military and government personnel were informed of the hush-hush arrangement. It was better for both countries to keep all but those with a need to know in the dark.

In Yokosuka's military seaport, the *Tunny*'s crewmen took cloak-and-dagger precautions against blowing open the secret. Their basic ruse was to claim to be from the USS *Perch*, a conventional diesel-electric boat. They were even dispensed jackets with the other vessel's patches to wear ashore.

From Yokosuka the men of the *Tunny* sailed on to the North Pacific, where they lurked beneath the frigid waters, ready for a possible order to fire the sub's payload of two Regulus cruise missiles. If the desert skirmish in Lebanon had flared up into World War III, the *Tunny* would likely have launched the opening strike at the Soviet Union—and it would have been done from behind enemy lines.

Within a couple of years, Regulus-armed subs like the *Tunny* were phased out of service. Modern nuclear submarines carrying long-range Polaris ballistic missiles rendered them obsolete and replaced them on deterrent patrols. But the *Tunny* faced more than obsolescence. Because of its political sensitivity, her vanguard mission went unheralded for decades, any hint that it had occurred buried in classified files. Only in 1998 would the U.S. Navy distinguish the accomplishment of the *Tunny*'s crew by presenting them with the Submarine Deterrent Patrol pin, the linear successor to the Submarine Combat Patrol insignia awarded for submarine patrols during the Second World War.

For Frank Slattery, Mac Maclaren, and the rest of the *Tunny's* crewmen, however, recognition wasn't very important. There was a reason being on submarines was called the silent service, and they understood that. For them, it was good enough knowing they'd been the first.

III

In October 1967, seventeen years after Francis Slattery entered Annapolis as a cadet, he was given command of the USS *Scorpion*, a sleek, state-of-the-art Skipjack-class nuclear attack submarine. It was a laudable accomplishment for someone still in his thirties.

Since his tour aboard the *Tunny* ended nine years earlier, Slattery had gotten more than enough seasoning to qualify him for the role. He'd spent two years at nuclear power school and then, according to his naval career summary, "filled a variety of positions at the submarine school and submarine base, including classified material officer and advanced nuclear propulsion instructor." His next submarine duty had been on the USS *Nautilus*. Although Slattery had already earned his gold dolphins—the warfare insignia of an officer qualified on submarines—aboard the *Tunny*, he was still required to requalify on the ultramodern *Nautilus*. Only two months after coming onboard he was on a spy run in the Barents Sea when K-19 barely avoided ramming the sub. Slattery was unaware how close he and his crewmates came to losing their lives that day, and could not have imagined that the mere fact of their survival had left a smoldering rage in the heart and mind of Admiral Sergei Gorshkov.

In his half decade on *Nautilus*, Slattery would continue gaining experience in nearly every facet of the boat's operations. A year at the Naval War College and interim duty with the Division of Nuclear Reactors followed the completion of his tour aboard the boat.

Slattery's portfolio looks even more impressive within the context of the times—a transitional period when the U.S. submarine fleet was being shifted from World War II era diesel-electric boats like the *Tunny* to the new generation of nuclear vessels. As the diesels were retired from service, there was an excess of potential skippers for relatively few service-ready nuclear-powered subs, and only the brightest and most able candidates were fast-tracked to command of the SSNs.

Slattery was quick to make a solid impression on *Scorpion*'s crew after earning his commission, perhaps aided by their underlying readiness for a change in command. While generally respected, his predecessor, Commander James R. Lewis, was a detached, by-the-book figure who'd kept himself at an unapproachable distance from the enlisted men. Slattery's lively sense of humor and air of accessibility were welcome contrasts.

Under his capable leadership, *Scorpion* would depart Norfolk for a lengthy deployment on February 15, 1968. The trip would take it first to the Caribbean, then the Atlantic, and finally into the Mediterranean on a string of antisubmarine warfare exercises and patrols scheduled to last well into the spring.

But that was still in the future for Commander Slattery, who would first lead his new boat and crew through several months of yard refits and maneuvers a good deal closer to home.

IV

In 1968, the communications hub for all submarines deployed in the Atlantic was a squat gray concrete building in the headquarters of the Submarine Force U.S. Atlantic Fleet (SUBLANT) at Naval Station Norfolk, Virginia.

A key member of the message center's staff was a thirteen-year naval veteran, Warrant Officer John Anthony Walker, Jr. As a radio operator, Walker had a gleaming reputation—but it hadn't always been like that for him. His teenage years in Philadelphia were marred with troubled family relationships and brushes with the law, and that had made the day he'd walked into a Navy enlistment office a critical turning point in his life.

After basic training, Walker had breezed through radioman's school and hoped for an assignment on submarines—his older brother, Arthur, had been a submariner and loved it. But Walker failed to pass an eye test for submarine duty and wound up on surface vessels for several years. Eventually, though, the Navy lowered its vision requirement for sub school and Walker, who'd retaken the eye test three times, was able to enroll.

No one who knew him was surprised he'd gotten his wish. He didn't like falling short of his goals. There was an obsessive quality to his determination; John Walker had, in his own words, "high aspirations," and his personal satisfaction was inseparable from the need to show people what he could do. For him success meant nothing unless he could prove himself in the estimation of others.

With his intelligence, driving ambition, and friendly temperament, Walker made quick strides in his naval career. Four years before his assignment to Norfolk, he'd received a security clearance to work with top secret and cryptographic materials while aboard the nuclear-powered submarine USS *Andrew Jackson* (SSBN-619). When, in the summer of 1965, his superior officer on the *Andrew Jackson* was transferred onto the Polaris nuclear ballistic missile submarine USS *Simon Bolivar* (SSBN-641), he asked Walker to join him on the boat as the leader of its radio crew. Walker accepted, seeing it as a chance to both gain experience and advance in rank. He had earned the absolute trust and recommendation of his bosses and—at least outwardly—become the very portrait of a career Navy man.

It was during his stint on the *Simon Bolivar* that the sub's skipper briefly allowed Walker to scan a bound, three-inch-thick document that had the highest level of security classification. When he'd read the title on the book's cover—Single Integrated Operational Plan—SIOP—Walker was certain only that it related to his having to log a change in the sub's patrol route. What he realized was that he'd been given access to the complete U.S. blueprint for a possible nuclear war against the Soviet Union. Right before his eyes was the country's attack plan broken down in minute and intricate detail—troop and naval dispositions, the coordinated flight paths of bombers to the USSR, the order in which Eastern bloc nations and cities would be targeted, even the trajectory of every missile to be fired from land or sea.

Walker would lock the SIOP document away after holding it in his hands for just a few minutes. But whenever he thought about it—and that would be often—his brief glimpse into America's strategic planning for the inauguration of World War III made his pulse race.

While continuing to hold the favor of his superior officers aboard *Bolivar*, Walker rubbed many of his fellow chiefs the wrong way. As the ship's security officer, he was responsible for processing clearances, giving lectures on the physical security of classified information to the crew, and control of the handling of classified, top secret, and cryptographic material. Nobody doubted his proficiency at the job or the fact that he had a good brain in his head. But his conceited attitude grated on the men.

Word was also getting around that Walker's intellect hadn't imposed any rational checks on his free spending. Shortly before his transfer to Fleet Headquarters in Norfolk, he had gotten into a serious cash bind and was asking shipmates for loans to help bail him out of trouble. Radioman First Class Dennis Solheim was one of them.

Solheim's acquaintance with Walker spanned about half a decade. When they met in 1962 as members of the *Andrew Jackson*'s commissioning crew, Solheim was an E-4 third class radioman, and Walker already a better-paid radioman first class. The sub's final construction period was at the Mare Island shipyard in northern California, where their families had attended a lot of the same parties and functions and gotten friendly. John and his wife, Barbara, had four kids, and Solheim thought they seemed as normal as any other family.

Right before construction on the sub was finished, the crew moved their families to their new homeport of Charleston, South Carolina, and then went back west to bring the boat around from Mare Island. With almost a month to spend on liberty waiting to set sail, Solheim, Walker, and several crewmates hit a well-known submariner's bar, the Horse and Cow, in San Francisco. It was then that they were exposed to an unsuspected side of John's personality as the husband and father of four wasted no time shaking free of his marital vows and trying to pick up women. He left with one of the least-attractive girls in the place, something that contributed to the riding he took aboard the ship the next morning.

Walker shrugged off the comments. He seemed to think he'd put one over on everybody—the girl he'd slept with most of all.

"While I'm getting laid, you guys can spend your time and money on the good-looking women and not get anyplace with them," he said. "And besides, the ugly ones pay for the drinks and room."

Walker's bluntness offered a glimpse into his cavalier feelings about infidelity and sexual relations in general. To reduce the length of a ballistic missile submarine's port stays and keep it deployed as much as possible, the Navy would man it with alternate crews for sixty-day deterrent patrols. These were called Blue and Gold crews after the Navy's official colors. Both Walker and Solheim were on the *Andrew Jackson*'s Blue crew, among whom it soon became common knowledge that Walker would try seducing the wives of Gold crew members whenever they were out at sea. Solheim heard that John and Barbara had their share of blowups about his roving attentions, though it sometimes seemed that she gave his betrayals a certain level of tolerance—and possibly let herself be talked into participating in his swinger's lifestyle.

At an after-patrol party at the Walker house, he tried persuading the couples in attendance to swap both their house keys and spouses. The husbands, he explained, would put their keys in a bowl near the door, and the wives would pull them out at random as they left for the night, and go home with whoever owned the keys she found in her hand. Walker dropped the idea only after he saw it wasn't flying too well with his guests.

Walker's pliable moral standards did not, however, translate into any leniency in his parenting habits. On the contrary, the Walkers' harsh discipline of their children raised eyebrows. One night when Solheim was over for a visit, John ordered the kids to get ready for bed and the household instantly started to resemble a Marine boot camp. John and Barbara had three girls and a boy, all between the ages of two and nine, and as an appalled Solheim and his wife watched, John made them fall into formation for rigid "inspection and evening instructions" in the exact manner of a drill sergeant. Then he ordered them to march to their rooms in lockstep. Walker told Solheim that if the kids made the slightest noise after "lights out," he would take a belt to them and make them stand in a locked closet for an hour before they could return to bed.

After several patrols with Walker on the *Andrew Jackson*, Solheim was transferred to the *Simon Bolivar* as the new Benjamin Franklin–class ballistic missile sub got some final attention from the yardbirds in Newport News, Virginia. The two men lost touch following Solheim's reassignment, but six months later—in July 1966—Walker turned up on the *Bolivar* as a chief petty officer and leading radioman. This was when Solheim came to feel Walker had changed, as if the sordid personal life he'd always managed to keep from affecting the performance of his duties was consuming him from the inside out, even eating away at the likable, amusing front he'd shown his superiors in the past. Many crewmen found his ego intolerable. Solheim sensed that he regarded himself as a "James Bond type of super-spy" who was better than the average person at manipulating a situation or outsmarting others.

Solheim's observation was more perceptive than he realized. What neither he nor his *Bolivar* shipmates could have known was that Walker was, in reality, a spy at that point—although, unlike the heroic Bond character, he had chosen to work for his country's enemies.

Not long after Walker reported aboard the *Bolivar*, his brother, Arthur—who had earned an officer's bar in the Navy, and would soon have an instructor's assignment at Norfolk—asked John to help bail him out of a serious bind. He'd gotten in hock with some loan sharks, couldn't make his payments, and was desperate to get them off his back.

If it was money he'd wanted, Arthur had called at the worst possible moment—and must have known it. John not only didn't have any to lend him, but had made a shambles of his own finances with a business investment that was well beyond his means. Like his previous boat, the *Bolivar* was homeported in Charleston, and John's family had remained there through her yard period. During that stay he'd bought a four-and-a-half-acre property in Ladson, South Carolina, about a fifteen-minute drive from Charleston, and had begun remodeling the old home that stood on it into a restaurant/bar he called the Bamboo Snack Bar. As the place was being redone—Walker installed a commercial oven, grill, bar counter, and dining area—his family moved out of the Navy housing on base and lived in a house trailer on the property. But even before the Bamboo Snack Bar's doors opened there had been problems with the venture, starting when John's partner—another radioman on the *Bolivar* named Bill Wilkinson—backed out of their deal and took his share of the financing with him. Arthur had eventually replaced Wilkinson and thrown in a thousand dollars, but the expenses of setting up the bar continued to compound. A second mortgage on the Ladson property and various business and personal loans left John over $16,000 in debt.

Seeking a way to avoid bankruptcy, Walker approached Dennis Solheim for a handout shortly after they reconnected aboard the *Simon Bolivar*. But Solheim didn't have the spare funds, and Walker had gone on to solicit loans from other shipmates without success.

Around the fall of 1966, Solheim was transferred to New London for instructor duty and again lost track of Walker and his family. He heard nothing more of John and Barbara until almost twenty years later, when their names hit the news and became notorious.

Although it never turned a profit for him, Walker did manage to open the Bamboo Snack Bar and keep it afloat. He'd also gotten his brother off the hook with the loan sharks. Both these things were accomplished through acts of treason.

At some point while working aboard the *Bolivar*, John filched some low-priority classified documents for his brother, who in turn sold them to one of the many KGB recruiters that would circulate around naval port cities sniffing out men they believed were candidates for subversion. But once he'd taken care of what he owed the loan sharks, Arthur got the jitters and backed off from providing any more secret material to the Russians. John, however, decided to go on dealing with them on his own.

He would have denied his motives were at all psychologically rooted. He refused to draw correlations between his father's neglect, cruelty, and drunken rages and his own behavior. He would have scoffed at the suggestion that anything he did as an adult might have sprung, even in part, from some unfulfilled boyhood need for paternal attention or approval. John Walker was not an introspective man, and claimed his treason was strictly a financial expedient. He was buried in debt, and had turned to selling secrets to the Russians as a way to ward off his swarming creditors. Inner demons? John admitted to having none—or at least none that held sway over him. He insisted it was all about the easy money.

During one of the *Bolivar*'s port stays, he approached a KGB agent—likely Arthur's original contact—with the monthly list of key codes for an American encryption machine known as the KL-47. A fairly old device that was being phased out in favor of the state-of-the-art Orestes KW-7 cipher box, the KL-47 was still widely used for naval communications, and the acquisition of its key list therefore remained a substantial intelligence score for the Soviets. It was proof that Walker could deliver choice goods.

Walker had followed up by providing the KGB with KL-47 technical and repair manuals that he copied from the *Bolivar*'s radio shack, and eventually with readings from a sophisticated, palm-sized instrument the KGB had given him to scan the inner circuitry for the KL-47 rotors—Bakelite plastic wheels with alphabetic characters that transcribed plain text messages into cipher text.

Soon, Walker's lifestyle had gone well beyond the bounds of what he ought to have been able to afford on his $120 a week sailor's pay. Besides tooling around in a new red British MG sports car, he was getting ready for the grand opening of the Bamboo Snack Bar, taking his family on regular beach trips to the Isle of Palms, and all the while carrying on multiple extramarital affairs.

Sometime around the end of 1967, Walker discovered that he was being transferred to SUBLANT, the very nerve center of Atlantic Fleet communications at Norfolk. As a watch officer there, he would serve directly under Lieutenant John Roberts in the message room. His job was to read every classified incoming and outgoing communication to or from fleet submarines and then make sure they were properly routed, giving him easy access to the sort of top-level security messages the Soviets coveted. Seeing dollar signs, he quickly gave them a heads-up.

Management of his case was now passed along to the KGB's Line PR, a political intelligence department that operated out of the Soviet embassy in Washington, just blocks from the White House. The first of his face-to-face meetings with his new handler occurred outside the Zayre department store in Alexandria, Virginia. As arranged, Walker was waiting in front on the street, pretending to window-shop, when the tall, dark-haired Russian agent approached from behind and told Walker to take a stroll with him. As they went along, the KGB agent asked Walker for the materials he'd brought, and Walker presented him with a shopping list of intelligence he could obtain from the command center. He'd added the key list for the new KW-7 crypto box near the bottom of the sheet of paper, almost as if it was an afterthought. In fact, it was done for a calculated effect. He had expected that the agent would be particularly impressed by that item, and wanted to see his reaction when his gaze landed on it.

Walker wasn't disappointed. One peek at the shopping list and the tall, dark-haired KGB man was sold. His eyes eager, he'd stared at the bottom of the list for a long moment, then asked Walker to continue on with him for a number of blocks while they established their working arrangement. Among the things they discussed were payment terms, security precautions, and what Walker was to tell American interrogators about the timing and circumstances of how he'd started spying if he were ever arrested.

With the ground rules laid out, John Walker was essentially put on the KGB's payroll. He would earn between $500 and $1,000 a week for top-secret documents from SUBLANT headquarters, with bonuses of several thousand dollars for exceptional pieces of intelligence like the KW-7 Orestes key codes and any manuals relating to the cipher machine's use.

Finally the KGB agent let Walker know that they would have no more personal meetings—the risk of continuing them was too great. Before melting into the crowd on the busy sidewalk, he handed Walker an information packet that explained the dead drop method by which their future transactions would be conducted.

In the packet, Walker discovered a map and handwritten directions to an isolated wooded location where he would leave his next batch of material on a predetermined date. At the drop site he would find his payment and another packet with a map and note about the following dead drop. He would also receive a sign to leave behind as confirmation that he had made the drop. This could be a marker on a utility pole, a notation on a specified page in a telephone book at a roadside restaurant, or something else of that nature. A set time after the drop, the KGB man would drive to the site, look for Walker's sign, and recover the materials. He would then place a marker that indicated he'd made the pickup. Later, Walker would double back to seek out the marker. If he spotted it, he would know all had gone as planned.

And so the pattern for an ongoing succession of dead drops was set. Although he acknowledged it was best to play it safe, Walker actually might have preferred going on with the direct meetings. He'd gotten a visceral charge out of it, and relished the expression on the Soviet agent's face as he scanned the shopping list. To him spying was no more than an adult game, and having the power to turn over the keys made him a master player. Not just in *his* eyes, but in those of the Russians.

In the months after the first of the dead drops, there had been a refinement or two to the process. Walker had started out bringing large plastic trash bags filled with documents that he'd photocopied late at night in the Norfolk communications center. But using the copy machine was dangerous. If someone noticed him duplicating classified materials, it would be tough for him to explain. As a better alternative, the Russians had given him a Minox camera about the size and shape of a pack of chewing gum. Like the rotor decryptor he'd been using on the *Simon Bolivar,* the

Minox was designed for one-handed operation. Walker would photograph the documents at headquarters with the camera, or briefly slink off with them, take his pictures in the security of his home, and return them to the SUBLANT crypto vault before their absence was noticed. He would then place the undeveloped rolls of film in Coca-Cola cans and bring them to the dead drops. These containers were less obtrusive than the large bags of paper documents, reducing the odds of anyone stumbling upon them in the woods. They also weren't as cumbersome for the Soviets to examine and then pass along to their Moscow superiors.

Walker would find the spying effortless and lucrative. His money problems seemed like something from another existence. He had rented a three-bedroom luxury apartment in Norfolk's swankest neighborhood and bought a new twenty-four-foot sailboat he named the *Dirty Old Man*.

At a party Walker threw on the boat for some younger sailors, he met a sexy college girl named Jimi. Jimi-Jet, her friends called her. The nickname alluded to the fast, wild way she lived her life, and Walker had gotten to know firsthand what that meant. His relationship with Jimi-Jet soon consumed him. He would sneak off with her on weeknights, take her out on the town, show her a good time. When she asked how he could afford the nightclubs and expensive restaurants, Walker said he was in the Mafia. He liked projecting an outlaw image, and it seemed to excite her.

Meanwhile, Walker would tell Navy colleagues who wondered how he was living so well that the Bamboo Snack Bar was raking it in at the door. Convincing them that his investment in the bar had panned out was more than a handy cover story, it gave him a sense of superiority. The men at the base would believe him a smooth operator, a foresighted entrepreneur. He wanted them to think he was their better and didn't give a damn that all of it was a lie. Lying was not only part of the game, it enhanced his enjoyment as a player. He saw his skill at getting his colleagues to believe whatever he told them as proof that he could deceive anyone and attain anything he chose.

After years of financial ups and downs, Walker felt he was now in a position to have everything he wanted. The world was at his fingertips.

V

Kincaid, Illinois, is in the heart of coal-mining country, and twenty-two-year-old Vernon Foli came from a large Italian Catholic clan whose men had made their living in the tunnels there—his own father and grandfather having labored for the Peabody Mining Company.

A miner's pay was high compared to what he'd earn from other jobs in the area, but the work carried a proportionately high measure of risk. The coal dust that got into his lungs would often cut his life short, assuming a shaft collapse, or some accident involving the heavy machinery used to tap and haul the coal, didn't kill him first. Each generation of Kincaid men, therefore, would sprout new dreams of getting out of town and finding easier and safer ways to support their families.

Vernie, as his wife, Barbara, called him, was the latest of the Foli males to entertain such hopes. Handsome and slim, with a thick head of wavy black hair—his mother always said he was a dead ringer for Elvis, and photographs bear out the resemblance—he'd gone to business college for a while, but that was before Barbara met him. Barbara wasn't sure why he made the decision to leave school; all she would remember was that by the time they started dating, Vernie had gotten a job at a mining equipment plant near the state capital. Though still tied to the mines, it kept him away from the cutting, drilling, and black lung disease that had taken its toll on so many of the guys he'd grown up around, and was buying him time to decide what he was going to do with his life.

Then, in the autumn of 1965, Vernon received his military draft papers in the mail. Suddenly his decisions were limited, his timetable for making them curtailed. The Vietnam War was gaining momentum, with the number of U.S. troops being sent to the region about to quadruple. Encouraged by his then-fiancé, Barbara, and his older brother, a Navy lifer who'd done duty on submarines, Vernon enlisted for naval service in October. He and Barbara got married practically the moment he finished basic training in Great Lakes, Illinois—in fact, the abundant crop of hair Barbara had loved remained nothing but buzz-cut stubble at their wedding, a small affair in which Vernon's brother, the career military man, stood up for him. Both wore their uniforms. They were proud they were in the Navy, and Barbara was proud of it, too. For their honeymoon, the newlyweds spent the weekend in a town maybe an hour's drive from Great Lakes, getting out for dinner and drinks with two of Vernon's pals from boot camp.

The Navy life, as Barbara would say, "had already consumed us."

It would very shortly bring them eastward to New London, Connecticut, where Vernie attended Submarine School. Earning his silver dolphins in February 1967, he served his first tour of duty aboard the USS *Redfin*, an aging Gato-class diesel-powered vessel that was decommissioned in mid-May.

Later that month, Interior Communications Electrician Third Class Vernon Foli was transferred to the USS *Scorpion* at Naval Station Norfolk.

The reassignment distressed Barbara in a way she found hard to express. Though reluctant to share her odd sense of trepidation with Vernon, she quietly arranged to see a chaplain while on a doctor's visit to the Naval Medical Center in Portsmouth, Virginia. Her pregnancy with their daughter, Holli, was nearing term, and she was huge, and about due for a routine prenatal checkup.

Before heading into the doctor's office, Barbara meant to stop and open up about her worries to the chaplain. Once alone with him, however, she took things a lot further, asking point-blank if he'd help pull her husband off *Scorpion*. The chaplain tried to allay her fears.

"I bet you're afraid because it's a nuclear-powered submarine," he said.

Barbara was clear about his meaning. In the 1960s, atomic power plants were the product of a technology that was still young and widely misunderstood—enough so to prompt thoughts of inevitable radioactive leaks, and deadly poisoning for those who worked around them. But Barbara knew the chaplain was wrong, and thought there was at least a measure of condescension in his dismissal.

"That *isn't* what I'm afraid of," she insisted, while conceding that the likelihood of increasingly long separations from her husband may have factored somewhat into her anxiousness. Bright and perceptive, Barbara was aware that nuclear submarines could stay submerged for weeks and potentially months on end, unlike the older diesel subs that would have to surface to refuel or draw oxygen into their turbines after much briefer periods at sea. For the Navy, this afforded the tactical edge of being able to send subs out on longer deployments, and to farther locales, than had been imaginable in the past. For a wife whose husband was stationed on a nuclear-powered sub, its implication was more basic and emotional—he would be away from home more than ever before.

But Barbara's bad feelings about Vernon stepping aboard *Scorpion* had deeper roots than she could articulate to the chaplain. Yes, they may have been connected to the prospect of the boat carrying him off for longer stretches than those to which she'd grown accustomed—but only in part. And no, she certainly wasn't harboring a dread of her husband falling victim to some kind of glow-in-the-dark contamination. There was something else to her misgivings. Something shapeless and indefinable she was at a loss for words to explain.

Be that as it may, Barbara left the chaplain wondering if maybe she'd been a little out of line requesting some sort of special treatment. In the end, it was irrelevant. Unswayed, the chaplain declined to press her appeal with Vernon's higher-ups. He would remain on *Scorpion*.

In Norfolk, the Folis leased a single-bedroom apartment off base in one of the military rental houses on the town outskirts, near the Naval Amphibious Base that's been the Atlantic Fleet's main amphibious operations launching and training center since the 1940s. This drab, low-income area offered nothing to resemble their hometown's neatly defined streets and avenues—never mind the green, tree-shaded neighborhoods of Norfolk proper. There were no sidewalks, curbs, or paved intersections. Just the run-down dwellings with their partially bald lawns divided by crumpled metal trashcans, beyond which a wide belt of dirt, sand, and pebbles eventually ran up against a potholed two-lane blacktop. Each house stood in a rough row of similar structures, one ground-floor apartment opening to the front yard, another to the backyard, the backyard facing the front of the next rental building in line. About five houses down from the place where Barbara and Vernon lived, the street dead-ended in a little cul-de-sac where wild grass and weeds rimmed out onto a tidal inlet fed by the Atlantic known as Little Creek.

About a year after the Folis moved into this area, a Chicago newspaper article would mention a woman carrying her infant daughter out into the water in a possible attempt to drown herself and the child. The woman, not named in the article, was Barbara Foli. While the report was accurate to the extent that Barbara had waded into the water with Holli, its speculation about her reasons for doing it couldn't have been further from the truth.

But that all would be in the unforeseen days to come. Immediately following Vernon's reassignment, Barbara, then several months pregnant, found herself overwhelmed with the commingled joys and anxieties of impending motherhood, and the sometimes difficult process of settling into being the wife of a submarine crewman—difficulties that were somewhat mitigated by the fact that Vernon had initially remained close to home. His transfer to *Scorpion* had come while the sub was at the Norfolk Naval Shipyard in Portsmouth for nuclear refueling and overhaul. Originally scheduled to be finished in June, the work became delayed by several hitches in its refueling—just the second ever performed at this yard. As the result of mechanical problems encountered during the three days of sea trials that followed the refueling, *Scorpion*'s yard period lagged into mid-October, when Francis Slattery was given command of the boat.

Then, after a brief trip to the Naval Submarine Base New London, Connecticut, for crew refresher training, and a forty-eight-hour inspection and minor maintenance dry-dock, the USS *Scorpion* had departed for the Caribbean.

At Naval Station Roosevelt Roads in eastern Puerto Rico, *Scorpion* was loaded with trial versions of the Mk 37 antisubmarine torpedo, the Mk 45 Astor nuclear-armed antisubmarine torpedo, and the Mk 14 antishipping torpedo.

The ten days of weapons trials that *Scorpion* subsequently conducted between Puerto Rico and St. Croix in the United States Virgin Islands constituted Vernon Foli's lengthiest stint at sea since he'd reported to the boat. They would be fairly uneventful. The exercise torpedoes carried no explosives in their warheads. Instead the warheads had inflatable bladders that would allow them to float to the surface and be recovered for refurbishing and reuse after their test runs. Because these REXTORPs, as they were called, saw extensive service, they would suffer a higher failure rate than standard explosive-bearing war shots. This fouled up some of the test launches, and may have contributed to the imprecise release of an Mk 45 by a member of the sub's torpedo gang. But all in all, whatever snags arose during *Scorpion*'s torpedo-training were normal—the reason for peacetime exercises is to make sure the crew and weapons are ready for the real thing.

After the snafus were reported, *Scorpion* had some additional REXTORPs loaded into her tubes at Roosevelt Roads, and then went on to complete her weapons trials without further problems.

She arrived back at Norfolk in time for Thanksgiving. The sailors who'd pull duty on the holiday were mainly single, affording married men like Vernon Foli and his pal Jerry Pospisil a chance to spend the holiday with their families. If a single guy was lucky enough to find his name left off the duty roster, there was a good chance he'd get a dinner invite from a married shipmate. Cooped aboard a sub for weeks and weeks on end, a sailor would establish tight working relationships with his fellow crewmen. He'd come to know most everybody, but with some of the guys he'd develop a closeness. They were like family members, even brothers, and for a sailor whose relatives might be thousands of miles away, there was nothing better to do on Thanksgiving Day than enjoy a big holiday meal surrounded by the ordinary comforts and cooking smells of a married buddy's place.

Of course, the married guys appreciated the company, too. Often it was only a sailor, his wife, and his child at the table. No mother, no father, no Aunt Betty or Uncle Carl. A married crewman was often stationed far from his extended family. So on holidays he'd gather his submarine family and they would share in some of the normalcy left behind with civilian life. Thanksgiving dinner was a needed dose of the familiar for all of them.

Every so often, though, a Thanksgiving duty roster might require that one of the submarine's married hands take the watch. Generally this had to do with shortages of trained men, as the nukes—nuclear engineers who ran the reactor—would grumblingly attest. In these instances, the family could come aboard and eat with the crewman. For sailors on duty and anybody else who showed up, the mess always served a special meal of turkey with all the usual dressings—stuffing, gravy, cranberry sauce, mashed potatoes, corn, and even pumpkin pie for dessert. It wasn't rare for a guy to hear his wife comment about how good the food was. Now I know why you're gaining weight, she'd wisecrack. Must be nice to have somebody do all the cooking for you.

That Thanksgiving it was Barbara Foli who did the cooking for her husband, Vernon. They spent the holiday at home. She'd planned a dinner that included recipes for dressing and fancy sweet potatoes from some of her cookbooks, and was especially proud of a cornbread stuffing prepared from a recipe she'd found in a *Hints from Heloise* paperback.

Years later, Barbara happened upon that page with the cornbread stuffing recipe, noticed it was soiled from bits of food, and was reminded how she'd left it open while preparing the recipe. Swept with a wave of melancholy, she browsed through the other cookbooks in her collection, and opening one to the front page, saw a note Vernie had planted for her to find as a future surprise.

I love you, it read simply.

VI

Scorpion had a quick turnaround after the holiday. On December 4, 1967, the sub headed out for more weapons accuracy and systems tests, although now she would remain in the local waters of the Virginia Capes Operating Area.

It was during these trials that an unusual mishap occurred in the torpedo room. The Navy would conveniently seize on this incident much later to tarnish the names of *Scorpion*'s torpedo gang—and, indeed, her entire crew—for decades to come.

A day after the trials kicked off, Torpedoman First Class James M. Peercy, Torpedoman Third Class Mark Domanski, and several handlers were firing two Mk 37 REXTORPs when one of the torpedoes failed to accept its electric launch command. Under normal circumstances, this firing signal was an impulse transmitted along a cable—known as an A-cable—running through the firing tube to the torpedo's motor.

When the torpedo didn't launch, the sailors assumed it was dead in its tube and moved on to successfully fire a second torpedo. But moments after that torpedo shot into the water, Peercy and Domanski heard the first fish's motor activate inside the tube. It had, they knew, gone into a hot run. Their decision to launch was a significant judgmental error.

When a torpedo was armed and ready—as it might be during patrols or combat situations—a hot run had to be quickly and properly dealt with. If the torpedo blew in its tube and ruptured the submarine's pressure hull, the self-inflicted wound would be calamitous.

But no U.S. sub had ever gone down because of a hot run. While at sea, a submarine crew is either on patrol or conducting drills. Torpedomen rehearse emergency procedures countless times over, doing so until their reactions are practically muscle memory.

"Firing a torpedo, hot run torpedo, fire in a torpedo tube, auto fuel spill . . . it's like even if it would happen, it wouldn't come as a surprise," said Joe Verse, who served as a fire control technician and qualified chief of the watch on *Scorpion*'s sister ship the USS *Sculpin*. "Submarine people are the best-trained people in the world. They don't, in time of emergency, panic. I've never seen anybody panic, you just do your job."

And in case somebody didn't do his job, for whatever reason, the Mk 37 had redundant safeguards against human error. If a war shot received an accidental firing signal while stored in a rack, it had a circular propeller guard back of the fins that would stop the props from spinning, overload a circuit breaker, and kill the motor. The torpedo also had a gyroscopic anticircular run (ACR) mechanism that would instantly deactivate it if the submarine executed a 135 degree turn—and it would have been standard procedure for a submarine to turn a full 180 degrees in the event of a torpedo going live in its tube. When the officer of the deck heard somebody shout "Hot run" over the underwater phone, he'd immediately hit a hard rudder and do that 180 to disarm the warhead. Meanwhile, in the torpedo room, the tube would be flooded with seawater to absorb any heat emitted by the torpedo's motor and eliminate explosive hydrogen released from its battery. Once the battery was dead, the torpedomen would drain the tube, bring the fish out, and disarm it.

All these safeguards were intended to prevent the launch of the war shot from its tube, and the consequent risk of having its homing mechanism kick into search mode. Then the torpedo would snake back and forth through the water, seeking to acquire a target on its active sonar. If that were to occur, there was a chance the torpedo could turn back on the submarine and take a fatal bite out of it.

Even in this scenario, however, a streamlined Skipjack-class nuclear attack sub like the *Scorpion* would have had ample time to take an evasive course. Upon launch, a wire-guided Mk 37 would travel to a point where it could intercept its moving target. Minor trajectory adjustments of no more than a couple of degrees this way or that were made possible by commands sent through the cable. When the torpedo was about seven hundred yards from its target, its sonar homing system would take over, pinging to locate the hull of a target vessel. But to safeguard against a torp's HBX-3 high-explosive charge detonating near a submarine that launched it, the warhead typically wouldn't be enabled until it had swum out beyond a quarter mile from the sub. Since the Mk 37 was fairly slow, with a top speed of 24 knots, a Skipjack would have easily outraced it, cutting away from it at the sub's own maximum speed, which was upward of 30 knots—close to 40 knots, some insisted, when engineers really poured on the rpms.

And there were additional precautions against a sub being struck by its own torpedo.

"You had above limits, below limits, and no limits," former USS *Scorpion* Torpedoman Robert McClain explained. In other words, a torpedoman could calibrate the torpedo for a specific stratum level—a limiting plane of trajectory above or below the depth where his submarine was positioned. Say you'd targeted an enemy destroyer a hundred feet above you on the surface. You would set the torp for a stratum level above limits at a hundred feet, preventing the torpedo from coming down any deeper than that, and then have the submarine slip beneath that hundred-foot boundary. Conversely, if you were firing at a submerged target a hundred feet below you—a hostile sub, in other words—you'd keep the torp's stratum level at a hundred feet below limits, and put yourself above that depth so it couldn't come back up where it could strike you. You could also shoot a torpedo at no limits—or without specifying its stratum level—and it would, as McClain said, "go anywhere it wanted to go." But a sub would only fire a torpedo in that manner if it were under clear and present threat of attack from another vessel at its own depth.

For a submarine to take a lethal hit from its own hot-running Mk 37 torpedo, then, an extraordinary number of things would have to go wrong.

Because the trial version Mk 37 fired by Peercy and Domanski bore no explosive charge, a full-scale detonation onboard *Scorpion* wasn't a concern. They knew that the torpedo was going to give off heat, and they were worried that the heat might damage the torpedo tube, a major repair. Their subsequent testimonies to a naval board that investigated the accident revealed that the malfunction caught them off guard, and that they'd released the torpedo fearing it would "get too hot" in its launch tube and possibly ignite a buildup of hydrogen gas leaked from the weapon's battery—a situation that flooding the tube would have easily prevented.

The accident exposed a flaw in the training of *Scorpion*'s torpedo crew. The Navy's insistence on repetitive, highly demanding drills for its submarine fleet kept sailors on their toes and ensured that incidents like Peercy and Domanski's occurred in training and not when it really counted—under risky patrol or combat conditions.

For Slattery, a new commander, the wasteful loss of a training torpedo must have been an embarrassment, as it would have been for the executive officer, Lieutenant Commander Robert R. Fountain, who had once been the weapons officer, and took great personal pride in a tightly run, well-disciplined torpedo room.

Within a couple of months, Peercy and Domanski would be rotated off the boat along with two other members of the torpedo gang. Replacing Peercy as senior man was Torpedoman's Mate First Class Donald Yarbrough, a twelve-year veteran who had served on four other submarines. Yarbrough had undergone specialized training in torpedoes and, despite being known for his hell-raising ways while on liberty, would impress his superiors with his experience and competence.

VII

Owed a couple of weeks' shore leave, Vernon Foli was able to take it shortly after *Scorpion* returned to base from her torpedo-firing exercises. He and Barbara were making a trip to visit their families in Illinois, and they left as soon as he got home from the boat, loading their six-month-old daughter, Holli, and luggage bags into their battered little Volkswagen Karmann Ghia.

The moment they got into the packed car, Vernon jammed his foot down hard on the gas pedal and sped off onto the highway with a whoosh. Barbara was startled. *My God!* she thought. Her husband had seemed in a decent enough mood, but the sudden, aggressive speeding was unlike him, a side of his personality she didn't recognize. It gave her a bit of a fright.

"Vernie, calm down," she said as he tooled along the road. "What's wrong?"

He never really answered. It was impossible to explain how combat simulations at sea got you going. Impossible to talk about the mix of adrenaline and tension that wound a submarine crewman tight inside. Unwinding the spring wasn't something you could do at will, not any more than tightening it up again was easy once you were back at sea. It was a different world on a sub. There was nothing routine about human beings traveling—and knowing they would possibly have to do battle—underwater. A different world, and the realism of the drills would remind a sailor of its precariousness, take him right to the edge. Anything he did on the boat could have dangerous consequences if it wasn't done right.

How did you describe that feeling to someone that hadn't experienced it? Even—or maybe especially—when the person was your wife?

After a while behind the wheel, Vernon settled down and eased his foot off the pedal. Soon he was pretty much back to himself. The couple's visit went well, and they felt lucky to be together.

They returned to Norfolk in time for Christmas. In mid-January, Vernon departed aboard *Scorpion* for an annual round of antisubmarine war games off the Florida coast. These exercises, called Aged Daddy V, would keep him away from Norfolk for about three weeks.

VIII

One mild, sunny February day after he'd come home from the Aged Daddy V maneuvers, Vernon brought a couple of his *Scorpion* shipmates over to the apartment near the Amphib base.

Barbara was there with the baby when they came into the living room, leaving the front door partly open behind them, all three of the sailors on liberty and wearing blue jeans. Vernie's friends were giving him a hand with something or other—*guy stuff*—and she figured she'd just leave them to their own business.

They were having a smoke and gabbing, maybe taking a break from whatever they were doing, when a snatch of their conversation reached Barbara's ear. She hadn't been paying much attention to them until that moment, but what she heard made her heart drop to her feet: they were heading off on a prolonged deployment. Leaving soon. And they would be gone for three months.

What? Barbara thought. *Soon? Three months!*

She stood looking at the three sailors. The smoke from their cigarettes hung in the air around them and filtered the sunlight streaming through the door from outside. It was all Barbara could do to restrain herself from asking questions, but they were talking away and she didn't want to interrupt. Amid discussion of their approaching departure, one of Vern's buddies said something about a popular clairvoyant, maybe Jeane Dixon, predicting another sub would go down that year. *Another sub?* Barbara supposed the first boat must have been the *Seawolf,* which had gotten into some sort of accident back at the end of January. But was the second one an American sub, a nuclear sub, or both? Barbara wasn't clear on it from the conversation. None of the three sailors seemed to be taking the prediction very seriously, and Vernie had produced a quick, dismissive chuckle when it was brought up. And then, after a minute, they had moved on to other scuttlebutt. That sort of calmed Barbara. If the guys didn't see it as important, she wouldn't either. Right now she was mainly waiting for Vernie's friends to leave the apartment so she could ask him questions about his departure.

When they were alone and Vernie eventually told her what he knew, she felt like a little girl ready to stomp her foot in defiance. His deployment was, after all, connected to the *Seawolf*'s scraping up against an underwater mountain somewhere off New England. She had heard about that on a televised news broadcast when it happened and never imagined that it would directly affect their lives. But *Seawolf* had been scheduled to rotate out to the Mediterranean ahead of *Scorpion*, and now it couldn't because of damages it sustained in the collision. Her husband's sub had been selected as its replacement.

It isn't fair, she thought over and over. *That was the other sub's planned trip, not* Scorpion's.

Of course, Barbara was aware her inner tantrum would not change anything. In a little over a week, *Scorpion* was leaving on a voyage that would take it to the distant Mediterranean.

IX

Prior to *Scorpion*'s deployment to the Med, Commander Frank Slattery had leaned on several veteran hands to assist him in learning the ins and outs of the boat.

Two of them were senior enlisted men: Chief of the Boat Walter "Wally" Bishop, and Senior Chief Quartermaster Frank "Patsy" Mazzuchi. The third was its executive officer, Lieutenant Commander Robert R. Fountain, *Scorpion*'s longest-tenured officer. Three months after Slattery came aboard, the exacting, doctrinaire Fountain was boosted up to a policymaking and management post in Washington and replaced by Lieutenant Commander David Bennett Lloyd. But Fountain had been an immense help to the commander early on, having gained an extensive and intimate knowledge of the sub in his two tours on *Scorpion*, starting with her post-shakedown period, extending through a total of six "special operations," or covert-intelligence-gathering cruises, and ending with a stretch in which he simultaneously served as her weapons officer, first lieutenant, diving officer, main propulsion assistant, electrical officer, and qualification officer.

Although Fountain's knowledge of the boat's vital systems may have been unsurpassed, no one could have better dealt with the sailors that kept those systems running than the crusty, squint-eyed, and notoriously coarse-tongued "Wally COB" Bishop, who'd been a member of her original commissioning crew—a plank owner in the vernacular of submariners. At the request of his captain and out of respect for his leadership skills, Bishop had been selected as chief of the boat in 1962 while a first-class petty officer, leapfrogging several chief petty officers. This happens so rarely that it has been noted in his official naval biography, and is a constant point of emphasis in the reminiscences of those who served with him.

A position unique to the submarine service, the COB is the highest-rated noncommissioned officer on the boat, bridging the gap between the commissioned men and the enlisted rank and file. The COB must grasp issues large and small from differing perspectives, relay the concerns of the crew to the brass, enforce discipline, smooth occasional ruffled feathers on both sides, and, in short, keep things operating efficiently on a daily basis. It's a tough job, and the morale of the boat hinges upon a COB's ability to pull it off. Walter Bishop's almost legendary skill at his job drew on an intuitive perceptiveness and strength of character that couldn't be taught, coupled with an understanding of the many differences between serving on subs and surface vessels. Since John Paul Jones raised the flag on America's first warship in 1775, the Navy had historically relied on custom and tradition to define the boundaries of personal relationships between officers and enlisted men. Rigid and proper social interactions were encouraged to enhance performance, and those that strayed from formal lines of protocol were believed to undermine the respect for authority. But the sheer lack of space aboard a sub forced officers and enlisted personnel to come into regular contact with one another. Packed into close quarters for weeks on end, living as well as working together, they could function as a unit only if a more relaxed etiquette prevailed.

There are common elements in the character of submariners that make this flexibility in behavior natural, starting with the desire to sail on a sub in the first place. You'll hear it time and again from these men: All my life, as far back as I can remember, I wanted to be on submarines. I didn't want to be in the Army, I didn't want to be in the Air Force. I wanted to be in the Navy and I wanted to be on submarines.

To be selected for duty aboard a sub, however, a volunteer must meet stringent psychological requirements, and must score in the upper tenth percentile of all applicants. In 1968, the scores required to enter the Nuclear Power Training Program were higher than those needed for admission to Annapolis. An enlisted man was likely to have had at least some college education, and many joined the Navy so they could benefit from the GI Bill and finish their education after fulfilling their military obligation. In fact, the majority of enlisted men were noncommissioned officers who'd gone through years of training before being assigned to a submarine.

Sailors would qualify for a particular watch station soon after reporting onboard a sub so they could contribute to manning the boat at sea. At the same time, they would undertake a broader qualification in submarines, a progression that often took a year or more of intense study, at the conclusion of which a sailor would have gained a comprehensive facility with every one of the sub's systems. The idea behind this rigorous training requirement was that every crewman would be capable of speedy damage control to save the submerged boat and his shipmates in a life-threatening crisis. It was truly all or none when it came to survival. If a catastrophic event occurred underwater, there was very little likelihood of any crewman abandoning ship. "It's kind of hard to push all that water off you," said one submariner. "You don't leave when you want."

To a sailor, enlisted or commissioned, qualifying on subs was an accomplishment that was a source of immense and lasting pride. It was only when you qualified on subs that you earned your dolphins. Once you wore the breastpin, you were family, a member of the Dolphin Brotherhood for life.

Chief petty officers like Bishop and Mazzuchi were the back-bone of the U.S. submarine fleet, responsible for guiding junior enlisted men, ensigns, and junior grade officers through the qualification process. "From the time they're eighteen years old till they're twenty-six years old they've [junior officers] never breathed a breath of the real world," said one former *Scorpion* sailor. "And you got these salty veterans in there like Wally COB, they were the ones that really held the crew together."

After reporting to his submarine command, a young ensign would be assigned to act as a division officer in one of its four departments: Navigation/Operations, Weapons, Engineering, and Supply. As he moved from division to division, familiarizing himself with all the systems of the boat, it was often a chief petty officer who'd show the ensign the ropes. On a sub respect was directly related to your skills and abilities. While at sea, every sailor aboard was assigned regular shifts at a specific station, and qualification on these watch stations was important. The bond between chief petty officers and officers was earned, and reinforced by a truth every submariner understood: the actions of any one man could mean life or death for the entire crew. A good submarine crewman wouldn't think twice about closing a hatch on a flooding compartment to save the boat, even if it meant the loss of a fellow crewman on the other side. Officer, enlisted man, it made no difference. All brothers of the dolphin shared the same risks.

The young guys on *Scorpion* looked up to Bishop as a larger-than-life character, the heart and soul of the boat. They would credit him with getting them on the right track on the *Scorpion*. They would say he corrected them when they were wrong, and punished them when they did something stupid. Practically to a man, they would say he made sailors out of them.

"The guy was part psychologist, father confessor . . . the kind of dad everybody wished they had," remembered Douglas Kariker, who spent almost two years on *Scorpion* as an interior communications electrician before mustering out to attend college in March of 1967. "I think a lot of the reason the crew was so harmonious and got along so well was because of his direct leadership. He probably could have been the CEO of a corporation in another life . . . his insightfulness about what was going on inside your head was unbelievable. It just seemed like he could put his finger on the pulse at any time and kind of tap into your brain when you didn't want him to."

The primary job of the chief of the boat is to do whatever is needed to keep the submarine running. In the five years Bishop had been chief of the boat, *Scorpion* had earned the Navy Unit Commendation and the Award for Excellence in Fire Control, Torpedo Firing, and Tactics. Three separate times during his term *Scorpion* received the coveted Battle Efficiency "E" hash mark awarded annually by the squadron commander to just a single submarine in a particular squadron.

Sanford N. Levy was executive officer on *Scorpion* for three years, under three commanding officers. He would insist that he owed a large part of his success to Bishop: "He made my job a snap. There was no discipline or other personnel problems in that crew. Chief Bishop by his demeanor and style demonstrated the most perfect leadership I have ever beheld in an enlisted man in the Navy."

Levy's right-hand man was Chief Mazzuchi. According to Levy, Mazzuchi was a skillful navigator. Born in Italy and raised in upstate New York by parents who barely spoke a word of English, he'd been in the Navy since World War II, when he made dozens of PT boat runs in the Pacific. Burly and gregarious, he could often be spotted capturing one of the young guys in the crew's mess to hawk them items from his wife's Tupperware catalogue. The old goats, who knew his pitch by heart, would give each other the elbow whenever they heard him launch into it: *C'mere boy, sit down, I want to talk to you.* He lived for his wife, Geneva, and three daughters. They were everything to him: his wife, the girls, and of course the submarine.

There was also a thoughtful side to Mazzuchi that would usually show during the long night watches. He'd never graduated high school but was a prodigious reader with a fondness for American history. Men standing the mid-watch, which lasted from midnight to four o'clock in the morning, would often find themselves gripped by his stories of daring pioneers and proud Indian tribes. For a lot of sailors, those watches were fairly mundane. You'd rove from compartment to compartment, take your readings, and make sure everything was functional. And with the boat shooting through the water like a bullet, and only the slight vibration of its movement and the steady hum of the ventilation system disturbing the background silence, Mazzuchi would spin you a tale of the Old West any chance he got.

Executive Officer Levy moved on to his own command in 1966—to be replaced by Fountain on his second tour—with a twinge of sadness. Climbing up the ladder in rank was something every officer desired, but parting with Bishop, Mazzuchi, and many of the other sailors on *Scorpion* was tough. Still, the way things went in the Navy, with sailors rotating onto different fleet boats, and holding reunion banquets when they were old and gray, Levy figured it was a safe bet he'd be seeing his shipmates later.

X

In Norfolk, *Scorpion*'s departure for its Mediterranean trip was slated for the morning of February 15, right after Valentine's Day, making the holiday a bittersweet occasion for the crewmen, their wives, and their girlfriends.

The instant she'd heard about *Scorpion*'s impending voyage, Barbara Foli had begun her secret countdown to its launch.

They rose early on February 15 and drove out to Pier 22, Vernon behind the wheel, and the baby in the car with them. Sick to her stomach from nerves, Barbara tried to pay attention to the directions. When she next made the trip she would be driving to pick up Vernon from the naval station after *Scorpion* brought him home. At least that would be a happy occasion.

Out on the pier, the couple lingered awhile giving each other so-long hugs, Holli between them, Vernon's seabag slung over his back. Barbara stood there feeling the shared warmth of their bodies and didn't want to move from the spot.

When they finally parted, and her husband turned toward the waiting submarine's gangway, Barbara felt a strange mix of helplessness and resignation. Vernon's long journey had begun. Left behind, watching, there was nothing she could do about it.

XI

Because of a dream, Sonarman First Class Bob Davis missed leaving with the sub.

After spending Valentine's Day—and night—with Davis, his girlfriend had woken up pleading with him not to leave the house. If he stepped aboard *Scorpion*, she insisted, something bad would happen and they would never see each other again.

Davis told his girl that she was being ridiculous. He had no intention of going AWOL. Definitely not over something as far-fetched as a premonition she'd gotten in her sleep.

His seabag packed, Davis had been ready to drive over to the pier when he discovered she'd hidden the car keys to keep him from going anywhere. It took some looking before he finally dug them up, hefted the seabag over his shoulder, and scrambled out the door to his car.

Tooling into the parking area behind Pier 22, Davis snagged a spot and hustled over to the pier just in time to see *Scorpion* easing out into the harbor. When the boat's roll call had come up short one man, the skipper had held up the sub's departure for fifteen minutes to wait for him. But he wouldn't delay any longer.

Davis had stood on the pier gesticulating toward the sub, his arms high in the air. It was too late, though. He knew it even before Commander Slattery raised the bullhorn to his lips from atop the bridge and instructed him to report to the squadron commander.

Instead of joining his crewmates on deployment, he would do a thirty-day stretch in the Camp Allen brig.

XII

In naval parlance, "special operations" means intelligence-gathering, itself an artful term for spying—and Communist bloc vessels, waterways, and port facilities were a nuclear attack submarine's main targets of surveillance.

Just a year before *Scorpion*'s trip to the Mediterranean, Frank Slattery's predecessor, Commander Lewis, as well as veteran Chief of the Boat Walter Bishop and several other petty officers and crewmen, were awarded a host of citations for professional skill and meritorious achievement for three surveillance missions up the Northeast Passage into the Barents Sea, near Russia's borders with Finland and Norway. These all occurred in an eighteen-month period between June 1965 and March 1967, when *Scorpion* had kept tabs on maneuvers—and, once, was sent with the specific purpose of observing the test-firings of submarine-launched ballistic missiles—conducted by the Soviet Union's Northern Fleet off the shores of Murmansk. Kept free of ice by a warm branch of the Gulf Stream known as the North Atlantic Drift, the naval facilities there were Russia's only year-round military seaports with direct access to the Atlantic. Stealing through the region's network of bays, channels, and shallow, cliff-walled fjords, *Scorpion* penetrated an aquatic hive of ship and nuclear submarine activity that

U.S. spymasters found irresistible. While doing so, she had been in more than a few tight spots.

On one recon, her presence was detected. After pinging *Scorpion* with their sonar, the Soviets stunned her crew by warning them off on the underwater telephone in perfect English. A sailor whose main station was in the command center would struggle to express the reaction aboard the boat: "It was scary as hell, but exciting. Everybody was concerned, 'cause it was no joke. But then again, you know, the testosterone, or whatever, just started pumping."

Her crew ordered into silence, *Scorpion* had swiftly gone deep and fled the area.

The 1968 trip to the Mediterranean would be the sub's first extended patrol under Commander Slattery. While her acknowledged mission was the development of undersea warfare tactics with NATO allies, covert intel collection always remained central to *Scorpion*'s operations, and she continued to acquaint herself with the Soviets throughout her deployment.

At that time the Med was a stalking ground for American and Soviet boats, whose personnel took regular turns at antagonizing one another above and below the water's surface. As this strategic naval corridor grew overcrowded with vessels from both sides, their run-ins occurred with increasing frequency. These close encounters served a purpose beyond merely easing the boredom of repetitive drills. The opportunities they provided for measuring the rival fleet's capabilities yielded tangible intelligence dividends.

In the cool stillness of the sonar shack, Sonarmen Bill Elrod, Michael E. Henry, and Harold Snapp Jr. would sit attentively at the bow-mounted BQQ-2 sonar's operating console, watching their displays, listening over their headphones, and matching the graphic waterfall patterns in front of them to the tonal voiceprints of known Soviet vessels. These noises would be sorted out from normal environmental background noise made by crashing waves above and so-called biologics—whales, dolphins, or the immense colonies of shrimp whose thousands of snapping claws reminded the sonarmen of bacon crackling away on a hot skillet. When the sonarmen picked up a contact they would communicate its range and bearings to the control room, where a member of the tracking party would sit at a plotting table and calculate the vessel's position relative to the sub. Using different-colored grease pens, he'd constantly update his coordinates based on information from various systems, drawing Xs and tracing lines across a long sheet of paper.

Often the sonar gang and radio operators would be joined by the spook riders. Depending on the mission, between two and four of them would accompany *Scorpion* on patrol, though their names weren't listed on the crew manifest. Usually they kept to themselves, hanging around the sonar or radio compartment and often talking to each other in Russian. Some of the regular crew assumed those conversations were just language practice. But the purpose of a mission was always need-to-know—at times guys weren't even sure exactly where they were sailing—and the riders would want things kept secret. That also explained why they spoke in a foreign language.

In quieter moments, the sonar shack might get visitors whose doings weren't so mysterious. For instance, a nuke. The electronics associated with crypto, sonar, communications, and navigation systems generated a lot of amps, and the compartments that housed them were kept at a low temperature to prevent wiring and equipment from overheating. On the other hand, *Scorpion's* engine room, aft of frame 44, did not have computers. The rudimentary analog machines used in 1968 lacked the processing capacity to regulate the functions of the sub's reactor and steam plants. As a result, there was no need to reduce heat to prevent stress on the equipment in the engineering spaces. Those spaces were full of high-pressure, superheated steam pipes, and the nuclear engineers would roast inside them. But once they exited the tunnel from the reactor compartment to the forward sections, the temperature dropped considerably. A nuke would open the hatch, step through, shudder as if he'd emerged into a chill mountain night, and then proceed forward into the nose cone.

To a nuke, the sonar shack was a pretty cool place. Cool in terms of its thermometer readings, cool in terms of attitude. Now and then when he was off duty, or between watches, he might drop by the sonar shack for a little while. This was what being a sub-mariner was all about, searching for the bad guys, finding them before they find you.

The nuclear-trained personnel considered the dark little alcove with its glowing screens the most high-tech area of the boat. To the sonarmen, meanwhile, the nukes were the smart guys, versed in the arcane mysteries of splitting atoms. There was a lot of mutual admiration between these two groups.

Chief Hospital Corpsman Lynn Thompson Saville was another guy who might appear in the sonar shack from time to time. In a broad sense, a corpsman oversaw the health and cleanliness of a vessel's crew, while also filling the role of its medic. Nearly all corpsmen were nicknamed "Doc"—when they weren't called pecker-checkers in jest. Nobody was putting them down; they were dedicated Navy men. But on a boat filled with healthy young males in their twenties, many of them single, the routine duties of a corpsman could be considered limited or underappreciated, depending on the eye of the beholder.

The fact was, however, that good personal hygiene was expected from the men on a nuclear submarine. Through no fault of their own, the crewmen on older diesel subs were unable to regularly wash themselves or their uniforms while on patrol. The water in their stores consisted only of what they had brought to sea with them, and conserving it was of the essence. Given the choice between scrubbing up and having enough drinking water aboard, sailors would rightfully let their sanitary habits suffer.

All that would change on the atomic boats. Their propulsion systems needed a high volume of distilled water for their operation, and the same process that turned seawater into steam for the turbines provided the crew with an abundant supply for drinking, cooking, and bathing. On *Scorpion* a sailor had no excuse for grubbiness. The last thing a seaman wanted was to see his name on the plan of the day with the word "scrounge" written next to it. Saville's ultimate authority, then, lay in his ability to hang that offensive tag on an uncleanly sailor.

The crew's having a disagreeable label of their own for the corpsman somewhat balanced the scales. A submarine sailor took an oath to his country and the military, a submarine sailor took an eighty-year oath to secrecy, but nobody ever made a submarine sailor take an oath of celibacy. When a corpsman gave him a checkup, he'd look for outward symptoms of sexually transmitted diseases that might just happen to appear after a shore leave. Hence, pecker-checker. Hence, too, the reason corpsmen were qualified on watch stations. When they weren't busy with minor medical problems, they'd pull their weight in different ways.

Before his tour on *Scorpion,* Doc Saville had served on the Skate-class USS *Seadragon,* which had been built with the earliest generation of nuclear subs. Even though he wasn't obliged to, Doc would volunteer to stand sonar watches on *Seadragon,* and the sonar gang swore he had one of the keenest sets of ears on the boat. Once Doc was in the shack with a sonarman named Barry Martin and reported a contact on a certain bearing. Martin searched and searched for it without success, fiddling with different frequency filters and playing with the volume on his control panel. Ten minutes later, he picked up the contact on the same bearing Doc said it was on. That left him dumbfounded. How Doc had heard it was something he'd never know.

Doc had reported to *Scorpion* about five months before she embarked for the Mediterranean, and that only happened as a fluke.

After his tour aboard *Seadragon* was over, he was supposed to be rotated to a new-construction submarine. But its production was delayed, and he'd instead been reassigned to *Scorpion*.

The sonar gang must have appreciated having him aboard. Like Doc Saville, they'd gained a reputation as being without rival in the fleet.

"They amazed me on a constant basis," said former crewman Jerry Pratt. "Wherever the Soviets were, we were."

This was something the Navy's intelligence collectors would doubtless consider before too long, when a mysterious group of Russian vessels out near the Canary Islands began to draw their intense curiosity.

XIII

In the era before modern e-mail and satellite communications, correspondence between the submariner and his relatives at home was a slow affair. Letters were sent and received during scheduled port calls, and occasional "family-grams"—short personal messages from a crewman's relatives usually announcing births or deaths—would be coded and transmitted to a boat on the regular submarine radio schedules. A crewman would spend hours writing to a family member knowing the thoughts he'd set down on paper might be many weeks old before reaching them.

When *Scorpion* Electrician's Mate Third Class Gerald Stanley Pospisil began penning the first of several letters to his wife, Judy Lynn, he was pretty sure he'd beat at least some of them back to her.

The thoughts and sentiments Pospisil expressed in his letters typified those of young sailors at sea, especially married men who knew the wives they left behind would have to share in the loneliness and stress of a long deployment. "It seems like we have been gone for ages already and it is only a little over two weeks," he reflected to Judy, who'd flown their infant son, Tim, to Nebraska on a family visit.

Besides being homesick, Pospisil was preoccupied with thoughts of his imminent return to civilian life. After years of solid military service, he looked forward to getting out of the Navy and starting a career "on the outside." He'd completed nuclear power school before his assignment to the *Scorpion* in 1964, and figured he'd be eligible for a job in the burgeoning nuclear power industry. The salaries were good, he'd heard. His father had bumped into an acquaintance, the wife of a former nuke who was pulling $1,200 a month at the decommissioned Hallam plant south of Lincoln, Nebraska, not far from the Pospisils' hometown of Wilber. In a couple of years her husband would be transferred to the big, modern Cooper Nuclear Station going up near Brownsville. CNB would eventually run the largest single-unit electrical generator in the state, and engineers with the unparalleled level of training provided by the Navy would be in high demand.

Still, the longer he considered it, the more Jerry grew convinced he'd eventually want to work for himself, and maybe find an interim job that would let him stay closer to Wilber. "Mom said in one of her letters that they were looking for a new manager for the bowling alley," he mentioned. "That would be a job that I would like much better than working for any power company."

For now, however, Jerry remained a Navy man. And as the deployment stretched on, he'd spend many of his free moments thinking about *Scorpion*'s return to Norfolk.

In an April 25 letter to his wife, Jerry indicated that was probably a month away—May 24 or 25—though he added there was a chance of the sub getting in late, depending when it was released from some exercises. "I'll take my bet on the later date," he commented. "I don't know what you would bet on, but I can just imagine the little cogs going 'round and 'round screaming, 'That god damn Navy. They can't even make a decision ahead of time and let anyone know.'"

Three days after Jerry wrote those words, *Scorpion* began its participation in the NATO/U.S. Dawn Patrol maneuvers in the waters off Crete.

XIV

The first of the two covert missions *Scorpion* was to conduct before heading back to Norfolk remains obscure to this day. What seems probable is that Commander Slattery received his orders while in Naples, Italy, where the sub made her final port call of the Mediterranean deployment. What's become known only after four decades is that it involved a rider named Tony Marquez—and that his particular area of specialization was SOSUS, the Navy's sound surveillance system.

Developed in the 1950s, SOSUS consisted of a vast network of hydroacoustical listening devices called hydrophones placed strategically in the Atlantic and Pacific Oceans, and connected by cables laid across the seafloor to naval shore facilities, or NavFacs. The sounds they would gather were recorded on continuous rolls of paper in graph lines that resembled EKG readings, and then analyzed by acoustic experts at the NavFacs who could differentiate between the frequencies produced by ships, submarines, or ocean noises—somewhat like the men that occupied a sub's sonar shack. Originally placed around the coastal United States and Hawaii in areas where Soviet subs were suspected of conducting operations, the SOSUS arrays were soon installed at probable submarine transit points from Europe to the Far East. So sensitive were the hydrophones that SOSUS could locate a vessel within fifty nautical miles of an emplacement, pick up and track aircraft flying over the ocean, even detect the sound of falling rain.

No mention of *Scorpion*'s SOSUS-related activities exists in public naval records, nor is there hard documentation of Marquez coming aboard to aid or oversee them. The names of spook riders on submarines—and the routes they sailed—received the highest possible level of classification; the less people knew about their work, the better. But there is evidence the mission involved calibration of a hydrophonic array. In theory, it wouldn't have been too complicated. A sound source buoy released at a specified location would transmit signals at an assigned sound pressure level, a mathematical calculation of the pressure a sound wave exerts on the medium it passes through, either air or water. The buoy, with its preset SPL emissions, would provide a known reference by which to measure the range and sensitivity of hydrophonic receivers at various underwater sites in the array. Each hydrophone's sensitivity was somewhat different due to environmental conditions, and knowing their exact levels would help SOSUS experts pin down an unfriendly submarine's position. It may well be that *Scorpion*'s task was to lay the buoys under the direction of acoustical scientists at one or more naval shore stations.

There is a chance, however, that she was on a very different type of mission. For much of the Cold War, large submarines carrying ballistic nuclear missiles were deadly security threats on both sides of the Iron Curtain. Slipping within range of a major U.S. coastal city like New York or Los Angeles, a NATO-designation Yankee-class Soviet ballistic missile sub could launch enough nuclear missiles to obliterate it many times over. Conversely, an American Polaris submarine with a payload of sixteen multiple-warhead nuclear missiles could pile an inestimable amount of destruction upon the Soviet Union.

By the mid-1960s, the Americans and Soviets were shadowing each other's ballistic missile submarines, or boomers, all across the oceans of the world. Combining data from reconnaissance satellites and SOSUS networks, the U.S. Navy had developed antisubmarine warfare strategies that would clue patrolling attack submarines to the presence of Soviet ballistic submarines in nearby waters. Implicitly, these submerged warfare techniques would direct the attack subs to where the Russian boomers could be followed and intercepted. It is possible *Scorpion*'s mission was a practice maneuver to assess and refine U.S. trailing procedures, or even an actual tracking operation.

What's certain is that *Scorpion* received her orders about two weeks after she pulled into Naples on April 10, mooring alongside the 2,250-ton support and maintenance ship USS *Tallahatchie County* in Claywall Harbor. Still crisp and clear to the eye, black-and-white snapshots taken from aboard *Tallahatchie County* show Commander Slattery looking down from atop the sub's tall metal sail, a megaphone in hand as he oversees the casting of her lines. The fluttering American flag at her stern—the national ensign—has been moved to the in-port position.

These were the last official Navy photos taken of *Scorpion* before her disappearance.

XV

American seamen saw Naples as the classic port city. The streets were chaotic and noisy. The water was foul. The women either seemed classy and gorgeous or old and fat. There were exotic sights, crowded trader's markets, bars full of marines and sailors drinking beer and letting off steam, and clubs where you could listen to a local band sing American or British rock-and-roll hits with Italian accents, while young B-girls sweet-talked you into buying them $5 cocktails that both they and the barkeeps knew were really just big glasses of Kool-Aid. The weather was cool, but not cold, and there was the awful, seedy harbor that sailors loved and hated at the same time.

Naples and the smaller towns around it, both inland and along the bay, were spots where you could buy gifts for your girl, wife, or mother that you couldn't find back home. Most of the guys got jewelry, especially the cameos carved from coral or seashells at the factories up in the hills near Mount Vesuvius. When a sub put down liberty, Mercedes cabs would arrive at the pier in droves, their sport-coated drivers soliciting fares among the sailors coming ashore. Twenty dollars paid for as many passengers as the cabbie could jam inside, and he'd spend the entire day hauling them all over the place. He'd drive them up to Vesuvius and Pompeii, to Torre del Greco, where the cameos were fashioned by hand. When the sailors were done buying things they couldn't afford the cabbie would drive them on to some restaurant where he'd claim the local celebrities and bigwigs ate so they could spend more money sampling the local pizza, lasagna, and ravioli. Once a crewman returned to his boat, he'd take the carefully wrapped cameo brooch or locket he'd bought as a present and stow it in his bunk tray with his other belongings. While at sea he might take it out after he hit the rack, and unwrap it, and turn it in his hands while he thought about home and how many days were left before he'd see it again.

Naples was also where you could get deals on Beretta .22 caliber pistols at the NATO base exchange and switchblades at local shops. Naval policies allowed sailors to purchase them, and it was customary for guys to pick up the weapons as novelties for themselves and the men in their families. For $35 or $40, you could buy a pistol and maybe a half dozen knives, a bargain that wasn't to be passed up. If a crewman was too strapped to afford a firearm at the exchange, he might ask a buddy from aboard the sub to lend him the cash for one.

Although Italy's political climate had grown uncomfortable as the USSR gained influence throughout the Mediterranean region, the flow of dollars from American sailors by and large made the Neapolitans receptive hosts: "The guys on here have really gone through some money . . . I'll bet [President Lyndon] Johnson would cuss the gold leaving the country just thinking about it," *Scorpion* crewman Jerry Pospisil wrote his wife.

Of course this wasn't to say that Soviet bills were refused or that they didn't buy their own kind of support. Russian backing of the Italian Communist Party, or Partito Comunista d'Italia, ran to the tune of millions of dollars in funds, with the KGB shipping party leaders off to Moscow to train them as spies and provocateurs. In 1968, over a third of Naples's electorate voted for the Communists, whose KGB advisors had taught them how to stir anti-American sentiment among a populace already mistrustful of U.S. nuclear strength. When the Communist Party leadership got wind of an atomic submarine coming into port, it would sometimes instigate rallies near the American base, cooking up propaganda stories about the sub's reactor bringing a threat of radioactive contamination to the city. These Communist rallies could pull large and disorderly crowds, and sailors were warned to steer clear of them. When protesters gathered, men on shore patrol duty would be instructed to stay at the edges of the crowd and make sure none of the American sailors mixed with it. If insults were flung at the sailors and fights erupted, the Italian police were liable to side with the protesters. Shore patrolmen were even stripped of their night sticks, helmets, belts, and flashlights to avoid further inflaming angry passions. Driven to the outer fringe of the rally on the back of a jeep, a guy on shore patrol would be told he'd be picked up at the end of his four-hour shift and given these parting words: "Do not get yourself in trouble."

Scorpion's visit to Naples was actually divided into two stays, one lasting from April 10 to April 15, and the other from April 20 to April 28. Wedged between them were more antisubmarine warfare exercises, and an eleventh-hour rebuff from the Turkish government that scuttled a planned call to the port of Izmir because of its citizens' mounting opposition to U.S. military interests. Needing a port in which to complete some routine upkeep before its final antisubmarine warfare exercises in the Med got rolling, *Scorpion* asked for and received permission for its second, unplanned Naples sojourn. This time, however, antsy Italian politicos bowed to the Communist Party's arm-twisting and asked that *Scorpion* drop anchor out in the water beyond the harbor landings. The Navy agreed. *Scorpion*'s officers, crewmen, and supplies would have to shuttle between the pier and the submarine on utility boats lowered from the destroyer tender USS *Shenandoah* (AD-26).

Besides some repairs and minor refits, Commander Slattery had the crew complete fresh paint jobs throughout the sub to clean up the rust and chipping that were evidence of her long turn at sea. With the aborted Turkish stay leaving them to wonder what other unpredictable changes of plan were in store, and their liberty dependent on the utility boat pickups, *Scorpion*'s homesick crew was plagued with nagging doubts about their chances of a timely return to Norfolk. In a letter home, Jerry Pospisil wrote of the disillusionment: "The last few days we have been painting like crazy. For what I haven't figured out. It is supposedly so we will get maximum liberty when we get back. Promises, promises. That's all we ever get. None of the guys ever even believe them any more."

They may not have believed the promises, but *Shenandoah*'s ferries to shore did periodically allow them to escape the confines of the sub. For the married hands this usually meant sightseeing, shopping for gifts, and an occasional pit stop at a bar. But a full third of *Scorpion*'s crewmen were single, and for those who didn't have anyone special waiting at home, watching the other guys buy things for their ladies only deepened their loneliness and isolation. Sure, the Hill, as sailors called the area climbing toward the center of town, was off limits. Everyone understood, though, that a few lire could buy ready companionship with the bar girls in the watering holes near the pier, or with the women who'd approach you on the twisty lanes and side streets leading up toward the Vomero's large public plaza. At the same time, the poor, desperate women the Joes picked up were receptive to many lines of trade, and always sought ways to double their profits with an open hand held out to KGB spies, who regularly used prostitutes and bar girls as informants in foreign ports with U.S. naval facilities.

This was something the KGB had learned to exploit. The average enlisted man didn't know a great deal of vital interest to Soviet intelligence, but old salts like Bishop and Mazzuchi would constantly warn submarine sailors not to discuss deployments and technical matters with the locals. The standard words of caution would go something along the lines of: *When they start asking those questions, just walk away,* although it was a rare sailor who could resist the urge to have a little fun with an overcurious lady of the night by cooking up a tall tale about some superheroic mission or outrageous new piece of hardware. In his mind he would envision the look on some Russian agent's face as he read a report about America's latest weapon—a flying submarine!

Those tall tales notwithstanding, there were trickles of genuinely useful information a sailor might let slip in unguarded moments, and a complaint about *Scorpion* being stuck in the middle of the harbor, or a dejected remark about the uncertain timetable for his return to the states, would have been morsels worth dangling in front of the Russian operatives.

In fact, *Scorpion*'s ETA in Norfolk was already looking questionable. Sometime during its second Naples visit, Commander Slattery had received orders for the SOSUS mission, and was a bit worried about the effect they would have on morale. At a naval officers' reception thrown shortly before *Scorpion* began its Atlantic crossing, Slattery and his executive officer, David Lloyd, shared their concerns with Captain James Bradley, the Navy's head of submarine intelligence, and the man who'd issued the orders. The crew was fatigued, Slattery explained. In most instances men had several weeks, or even longer, to psychologically prepare themselves for an extended patrol. But their stint in the Med had come with just twelve days' notice after the *Seawolf* was damaged in an underwater collision—and as *Scorpion* herself had been returning from a month-long antisubmarine warfare exercise in the Caribbean. Altogether, they'd spent the better part of the last five months at sea, and were ticking off days on the calendar till their homecoming. Slattery felt that a delay would be tough for them to swallow.

But while he was honest about his reservations, Slattery knew it was risky voicing them to a superior. The sub was Slattery's first command, and he'd only held it for several months. As a young skipper in an intensely competitive career environment, it would have been unwise of him to argue too strongly. Once orders were handed down from a higher-up, there was very little chance they'd be rescinded.

As Slattery and Lloyd expected, Bradley listened politely but didn't back off. The war games that were to have followed *Scorpion*'s visit to Turkey remained on tap for the first week of May. After their conclusion, she'd move on toward Gibraltar with Marquez, the SOSUS expert, aboard. Since the mission was to be conducted en route to Gibraltar, the odds were good that it wouldn't result in *Scorpion* losing much headway. If she wasn't home as scheduled on May 23, her return would still surely fall within days of the mark.

XVI

On April 28, *Scorpion* departed the Gulf of Naples and took an easterly course for her hunter-killer exercises in the Aegean Sea. Code-named Operation Dawn Patrol, they were conducted over a ten-day period that passed smoothly overall—although there would be a tense incident with a Soviet destroyer in early May, after the sub surfaced to exchange messages with another U.S. boat, the Tench-class diesel USS *Cutlass*.

The warship's appearance in an area where *Scorpion* was running NATO ops was no coincidence. *Scorpion*'s trackers excelled at their jobs, and she'd been a major nuisance to the Russians right up into her last few weeks in the Med. For their part, Soviet captains were known to stake aggressive territorial claims by provoking face-offs with U.S. subs, and in this instance wanted to make a clear point.

The destroyer had been hunting *Scorpion* through the waters near Crete when it made its move. Guns trained on the sub, it made several feints at ramming her hull, one rush bringing it to within a hundred feet of the submarine's prow. But *Scorpion*'s crew didn't blink, and a call from her radio room brought a task force of American fighter aircraft roaring in to warn off the destroyer, which finally pulled away to end the confrontation. "It took us two days to get rid of that big tin can," wrote twenty-two-year-old Torpedoman's Mate Third Class Robert Violetti in a letter home to his mother.

The remaining days of the Dawn Patrol operation passed without incident. On May 10, *Scorpion* was officially detached from the U.S. Sixth Mediterranean Fleet and shifted over to the control of SUBLANT's Submarine Group Naples. She was now headed off on her SOSUS assignment and her eventual trip home.

3. BAITED

"While our civilian population worried about Armageddon, submarine crews at sea did all they could to stave it off, living on the edge constantly. On the strategic level of this epic struggle, no one did more than our submarine force, the submarines and their crews, to win the Cold War."

—*Rear Admiral Robert R. Fountain USN (Ret.)*

I

LOCATED IN THE ATLANTIC OCEAN OFF THE AFRICAN coast, the Canary Islands are a familiar sight to seamen plying the ancient maritime trade lanes between Europe, Asia, and North America, routes that are likewise known for their historical importance to naval strategists. In early April 1968, the curiosity of U.S. intelligence experts was aroused when their reconnaissance flights and Keyhole photographic satellites spotted a group of three Russian surface vessels and a NATO-designation Echo II nuclear-powered guided missile submarine conducting mysterious actions in the open sea, about four hundred miles southwest of the volcanic island chain. A month later, the flotilla continued to linger in the area, baffling analysts with its movements.

At the time, Russian exercises were mostly restricted to sheltered inlets, bays, and rivers closer to their homeports and guarded to the best possible extent from the scrutiny of America and its NATO allies. But now the Soviets were floating weather balloons, or what appeared to be weather balloons, in full view of American observers.

The nuclear sub only made things more interesting. With its complement of eight Shaddock antiship missiles, an Echo II—designed for the sole purpose of attacking American aircraft carrier battle groups—would be a valued target of surveillance to the Anti-Submarine Warfare Force, Atlantic Fleet (ASWFORLANT), whose air and naval units were already monitoring Russian submarine activities in the wide swath of ocean between the Canaries and the Azores. Code-named Bravo 20, this operation had been underway for a while, often with the participation of SUBLANT's nuclear fleet boats.

Rear Admiral Philip A. Beshany, deputy chief of submarine warfare operations, would later say that the focus of new concern was the possibility of the Soviets developing a way to support their warships and submarines without requiring access to foreign bases for supplies. Most authorities on Soviet marine operations, however, came to dismiss his explanation. Refueling and resupply at sea had been taking place since before World War II. In wartime, a lumbering support ship wouldn't last more than a couple of days before it was discovered and sunk. On its face, it made little or no sense that the ships traveled 1,500 miles out of the Mediterranean to perform experiments that could have been done in friendlier waters. And what of those balloons?

Intelligence experts in Washington were convinced there had to be some other reason for the conspicuous presence of the ships—and some means of determining what it was. The Special Naval Collection Program (SNCP) oversaw and directed a range of submarine espionage operations under the code name Holystone, and checking out the oddball Soviet flotilla fell under its purview.

In those days, America always kept five to seven submarines in the region of the Mediterranean. Their six-month tours usually overlapped, with one sub transiting the Great Circle Route between the Mediterranean and the continental United States every four weeks. It would be easy enough to divert to the Canaries a submarine on its way home. And the Soviets were aware of this.

The Soviets also held some other critical pieces of information, namely the means and patterns of U.S. aerial reconnaissance in the region. Their radar could detect U.S. spy planes long before they came into visual range. They knew the exact orbital schedule of the KH-8 photo intelligence birds. And, as was often the case in those days of tag-you're-it Cold War intrigue, their American intelligence counterparts knew they knew.

While Soviet vessels normally conducted their experiments at night when observation was most difficult, the maneuvers near the Canaries were peculiar exceptions. The flotilla would launch its balloons in broad daylight and wait until the last minute to bring its movements to a halt, breaking off right before U.S. naval aircraft or satellites approached—almost as if wanting to be noticed. This behavior added to the questions surrounding the flotilla's presence. Were the ships playing a game? Taunting their observers with false attempts to avoid detection? If so, why? What other activities might the Russians be concealing with their shadow dance?

A former *Scorpion* sailor who'd been aboard the boat for several Cold War Holystone missions into Soviet territorial waters would compare the tantalizing ship movements to a matador's waving of his red cape in the bull ring: Hey look, here I am, come and get me!

Indeed, Washington's intelligence experts were far more intrigued by the flotilla's peculiar actions than its composition. Of the four vessels only the sub was designed for battle. Two of the others were hydrographic survey ships, the third a rescue and support tug. All three surface craft had acoustical signatures—distinct sonar voiceprints—that had been recorded by past spy missions and were easily identifiable to ASWFORLANT's sonobuoys, making them of little or no intrinsic military interest. Moreover, if unusual electronic activity—radio transmissions from the Soviet vessels, for instance—had been a major concern to analysts, it would have been standard procedure to dispatch an EC-121 or P-3 Orion reconnaissance plane that could observe the ships from the air.

But a submarine held a significant advantage over the floating buoys and spy planes: it could steal up on the Russian ships for a close-up look at whatever was going on with them. Checking out the Echo II would essentially amount to an added bonus.

Although some Navy officials later insisted that getting a sub out to the area was routine, their assertion was contradicted by one of the principals involved in the intelligence-gathering process, a ranking officer who'd kept an eye on the Russian vessels for weeks.

"We recognized the high desirability of getting over there and taking a look at them," Captain Walter N. "Buck" Dietzen recalled. When the flotilla was spotted, Dietzen was the Pentagon assistant to Rear Admiral Philip Beshany, deputy chief of naval operations for submarine warfare. "I was salivating in the [Pentagon's] corridors to find out what they were doing," he would add.

The desire of which Dietzen spoke would soon translate into a direct, highly classified order that came down to the USS *Scorpion* from the Navy's top-most echelons. Even today, one can see why she was picked for the mission. With her speed and quiet stealth, the Skipjack-class submarine was ideally suited for snooping on the Soviet vessels. She had done that sort of thing often enough, and would be in their general neighborhood anyway.

Vice Admiral Arnold F. Schade, commander of the Atlantic Fleet's submarine force, would have the communiqué sent out to *Scorpion* from the message room at operational headquarters in Norfolk.

It isn't known whether John Walker Jr. was on duty at the time. It's also moot. Walker had easy access to the vault where the coded dispatch was filed, and would have been aware of it.

He was always on the furtive lookout for exactly that sort of thing.

II

Whether aboard a submarine or surface vessel, sailors didn't have many ways to spend their downtime while traversing the high seas. Among *Scorpion's* crewmen "best beard" contests were a standby, since shaving was not a requirement during patrols. The winners would receive cash prizes, with judging of the contest held toward the end of the deployment. There would be many categories—bushiest beard, fullest beard, and most artistic beard.

Gregg Pennington, a former *Scorpion* nuke, remembered some of his shipmates getting creative in their efforts to relieve the monotony. On one patrol, they decided to fashion rings out of English half-crown coins they'd picked up on liberty in Holy Loch, Scotland. This took patience, resourcefulness, and no small measure of clandestine assistance from various quarters throughout the sub. Spoons vanished from the galley and magically reappeared in crewmen's pockets. Using them as makeshift jeweler's hammers, the men would tap the inside curves of the spoons on the edges of the coins until they flattened out to a desired width. Next, machinist's mates were enlisted to drill out the centers of the coins. As a finishing touch, the amateur ringsmiths would impart a sparkling smoothness to their handiwork with small metal files.

Generally, though, the men would find more mundane diversions. When a sailor completed his watch and needed to unwind before turning in, he would grab a bite to eat from the galley and then kill a couple of hours playing card games, checkers, or Acey Deucy with some of the other off-duty crewmen—either that or catch a movie in the crew's mess. As a rule the interior communications electricians would run the movies. The IC men were responsible for a wide range of equipment, including the ship's projector.

Before going off on deployment, a vessel always loaded up on film reels from a movie exchange on base. Since a nuclear-powered sub would be at sea for two or three months at a time, it brought along between sixty and seventy movies, ensuring that a new film could be screened every night—at least during those first couple of months. If you got a really good film, it might be shown two or three times a day. As long as the sub wasn't in dangerous waters, and the IC man got permission from Control to burn a flick, it didn't matter how often the movies were shown.

The film exchange process was uncomplicated when ships were in their homeports. After a vessel returned from patrol, a member of its crew would bring the reels in, and someone from a departing ship would promptly check them out again. You couldn't be too choosy if you were assigned to acquire the movies but you'd try to get hold of the latest ones to be had. *Victory at Sea*, produced for NBC television in the 1950s, was a perennial favorite. Presented in twenty-six half hour installments, its tales of World War II naval battles bore stirring titles like *Melanesian Nightmare, Full Fathom Five,* and *Suicide for Glory*. For Navy crewmen the action hit close to home.

Even so, a steady diet of the same films would get miserably boring if a patrol ran longer than expected—as was frequently the case. Whenever feasible, then, movie swaps would be arranged at the sub's various ports of call, with the reels sometimes changing hands on the ship's tender. Seldom were the times when they were passed on between vessels at sea, a maneuver that was hardly as effortless as requisitioning them from an onshore exchange. If a ship-to-ship transfer did take place, it usually would be the incidental benefit of a relay with a far more serious—and perhaps even secret—military purpose.

Scorpion was on a westerly course toward Gibraltar and the Atlantic when her sonar picked up the USS *Bigelow* (DD-942), a Forrest Sherman–class destroyer out of Naval Station Mayport, Florida. About to begin a Mediterranean deployment, *Bigelow* was doing fuel-testing with the jet aircraft fuel JP-4, which contained additives the Navy hoped would improve the all-weather efficiency of ships' boilers. But the volatile JP-4 burned at such a rapid rate that the experiment failed, and *Bigelow* had needed to stop and replenish in Bermuda, and then again in the Azores, where it would spend two days taking on fuel and burning it, as Electrician Third Class Lawrence Brooks said, "almost as fast as they pumped it from the truck."

Riding gently on the clear, calm waters of the Atlantic under a daytime sky, the *Bigelow* was approaching the Strait of Gibraltar when a call to General Quarters blared out over the 1MC, or shipboard intercom. The GQ kicked the vessel into a state of combat readiness and, suddenly, all hands aboard, on duty or off, were hustling to battle stations. Guns were loaded. Torpedoes and missiles were readied for launch. Only a handful of men on the destroyer besides the officers would have had time to be informed what sort of hostile, or potential hostile, had been encountered. When the alert sounded, no explanations were given. Everyone and everything geared up for action.

Terry R. McCue's duty station during GQ was the radio room. Sitting at his console, his headphones on, he was among those aboard the *Bigelow* who knew nothing of the reason for the high alert. His job, like that of the other radiomen in the shack with him, was simply to remain at his station, isolated from the rest of the crew, and await whatever orders might come down from his superiors.

He would not remember how long the GQ lasted. But after a while the all-clear sounded and was received with a sigh of relief in the shack, as it was throughout the rest of the ship.

Later, McCue would be told that the GQ sounded due to contact with an American nuclear sub, the USS *Scorpion*. After she was identified, the alert was called off. According to his information, *Scorpion* was headed out of the Med for home on a track almost directly opposite that of the destroyer.

Lawrence Brooks, who was stationed in *Bigelow*'s IC room, remembered the sub and the destroyer engaging in some drills—approaches, evasive maneuvers, and so on. The possibility exists, then, that *Bigelow*'s commanding officer had gotten advance notice that he'd be crossing paths with the submarine and called battle stations so his crew could bone up on antisubmarine warfare tactics. Or it may be that the operations were conducted on the spur of the moment after the submarine was determined to be nonthreatening. Be that as it may, soon after each established its identity using its radio call name—*Bigelow*'s was "Decipher," and *Scorpion*'s was "Brandywine"—the two vessels rendezvoused on the surface. Their captains had arranged for a highline transfer.

Yeoman First Class Ed Washburn was the skipper's phone talker on *Bigelow*'s 1JV, a sound-powered phone circuit from a lookout station to the control and command center. That placed him with the captain on the destroyer's bridge, and among the sailors who saw *Scorpion* make her portside approach, matching speed and direction with *Bigelow* like a leviathan that had risen from the deep, sheets of foam streaming off her curved black flanks, a small group of men gathered on the narrow bridge atop a sail bearing a light gray Atlantic camouflage scheme. Beneath the men were her diving planes. The distinctive dorsal fin that marked her as a Skipjack nuclear attack sub was behind them, projecting down her spine to the aft section.

Then Washburn heard the call over the ship's intercom. "*Scorpion alongside!*" And echoing across the water from the sub: "*Bigelow alongside!*"

With the vessels about a hundred feet apart, their skippers

greeted each other using their bullhorns. Then a boatswain's mate on *Bigelow* attached a large pulley to an anchoring pole on the deck as his counterpart aboard the submarine did the same. *Scorpion* displaced 3,500 tons of water submerged, and over 3,000 on the surface. The fully loaded destroyer displaced 4,050 tons. That resulted in a massive combined displacement of seawater as the ships moved side by side, much of it squeezed into a pressurized channel between their hulls—and the longer they stayed close together the more agitated that channel would become.

As Yeoman Washburn watched from the destroyer's bridge, one of *Scorpion*'s crewmen fed a propellant charge into the breech of a line gun—it resembled an ordinary rifle, but had a metal canister under its barrel, and a large, ball-shaped projectile fitted over the bore. The stock braced against his shoulder, he aimed for the *Bigelow* and pulled its trigger. There was a loud explosive crack and a belch of smoke from the gun as the ball rocketed from the barrel and the line attached to it came whipping out of its metal canister.

A moment later, the ball landed on the destroyer's deck and was snatched up by one of its crewmen. On *Scorpion*'s bridge, someone tied a rope to the end of the line, and the entire rig was pulled onto the destroyer—a task that required several sailors, not only because of the rope's added weight, but because that heaviness caused its slack to tumble into the sea as it was paid out and become saturated with water, taking on even greater weight.

But the rope wasn't all that had to be pulled onto the destroyer. Once most of it was across, a steel cable was attached to the line on the submarine, making it still more of a burden as it was hauled aboard *Bigelow* and then drawn through the big pulleys on both vessels.

The highline now established, a trolley basket was hooked to a third, smaller rolling pulley mechanism, or block, and sent across to the *Bigelow* with its first load of films in either canvas or plastic sacks. Again, it would take a number of men to pull the basket across from ship to ship.

For a highline transfer to succeed, the cable must remain taut and the vessels on station. But that is far easier said than done. If *Scorpion* and *Bigelow* were moving at the recommended speed of 12 knots, a 1 degree course variation by either vessel would have moved them twenty feet sideways per minute. To prevent this listing, they needed to maintain a constant position and engine speed—something that took careful eyeballing from the conning officers, and a deft, continuous series of adjustments from their steering personnel. Meanwhile, as the trolley rolled from ship to ship, the seawater between them brewed ever more agitatedly around their keels, making the vessels pitch and yaw, tossing cold geysers of spray onto their decks.

From where he stood at the rail of the destroyer, Ed Washburn, who'd never before witnessed a highline transfer, found it a tremendous thrill. Sailors weren't used to seeing another large vessel come that close to them at sea. If even a minor foul-up occurred, he knew the line might sag into the water and dunk the trolley—films and all—into the swift, roiling pressure currents between the sub and destroyer. A bigger mistake and they would grind up against each other in what might prove the maritime equivalent of a fender-bender, or worse, a seriously damaging collision.

It was, in fact, an effort that hardly seemed worth its risk if all that was exchanged were some movies for the crews' entertainment. Washburn and his shipmate Phil Pagnoni, who took a snapshot of *Scorpion* from the bridge, would wonder in later years if some other material accompanied the movies across the line—and if the *Bigelow*'s rank and file simply weren't made privy to what it was. Could the movie exchange have been an afterthought, or even a clever ruse to obscure the sharing of a very different type of cargo? From his yeoman's experience, Washburn knew of all sorts of intel that Navy vessels would not transmit via radio if there was

even a suspicion the Soviets might be able to intercept it. A movie
transfer that appeared to be hastily arranged via the ship-to-ship
communications could well have been meant to throw potential
snoops off the true reason for the highline. Considering the top
secret mission that had occupied *Scorpion* since May 10, it is possible that Washburn guessed correctly, and that the highline transfer
was actually carried out to expedite the delivery of intelligence to
higher-ups in the Mediterranean.

Whatever its purpose, the exchange went off without a hitch.
With the lines disconnected and hauled back aboard *Scorpion*, the
men standing on the bridges of the two vessels gave each other
waves of farewell, and then resumed their respective courses.

As he watched the submarine pull away into the distance, and
then slide beneath the water until all sight and sound of her was
lost, Washburn was figuring he would remember that day for the
excitement of the transfer. He could not possibly have guessed at
the tragic associations it would soon bring to him and the almost
three hundred other sailors onboard the Mediterranean-bound
USS *Bigelow*.

III

At about 7:30 P.M. Greenwich Mean Time on May 17, six days
after detaching from the Sixth Fleet, *Scorpion* was somewhere near
Gibraltar when her radio mast pierced the chop to pick up a continuous, cyclic stream of UHF messages that submariners called
the skid—verbal shorthand for "schedule," as in scheduled transmission.

This coded broadcast loop would be recorded, decrypted, and
checked for dispatches that pertained to the receiving vessel. If
there were messages on the skid for *Scorpion*, this would be her last
opportunity to check it for a while.

The transmission carried bad news from Norfolk for one of the crewmen: twenty-five-year-old Sonarman First Class Bill Elrod's pregnant wife, Julie, had experienced a miscarriage.

Commander Slattery considered the sonarman's personal situation along with a potentially serious medical issue that had cropped up involving another crew member, Interior Communications Electrician Joseph Underwood. Over the past few days Underwood had developed an upper respiratory infection, and Doc Saville's antibiotics weren't doing anything to knock it out of him. The congestion in his lungs had gotten severe enough that Underwood was hacking blood, and Doc worried he might have contracted tuberculosis. If his ailment proved to be TB, it could become a serious problem, spreading through the sub to take down her entire crew, many of whom were already reporting flulike symptoms.

Slattery had a decision to make. The sub was just hours east of Naval Station Rota, Spain—a base in the province of Cádiz on Spain's southwestern Atlantic coast, beyond the Strait of Gibraltar. Rota had supported U.S. and NATO ships for over a decade, and *Scorpion* had spent some time there on her way into the Med two months earlier. Transferring Elrod and Underwood off the boat at Rota would solve both the humane problem and the health problem. As importantly for Underwood, Rota's large military hospital had the staff and facilities to test for TB and treat his symptoms.

By 9:00 P.M., *Scorpion* had made a swift passage from the Med into the Atlantic. In her crew spaces, men bent over sheets of notepaper and dashed off letters to their families, their penmanship scratchy and uneven from their own haste to put down their thoughts and the shaking of the boat as it sliced toward Rota at 18 knots. The crew had been told they would be stopping at Rota to discharge Elrod and Underwood via tugboat, and that a sack of mail would be leaving the sub with them.

What Commander Slattery hadn't announced was the imminent departure of a third man—one who wasn't even officially ever aboard *Scorpion*. His mission with the SOSUS project complete, Tony Marquez had been due to report to Norfolk along with the ship's company. The unscheduled stop at Rota gave him another option. Slattery invited him to stay with the boat or leave with the others.

Marquez was a skimmer, someone whose background was as a sonar tech on surface craft. This was his first experience traveling aboard a submarine, and he preferred making his way to the States by more routine means of transport. Also, given his status as a rider, he'd likely have been informed of a development most of the crew did not yet know—namely that *Scorpion* would not be heading straight home after departing Rota. Admiral Schade's orders to detour to the Canaries had been transmitted on the skid, and that surveillance was bound to extend the sub's voyage home by several days at the very least.

All that weighed, Marquez decided a short air hop from Rota to the States would suit him fine.

"I've had enough'a you guys," he said with a laugh. "I'm gonna fly—it'll get me back a lot quicker."

Commander Slattery and his officers couldn't have argued with him. They'd already been handed one last-minute assignment en route to Gibraltar. Now another had come down right on its heels, a second unexpected mission just when they and their tired crew were set to go home. It would surely add to the general discontent onboard the sub, but there was nothing to be done about it. You didn't get to choose your orders, and they were understandable from Schade's perspective. The opportunity to investigate the Soviet flotilla wouldn't last forever, and it was important to send a sub out there right away. *Scorpion* was close by, her men were topnotch, and that made her the obvious choice.

Sometime between midnight and 1:00 A.M., *Scorpion* surfaced off Rota outside the breakwater at the harbor entrance. Water streaming from her bridge, she was "on the step," her stern planes in a 10 to 15 degree dive position to stabilize her on the surface. Within minutes she was met by the tug, and the two regular crewmen and Marquez disembarked with the mail sack and a separate bundle of classified communications.

Scorpion was ready to slip underwater and head off toward the Russian grouping.

Almost.

IV

Before going ashore to Rota, the men discharged from *Scorpion* would transfer from the tug to the submarine tender USS *Canopus* out in the harbor. On *Canopus,* they received temporary berthing and, in Underwood's case, prompt medical attention. Engineman Second Class Tom Carlough, who had completed his service period on *Canopus* and was preparing to leave for Air Controller School at New London, Connecticut, later that morning, recalled hearing that three sailors had come aboard because they were too sick to make the Atlantic crossing to the States.

Once on the tender, Underwood was examined by Submarine Squadron 16 Medical Officer Andrew Urbanc, who decided to assign the communications man a bed in sick bay and monitor his condition. After a few days of treatment and observation Underwood's health showed great improvement and he was cleared to return to the States. The infection he'd contracted wasn't TB after all.

Finding a flight home for the *Scorpion* sailors would be no problem. As the gateway between the Atlantic and the Mediterranean, Rota was ideally suited for maintenance and resupply of Polaris ballistic missile submarines. Their Blue and Gold crews would often make the change at Rota while a boat was tied up and having work done on her. A regular slate of flights carried the Polaris replacement crews between Rota and the United States.

Soon, Elrod, Marquez, and Underwood were winging home

from the Spanish naval base, its palm trees and warmth left behind. Though Marquez may or may not have taken the same flight as the other two men, he would remember a conversation with Elrod in which he learned of Julie's "fetal distress."

The trip from Rota to Norfolk took about nine hours. Before the Navy even announced *Scorpion's* arrival date, Elrod and Underwood were in Norfolk waiting for their shipmates.

V

The Soviet embassy in Washington was an old, gated stone mansion on 16th Street, just four blocks north of the White House. The residency doubled as the KGB's Washington station, with over a third of its one hundred staffers serving as spies operating out of offices crammed into its fourth and uppermost story.

Between 1967 and 1970 three agents at the station would spend much of their time with the material obtained from John Walker before it was forwarded overseas to Lubyanka, the KGB's main headquarters in Moscow.

One of the agents was Yuri Linkov, the tall Russian who had met Walker outside the Zayre department store to lay the groundwork for their working relationship, and would remain his handler for years to come. Though Walker during that time didn't know his name, Linkov scouted their dead drop sites, retrieved Walker's packages of classified documents, and drove them back to the embassy for inspection.

The man to whom Linkov directly reported was a Leningrad native named Oleg Kalugin. With his sharp, handsome features, astute blue eyes, and blondish hair swept back from his high forehead in a widow's peak, the thirtyish Kalugin was a linguist and journalist who had spent a year studying at Columbia University in New York, and held diplomatic status as the embassy's "second secretary and press attaché," a cover that aided him in cultivating relationships with many members of the U.S. news media. In his capacity as head of Line PR, the Soviets' political intelligence department, Kalugin managed the cases of some of the KGB's most valuable moles in the American government and military. John Walker was of unrivaled value among them.

Day by day, hour after hour, Kalugin would sit behind the closed door of his office to review the bountiful top secret documents supplied by the industrious Walker, drawing upon his fluency in English to translate, sort, and organize them. Each and every one of the dead drops Linkov mapped out had required Kalugin's authorization, subject only to a final nod of approval from the station chief himself—the third major KGB figure involved in the Walker operation, Boris Aleksandrovich Solomatin.

Solomatin, who held the official role of counselor at the embassy, was a chain-smoker with a strong taste for alcohol and espionage. Shrewd and untiring, he routinely worked twelve-hour days and had little tolerance for any agent who fell short of his personal example of doggedness. In the two years since Kalugin had been assigned to the Washington station, he had impressed Solomatin with his own diligent work ethic and attention to detail. It was to the gruff, old-guard Communist ideologue that Kalugin largely owed his rise to the top of the political intelligence department.

In reviewing the deluge of Walker material, Kalugin and his boss gave foremost emphasis to the prioritization of individual pieces of intelligence for delivery to Lubyanka. The total of each haul was too voluminous to be sent in its entirety. It only made sense, then, to send the timeliest material first via coded telegraph, and courier the rest to Moscow in sealed diplomatic pouches, which were exempt from international customs inspections. In this facet of the Walker case, Kalugin relied heavily on the senior officer's judgment. Despite his fluency in English, the military jargon and shorthand used in the documents could be confusing to him on occasion. Solomatin, however, possessed an unfailing, even uncanny ability to get to the nub of it, perhaps owing in part to his own background as a soldier.

It was probably Solomatin who, with Kalugin's input, invented Walker's cover story. As imparted to him by Linkov, the story went like this:

Walker would maintain he'd begun his career as a spy in December 1967—as long as one year after it really started—when he took an impulsive cab ride to the Russian embassy in Washington. There was an elaborate part of the account straight out of an espionage novel—and perhaps of Walker's own invention—that involved him slipping through the embassy's electronic gate as it was about to close behind an exiting diplomatic car, shouldering past a guard, and walking through the building's front door. He would then say that he'd pushed right up to a female receptionist and insisted on speaking to the man in charge of security.

"I'm a naval officer," Walker would claim to have told the man when he appeared, flashing the KL-47 key lists in his face to establish his credibility. "I'd like to make some money and I'll give you some genuine stuff in return."

Walker fit the KGB's recruitment profile of a spy almost to the letter. He was greedy, in a financial predicament that made him susceptible to being compromised, and egomaniacal. The Russians knew that their cover story portrayal of him as an audacious rogue—someone who had disregarded Soviet embassy security to assert his presence upon the KGB—would appeal to his massive ego.

They also would have considered him bright enough to understand that the Russians wouldn't have bothered to cook up their artificial version of events and its accompanying chronology without good cause, and that deniability would be at the heart of their motivation. Just to make sure the point was driven home, Linkov may well have stressed that his adherence to the story would be to the shared benefit of all parties involved in their dealings.

Timing was a critical element. Walker was never to divulge that he'd provided information about the KW-7 Orestes unit before 1968. It is doubtful Linkov would have given Walker specific reasons why, and even unlikelier that the handler was high enough up the Soviet intelligence ladder to know why himself.

And so Solomatin and Kalugin had sifted through Walker's regular intelligence dead drops, immediately flagging the Orestes material for expeditious cable to Moscow. Information on longterm strategic planning would be of secondary import, but there wouldn't have to be much delay getting it to Lubyanka. Envoys constantly shuttled to and from Moscow and the United States. Once the haul of important information from a dead drop was identified, it was possible that no more than a day or two would separate the cabling of a high-priority U.S. key list or deployment order, and the hand delivery of a CIA or NSA white paper on America's long-range geopolitical goals.

The Orestes key lists and technical literature, which included up-to-date instructions for modifying the cipher boxes issued after North Korea seized the USS *Pueblo*, would have been immediately available to the Soviets. The Orestes employed the most modern technology available to the U.S. code makers, replacing the older encryptor's rotors and wiring with punch cards and transistors. At some point around 1967, it had become the primary encryptor for all four branches of the U.S. armed services—the Army, Marine Corps, Air Force, and Navy. It was used by America's military forces in Vietnam, by its intelligence community, and by its NATO allies. The Fleet Broadcasting System, which transmitted ship-to-shore operational orders to every Navy vessel at sea, had replaced the KL-47 with Orestes boxes on 80 percent of its surface ships and almost all the vessels in the Atlantic Fleet Submarine Force.

At each dead drop, John Walker would provide the Russians with a copy of a four-page booklet that was distributed to U.S. and NATO communications centers and contained roughly a week's worth of Orestes key codes, with a new code to be input on a daily basis.

As early as February or March of 1967, Walker would pass on the information about fixes being made to the Orestes boxes. Around the same time, he would have turned over all the messages in SUBLANT's vaults regarding the Pentagon's interest in the Soviet flotilla off the Canaries.

Later, he supplied the Russians with Admiral Schade's orders detouring *Scorpion* to investigate the vessels—orders that had been sent from his Norfolk headquarters and may well have been placed directly in Walker's hands for transmission to the submarine. He also turned over the decoded printout of a long, patchy situation report Commander Slattery transmitted from aboard *Scorpion* to confirm he was on track to investigate the Soviet grouping.

In that series of messages was *Scorpion*'s last known position, and the route she was taking to her surveillance station.

VI

The North African nation of Algeria is five hundred miles east of Rota in the Mediterranean passage. Once considered NATO's southern flank, the Mediterranean in the 1960s had come up for grabs in the struggle for Cold War dominance as the Soviets' regional foothold expanded. Only three years after *Scorpion*'s activities with the Sixth Fleet, NATO commander Admiral Horacio Rivero Jr. would declare that "The Mediterranean, which was for NATO part of the zone of the interior, a rear area, is now within the battle zone."

That "battle zone" extended from Egypt in the eastern Mediterranean to the Strait of Gibraltar. In it Soviet-aligned nations had opened their arms to uncounted military and KGB advisors, missile bases, airstrips accommodating a hundred fighter and reconnaissance planes, and coastal naval facilities that berthed be-

tween forty and seventy assorted warships. Drawing support from
the Black Sea Fleet, the Soviet 5th Eskadra, or Mediterranean
Squadron, patrolled the Strait of Gibraltar with a contingent of
five hundred black berets—naval infantry—and thousands of regular navy personnel. The Eskadra's fluid size depended on operational and logistical requirements, with elements coming and
going between major Black Sea Fleet bases in Sevastopol, Bala-
clava, Poti, and Odessa.

Like American teenagers tricking out their cars with plastic fins
and spoilers, the Soviet Navy's ship designers were constantly
floating modified versions of older-class warships. U.S. observers
found it a headache keeping visual track of their movements—
even close up from aboard submarines, they were able to tell which
ship was which by using its sound signature better than they could
distinguish them from looking through a periscope. There were,
for example, a large number of Kotlin-class destroyers, and these
served as test beds for a variety of weapons systems. One variant,
the Bravvy, was itself the prototype for eight missile project con-
versions. Because of the protean size and composition of the
Mediterranean squadron, NATO's attempts to tally the vessels in
the region at any given time were, at best, inexact.

About when *Scorpion* left Rota on May 18, a Soviet warship
and an oil replenishment vessel embarked on a westward journey
from their anchorage in Algiers, roughly following the course of
the American sub. According to a Defense Intelligence Agency report on the Soviet Mediterranean Naval Force for the month of
February 1968, the combat vessel was a four-thousand-ton
Krupny-class destroyer measuring 455 feet from stem to stern. A
second unreported warship would either leave Algiers with the
Krupny or meet up with it at sea. This ship was a slightly larger
Kanin-class vessel. Both vessels carried a full load of supplies,
equipment, and armaments.

Finally, the DIA's Mediterranean supplement to its February

report lists two oilers: one Uda-class and one Kazbek-class vessel. The Uda-class ship was almost certainly the vessel dispatched with the warships. Ponderous Kazbeks were used for replenishment of battle groups, whereas the Uda had ample room in its storage tanks for the smaller task force it was to service.

The limiting speed of the three ships traveling in formation would have been set by the Uda, which is capable of doing 17 knots with its twin diesels cranked, fast enough for the Soviet group to have reached its destination according to plan.

In 1969, a Navy Court of Inquiry's findings of fact would determine that the Russian destroyers were around two hundred miles from *Scorpion* as she reached her final position of 35° north, 35° west in the middle of the Atlantic Ocean, southwest of the Azores. This would have put the sub far beyond the maximum range of the destroyers' artillery, missile launchers, and torpedoes—and therefore out of harm's way as far as the findings of fact was concerned. The U.S. and Soviet governments would later find this information to be very convenient.

VII

In the early hours of May 18, 1968, the Polaris ballistic missile submarine USS *John C. Calhoun* (SSBN-630) was about to leave Rota on covert patrol when several NATO-designation November-class Russian attack submarines were detected in the area.

The presence of the Novembers was no surprise. The easiest place to pick up a vessel's trail was at its start, and Soviet subs would often hide outside naval ports and attempt to shadow U.S. boomers—ballistic missile submarines—as they departed on operations. To thwart the pursuers, American attack submarines would be called on to run interference—make noise to mask the warships' acoustic signatures, get in the way of the enemy boats, anything that might confound them.

The *Calhoun*, a big, new 425-foot-long Polaris ballistic missile boat, would have been a prime target of Russian surveillance. Thus, with *Scorpion* already on hand to drop off Elrod, Underwood, and the SOSUS rider Marquez, Commander Slattery was asked to escort the *Calhoun* out of Rota's harbor as a precaution against the Novembers getting too close. *Scorpion* would then be free to swing south toward the Canaries.

The escort operation was uneventful as remembered by Bill Hyler, a nuclear engineer aboard the *Calhoun*. Hyler had known six members of *Scorpion*'s crew from his days at the Navy's Windsor, Connecticut, nuke school in 1965—Lieutenant Bill Harwi, and crewmen Richard Curtis Hogeland, Richard Englehart, Thomas Amtower, Steven Gleason, and John Sturgill.

When the two submarines parted ways in the blackness of the hours after midnight, leaving the safe harbor of Rota behind, Hyler didn't have any idea where *Scorpion* was heading, or even know that all those former classmates were aboard. But he was grateful the crew of another boat had put themselves at risk so that *Calhoun* could start off on her trip unmolested. He wouldn't forget this, which in a sense said everything about what it was to be in the Dolphin Brotherhood. It formed connections between men— some who'd met, some who might meet one day, and some who would never set eyes on each other—that would hold fast across time and distance, even to the furthest reaches of their separate journeys beneath the world's vast waters.

VIII

A few moments before 12:00 A.M. Greenwich Mean Time on May 22, 1968, *Scorpion*'s periscope and electronic intelligence mast slipped above the Mid-Atlantic swells to scan for possible threats. All was clear. Soon another antenna broke the surface, and with the boat leveled off at periscope depth, a communications techni-

cian down in the radio shack began to transmit her location and
headings to Naval Station Rota for relay to SUBLANT headquarters in Norfolk, Virginia.

As of one minute past midnight, the submarine's reported position was about 36° north and 25° west—coincidentally the same
waters where the legendary nineteenth-century ghost ship *Mary
Celeste* was first sighted absent her entire crew. Below her keel was
the East Azores Fracture Zone, an active tectonic fault line running from the Strait of Gibraltar to just north of Santa Maria island in the Azores archipelago.

A batch of additional coded messages would quickly follow the
radioman's situation report, streaming from his KW-7 Orestes encryption box. But the broadcast was hindered by static interference, and it wasn't until an hour later that Naval Communications
Station Nea Makri on the Greek peninsula chanced to acquire the
ultra-high-frequency signal. Unable to determine whether the
static was a random atmospheric phenomenon or originating from
some man-made electronic source in the vicinity of the sub, the
personnel at Nea Makri recommended that *Scorpion* continue
sending to them. They would then pass the messages on to their
intended recipient.

Meanwhile, *Scorpion* had picked up a mild southern drift due to
the Azores Current, which flows southeastward from the Grand
Banks, crosses the Mid-Atlantic Ridge, and then lazes east past
the African coast toward the Gulf of Cádiz. As the 0.5 knot current nudged the boat's starboard side, her veteran navigator, Lieutenant Commander John Stephens, compensated with a slight
northern course adjustment to keep her headed west past Santa
Maria toward her destination.

Now well south of the Great Circle track taken by U.S. submarines transiting between their stateside bases and the Mediterranean, *Scorpion* resumed her clandestine passage with what sailors
called a sprint-and-drift, a repetitive pattern of running fast and

deep for a while, occasionally stopping to go shallow and carry on transmissions with Greece, then diving and kicking up her speed a few knots again. At 3:03 A.M., *Scorpion* suddenly broke off communications with Nea Makri and could not reestablish a link—the radio interference had followed her course and gotten too thick. She was within hours of reaching her operational objective and about to enter an area lined with Soviet diesel subs and surface units.

In Norfolk, Lieutenant John Roberts was at the receiving end of the initial message that Nea Makri forwarded from *Scorpion* to SUBLANT. Roberts, who would have received the communication from John Walker, always recalled that it included these explicit words from Commander Slattery:

"We are about to begin our surveillance of the Soviets."

IX

Toward dusk on May 22, *Scorpion* was cruising toward the Russian flotilla now 150 miles distant. After her rendezvous with the *Bigelow,* Commander Slattery had put the boat on a westerly course toward her target, and she was steadily closing in on it at a depth of 350 feet and a speed of 15 knots. While capable of traveling much faster, *Scorpion*'s present clip represented her tactical speed—the best time she could make and still retain the ability to detect enemy vessels before she herself was noticed.

Her depth range was also restricted. Prior to her departure for the Mediterranean, extensive work had been completed on *Scorpion*'s high-pressure seawater systems and pressure hull, requirements of the SUBSAFE program, a detailed quality control effort that the Navy had initiated in 1963. But five years later, with the military struggling with the manifold demands of Vietnam and the Cold War, time and money simply ran out before all of the SUBSAFE modifications could be installed. Critical components in the emergency blow system were deferred to a future shipyard visit. To offset the risks this presented, *Scorpion* would become a LID boat—one that was limited in depth to a maximum of five hundred feet—and Slattery complied with these restrictions.

As *Scorpion* moved along, the sea around her was mildly unsettled, with an overcast sky and winds blowing at 10 to 15 knots. On the Beaufort scale this is a Force 4 open sea state, described as a moderate breeze with "small waves becoming larger, and fairly frequent white horses." Mariners use the term "white horse" when they speak of a fast-moving wave with a crest that is broken and white with foam. On land, Beaufort advises, the wind will make branches tremble, blow dust up into the air, and sweep loose sheets of paper off tabletops.

If the weather held until *Scorpion* came within sight of the flotilla, Commander Slattery and his navigators knew it would fall well inside the effective parameters for a visual surveillance, though the running whitecaps, swelling to heights of between three and five feet, would make it a little tough for the sub to keep station at periscope depth without broaching—a sudden change in the boat's angle. Probably Slattery intended to order a slow cruise to within observation distance during the evening hours, and wait there to take advantage of the calmer seas that dawn typically brought before moving in for a closer look.

Still, *Scorpion* needed to get within about ten miles of the ships, and optimally three or four. Even in broad daylight, the ships wouldn't be discernible to her periscope operators beyond twelve miles, when the curvature of the earth would make sea and sky appear to bleed into a wide, seamless horizon. At that distance, the sub would also be too far away from the Russians for her electronic intelligence, or ELINT, mast to be effective.

Rising to periscope depth, *Scorpion* would glide up toward the Russians at low speed and take up position on the eastern side of the ships, keeping the sun behind her so it didn't reflect off the raised observation scope's glass or mirrors. The men would shut down all nonessential equipment, and that meant everything possible. They'd go to low power on the reactor pumps and the fan. They'd wear soft-soled shoes, or just their socks. They would move in quiet, the sub's head-on course to the ships giving her the smallest achievable profile in the water and creating the least amount of noise, since most noise emanated from her baffles—the propellers and machinery at her rear.

In the dimness out beyond the grouping, *Scorpion* would hover at periscope depth, doing 2 or 3 knots, the men in her conn continuing to observe its vessels through their eyepieces. Though Slattery's main focus would have been watching the maneuvers of the vessels, the sensitive ELINT antenna skimming just above the surface would distinguish any radio traffic or potential radars in use.

"The diving officer was just biting his nails," said a former fire control technician and qualified chief of the watch on a Skipjack. "He didn't want to broach, if you broach you're dead. . . . It was a very tense watch. I would get off duty and be exhausted. It was not physical. It was the mental strain of holding that boat on depth without showing ourselves."

The trickiest part of the surveillance would come at sunrise. As the sky brightened and rays of light penetrated the clear blue water, *Scorpion* would slip deeper beneath the surface, move in toward the ships, and then under-run them, photographing their hull bottoms and exterior propulsion mechanisms with the periscope. That accomplished, she would ascend to circle the vessels, raising the scope for short periods to photograph their topsides and whatever personnel might be on their decks. When she'd gotten enough information—or in the unfortunate event her targets' suspicions were aroused—*Scorpion* would dive and race off at maximum speed.

All this, of course, lay ahead. Mazzuchi and his navigators had logged the boat's current position at 35° north, 35° west, about 530 miles south of the city of Horta on the island of Faial, in the Azores archipelago. The African coastline, and the deserts of Morocco and the Spanish Sahara, were many miles west across the Atlantic. *Scorpion* would need to traverse a considerable stretch of open sea before she came remotely near the grouping.

The sound of an acoustical probe in the surrounding water, then, brought a jolt of shock and confusion to those aboard the sub. Every member of the crew could hear the pinging through her two-inch-thick metal hull. To a man, they grasped their immediate plight.

At their console forward of the control room, the sonar gang reported what Commander Slattery, in essence, already realized. An active sonar contact was close in.

Scorpion was a Skipjack-class submarine. That made her one of the fastest undersea vessels in the world—and Slattery ordered a retreat at once.

But it was already too late. The Soviet trap had been sprung. There would be no escape.

4. PIER 22

"Most submarine wives know that if it is overdue, it is gone."

—*Joan Cowan, widow of USS* Scorpion *crewman
and eighteen-year submarine veteran Machinist's
Mate First Class Robert James Cowan*

"All we ever wanted was an explanation. After the disaster
everything was covered up."

—*Barbara Barr Gillum, sister of* Scorpion
casualty Joseph A. Barr

I

ON MAY 9, 1968, ELEVEN DAYS AFTER *SCORPION* LEFT the Bay of Naples to participate in Dawn Patrol, Jerry Pospisil summed up in a single letter his yearning for home, his weariness with being at sea, and, in characteristic enlisted man's fashion, his determination to avoid getting short-shrifted on any portion of his leave:

> *This will be the last letter for sure. . . . I am not sure whether this will get mailed this afternoon or tomorrow. It will go by helicopter from the boat to either Crete or some carrier. From there it*

will go to you. I guess that it is possible that it won't get mailed at all, but I will write it with hope. I only wish that I could hide in the envelope along with the letter. This boat is really getting my goat the last couple of weeks. I'll be glad to get the heck off of here. I believe I told you about the leave policy the captain put out. They want me to write a letter stating that I will return to the ship on assigned duty days. If I wrote a letter like that, they could switch my duty days anytime they wanted, and I would end up with no days off. If I do write a letter it will be to the XO [executive officer] and not the engineer like they want. I told [Chief Electrician's Mate] Daniel Peterson I figured that the boat owed me the 15 days leave and, since I was going to come in every 3rd day, that as long as a duty electrician was aboard I should only have to come in for my watches.

After some further explanation of the restrictive policies that might cut into his leave, Pospisil broke off writing until the next day—May 10—when he made new mention of rumors circulating aboard the boat and expressed a deepening uncertainty about when he'd arrive in Norfolk.

There are so many rumors going around again today it is hard to tell when we will get in. The 24th is the earliest and the 30th is the latest. I will have duty on the 25th and 28th, so if that happens to be one of the dates we get home you might just as well stay at home and just wait for me to call. Then in the evening, you can come down.

Pospisil did not elaborate on the rumors, or offer any explanation for the possible delay in his arrival. But the timing of his remarks was curious, coming the same day *Scorpion* received word that it had completed its role in Dawn Patrol and could start on a homeward route. If anything, Pospisil's finding out that the anti-sub maneuvers had been wrapped up should have encouraged him that his return voyage was close to being on its original schedule.

Of course, enough had been going on aboard *Scorpion* to keep speculation flying. There was the presence of Tony Marquez, the SOSUS man. And Pospisil may have heard about the boat's covert mission to the Azores, or at least gotten wind that the sub would be diverting south once it passed Gibraltar and entered the Atlantic.

That was how it went on a submarine. Certain guys found out about things sooner, others later. Some of the enlisted men had to receive encrypted messages and decode them. Galley stewards would hear officers talking during meals and meetings. The scuttlebutt would start to bounce from section to section, and gang to gang. Pospisil was in the engineering crew and there was no need for him to know the details of reconnaissance or SOSUS missions. Every now and then an officer or one of the chiefs would come back into engineering and tell the guys that the boat was doing something special and that they'd have to watch the noise, but other than that they were kept in the dark. That was how operational security was maintained.

It's also possible Pospisil had heard the rumors back in Naples and decided not to hint at them to his wife, knowing that would only worry her—and that his mail was subject to heavy censorship anyway. After all, he'd made no mention of the sub's sticky encounter with a Russian surface warship during the Dawn Patrol operations.

On May 17, Pospisil wrote his final letter to Judy while *Scorpion* was steaming toward Rota for the debarkations of Elrod, Underwood, and Marquez. The entire crew had heard about Elrod's family tragedy and been advised a mailbag would accompany him aboard the tug coming out to pick him up.

Hi Darling,

     I know you won't expect this letter. One of the guys' wives had a miscarriage and lost a baby so we are transferring him to fly back to the states. This is [a] real quick transfer. We got the message about 6 P.M. and he will be transferred by around 1 A.M. I wish we would be real lucky and beat this mail home, but I know we won't.

     Arrival date is now the 24th at around 3:50 or 4 P.M. Naturally I have the duty the next day. We aren't going to be getting off early during the week either. My leave does start the 4th and end the 20th [of June].

     The boat will be going in the yard on the 10th and back out on the 20th. I will only have to go in to the boat about twice during this time.

     This letter may look like a little kid wrote it, but the boat is vibrating like a train. We departed the Med about 2 hours ago and are now back in the Atlantic heading for Rota. A couple of more hours and we will be on our way home at 18 knots.

     We still have a lot of water to cover so I hope we make it on time. If the boat doesn't fall apart we will make it.

     I look at your picture every hour and can't get you out of my mind. Sleep is getting short because no one can sleep due to excitement. It's funny that men get excited about something like getting in port.

     I don't have much time so all I can say is I love you and you'd better be ready when we get in. Miss you terribly.

Love,

Jerry

Pospisil was back to sounding confident that he'd make his May 24 arrival date, but it was doubtful he believed it. He would have still been hearing rumors about the diversion. There was, to be sure, a slim chance his impatience to get home had put him in denial of the odds; that he wanted so badly to make the original return date he'd convinced himself it was still somehow attainable even with the detour.

But Jerry was one of the more seasoned enlisted men aboard and had developed a healthy pragmatic nature. It's far more likely he just wanted to give Judy some encouragement. That's what guys did, and what was the harm? Why keep Judy's cogs turning?

The wives knew that anything their men put in the letters was subject to change, and always called the base info line to get updates on when a ship was coming in.

II

In 1968, Destroyer and Submarine Pier 22 was the narrowest of five or six piers jutting into the harbor mouth from Naval Station Norfolk. At the head of the pier, on its north side, sat the 535-foot bulk of the tender *Orion*—or Mother Onion, as sailors had playfully dubbed her.

Submarine tenders provided a complete range of maintenance and support services to the U.S. fleet, and *Orion* had been doing so for Norfolk's Submarine Squadron 6 since the early 1950s. A sub tender was at once a floating parts, repair, and resupply factory, and a way station of sorts that offered berthing, meals, and medical treatment for sailors waiting to go on reassignment. Spanning its length were large, specialized machine shops, weapons shops, electrical shops for sonar, navigation, and fire control equipment, optical shops to fashion lenses for periscopes, and foundries in which pipes, valves, panels, and other metal fixtures for a sub could be lathed, welded, and sometimes hastily improvised from scratch.

Robert McClain remembered an episode in the mid-1960s when the John F. Kennedy–appointed secretary of the navy, Fred Korth, was set to lead several top admirals on a tour of *Scorpion*. An attorney and financier by trade, Korth had been a longtime political wheel in the Democratic Party whose military service was with the Air Transport Command during World War II.

For COB Walter Bishop, this was relevant only because it meant Korth was a landlubber, whatever his official title might be. If the politico's show-and-tell was to proceed smoothly, Bishop decided, there would have to be some way for him to climb up from the bridge to the sail plane—a favorite exterior vantage for guests—without breaking his neck.

"We need a ladder, Fred Korth is coming onboard," he barked to McClain and some of the other hands. "Go to the tender and figure out how to make a ladder."

McClain snapped to it, and the guys in the metal shop came through for him, fashioning one out of stainless steel and adding a little chain ladder at the bottom so the bigwigs would have something extra to hang on to.

"And Fred Korth came up that thing, looked like a little monkey," McClain recalled with a chuckle. "Zipped right up there. And then we had a couple of admirals following him, and they were scared shitless."

While homeported, *Scorpion* always tied up to the mother ship about midway down the pier, on its south side. The USS *Shark* (SSN-591), another of the Navy's fleet of eight Skipjack-class nuclear submarines, would moor behind *Scorpion*. Occasionally the immense USS *Triton* (SSRN-586) would dock in front of her. When one or more of the subs were in port, cables could be seen running from plug-in connections along the concrete length of the pier, feeding power into the vessels when their reactors were in shutdown.

Once a nuclear-powered submarine pulled into its homeport it was hard to find anyone who wasn't eager for liberty—but the boat couldn't simply be left unmanned and unguarded at the pier. In-port watches were rotated daily and divided among the entire crew, enlisted and officer, qualified and unqualified in submarines.

During the day while *Scorpion* was in port, the crew would be onboard attending to repairs and routine upkeep. At the end of the day, they'd either go home or on liberty. This left the sub with those who had the watch and were onboard for the night: generally an officer, a belowdecks watch who'd roam the forward control spaces of the boat, and one maneuvering room watch responsible for keeping an eye on the shut-down reactor and maintaining electrical power for the boat from sources on shore.

With her reactor cooled and secured, the steam generators put in wet layup, and the bulk of her crew gone, the submarine would become cold and quiet. It was almost as if the life would go out of her—and in a sense, it did. Roaming her decks at night felt a little spooky.

Scorpion's in-port watches were toughest on the nuclear engineers, who were always short of qualified personnel to give them a break.

"After 1700, you were on your own," said a former *Scorpion* nuke. "For the next fifteen hours there was no one to relieve you for head breaks or go get anything to eat. I remember one time when I had to go to the head, and the only person qualified to relieve me was the captain. At about 0200 I asked the belowdecks watch to get him up to come relieve me, and he did it without question. At that time, asking to get the captain out of bed for that reason really scared me. All in all, it was better when we were at sea."

In May 1968, about a week before *Scorpion*'s scheduled return from her Med deployment, Barbara Foli began making plans to meet Vernon at the dock when the sub pulled in, periodically calling a special telephone hotline set up to provide Navy families with official estimates of ship arrivals. Her husband was among the crewmen who'd hastened to dash off letters home as *Scorpion* raced beneath the black surface of the Mediterranean toward Rota, and he'd tried to keep his message upbeat.

Vernon had always cared about his appearance, and told Barbara he'd been successfully exercising to shed some extra pounds. He'd also grown a mustache and could barely wait for Barbara's reaction to his new look. Vernon even sent along some photos of himself, but told her not to show them to anyone, since they'd been taken aboard the sub in a minor violation of regulations. He hoped to be home by Saturday the 25th, and would be giving her a little something special he'd picked up in Naples. While he admitted the guys were irritable and restless, he didn't get into any details, and Barbara put it down to their long months of being penned up together at sea. She'd never heard Vernon say anything negative about the sub or any of his shipmates. In fact, they'd always been a close-knit bunch.

Later, Barbara would wonder about the reasons for the crew's edginess. Might they have been related to *Scorpion*'s secret detour? It would have been just like Vernon to refrain from divulging the reasons, even circumspectly, in his letter, she thought. He was a loyal, trustworthy person, aware of his duty and obligations to the Navy. He'd never talk about things he wasn't supposed to.

At the time, though, the twenty-two-year-old Barbara remained optimistic that her husband's return was in the near offing. May 25 happened to be the day after their daughter, Holli's, first birthday, and she'd enthusiastically gone about making preparations to celebrate it—and Vernon's homecoming—together. Vernie loved eating ham more than anything except his mother's Italian cookies, loved it so much that when Barbara was nine months pregnant, she dreamed she gave birth to a roasted ham instead of a baby, something that hadn't seemed the slightest bit unusual to her until she awoke. Fortunately for Vernie—or so Barbara *hoped!*—she delivered a beautiful little girl, and not an oven roast, at the hospital. And she was sure Vernie wouldn't have any complaints about the canned ham she'd bought for their young family's reunion. In fact, she had opened it in advance of the occasion, figuring she could slice it up for sandwiches as soon as he got in.

Barbara was also busy prettying up for when she'd meet him at the pier. Eager to look her best, she had bought a spaghetti strap sundress and a hair fall of the type that was in style. Her mother's friend had shown her how to put the hairpiece in, and she had the summery outfit all fixed up and ready to go.

When a submariner's wife dialed Ship Arrivals on the phone— mention "the number" to her, and you didn't have to say *which* number, or explain any more about it, she'd know right off that was the one you meant—she would listen to a recorded tape of the vessels scheduled to return to port for whatever day you were calling, and extending on into the next week or so. The recording was regularly updated, and Barbara would sometimes check it as often as three times a day while awaiting confirmation of *Scorpion*'s expected due date. Since the Folis couldn't afford a telephone in their $35 a month apartment, she'd have to pack the baby into a stroller each time she checked, and then walk several blocks to use the pay phone in a small general store down alongside Ocean Boulevard.

On Monday, May 27, 1968, the families of *Scorpion*'s belated crew finally got a revised ETA over the Ship Arrivals number. *Scorpion*, they were assured, would pull into Norfolk at one o'clock that afternoon, two days later than expected.

It would be a soggy homecoming. Hampton Roads in spring can be one of the most temperate places in the country, its days warm and bright, the shore brushed with gentle saltwater breezes. But there is a fickleness to the weather. Some years as the incipient Atlantic hurricane season sucks moisture from the Gulf of Mexico and the Caribbean, and subtropical troughs whirl their way northeast to clash with cooler air masses, the Chesapeake Bay will rage with sudden, violent storms.

After a stretch of pleasant, sunny weather, a fierce northern storm front had swept in overnight. Awakening on Memorial Day, Norfolk residents looked out their windows to see a dense gray mantle of clouds across the sky as their yards and streets were lashed by heavy winds and a torrential downpour.

Barbara Foli would remember the horrible gale setting the tone for what would become one of the worst days she'd ever have to live through. She hadn't been feeling quite herself, anyway—several nights back, before Holli's birthday, she'd suffered an inexplicable spell, or whatever, that had kept her jumping in and out of bed for hours and thrown her into something of a panic—but waking up to that drastic, unexpected change in weather made it a struggle to pull her senses together.

It was just so dark out. So dark and wet and *ugly*.

Still, Barbara had her spaghetti-strap sundress ready, and had practiced doing her hair. With Vernie about to arrive, it seemed way too late to start choosing a whole new outfit, and she decided to fix herself up as she'd originally planned.

Dropping Holli off with a neighbor, she sloshed into her beat-up Karmann Ghia and headed out to the pier, the car's wipers *clock-clock-clocking* at their fastest, taking gainless swipes at the water coursing over the windshield.

At the parking lot, Barbara left the car and was promptly assailed by the wind blowing in across the river. It hurled rain into her eyes and tried to wrestle her umbrella from her hands as she opened it. Finally she turned against the driving gusts and walked backward toward the pier head.

On Pier 22 Barbara saw other women waiting in the rain. Some of them were huddled together in groups of two, three, and four. Others had brought their children, particularly those with older kids who'd gotten the holiday off from school. A few, like Barbara, had come alone.

Ruthann Hogeland, the wife of 22-year-old Electronics Technician First Class Richard Hogeland, was among the women who'd left the kids at home. She had last seen her husband in his hometown of Birmingham, Alabama, where the couple had gone to spend the previous Christmas with Richard's family. Ruthann had been expecting their second child, and because it was a difficult pregnancy, she'd stayed on in Birmingham after Richard's holiday leave ended.

On Sunday, January 29, 1968, Ruthann went into labor just as *Scorpion* was wrapping up her participation in the Aged Daddy V maneuvers off Florida's coast. The boat had pulled into Florida for the weekend, and Richard's brother was able to contact him there while the sub was in port.

Richard managed to get a few days' family leave so he could see his newborn daughter, but the tall, lanky southerner hadn't been able to afford the trip from Florida to Birmingham on his meager enlisted man's pay. Commander Slattery had loaned him the money out of his pocket, and told him to meet the sub back in Norfolk. A short while afterward, Richard would embark on the Mediterranean deployment with the rest of his *Scorpion* shipmates.

Now the welcomers tried to make the best of things. Festive balloons whipped about in the gusts, and colorful handmade signs and banners hung under the gunwales of the tender, where they might have some protection from the soaking downpour. Many of those gathered on the pier were optimistic the wait wouldn't go on too long.

Judy Pospisil was one of the wives who felt that way. She'd brought her eighteen-month-old son, Tim, and didn't really make much of it when the 1:00 P.M. arrival estimate passed without any sign of the boat. She'd been married to a sailor long enough to know it wasn't uncommon for the submarines to come in overdue, especially with the weather conditions bad as they were.

But not all the women were as confident. Barbara Foli had grown more restless as the day wore on. She'd found it difficult to talk or hear anyone else talk on the pier. The roaring wind drowned out everybody's voices, and that seemed to isolate the small knots of women, at least in terms of their conversation.

Whatever scattered, occasional murmurs Barbara was able to discern would arise from the women in one or another of the groups talking among themselves. Every so often she'd exchange a few words with someone, but she mostly just stood there in dismal silence, looking for *Scorpion* to appear between the dark roof of the sky and the rainswept water.

Aboard *Orion*, meanwhile, Bill Elrod, the sonar operator who'd flown home from Rota on bereavement leave, watched the wives standing around in the rain and sensed a growing anxiousness among them. He was probably unaware that the tender's skipper was also a bit concerned, more by the absence of any contact from *Scorpion* than by her lateness.

When returning to port from a mission, a submarine would maintain radio silence until it reached the hundred-fathom curve, at which point the edge of the continental shelf drops down in its abyssal descent like a canyon wall. As a safety precaution, the Navy had restricted subs from conducting submerged operations on the continental shelf—or, putting it another way, in waters shallower than six hundred feet. Contour charts of the sea bottom around the Virginia coast show the hundred-fathom line running from sixty to ninety miles offshore. At a marker approaching this range, it would be standard procedure for *Scorpion* to surface and confirm her arrival with a radio call to *Orion*. That message had not yet come in.

What did it mean? *Orion*'s Captain James Bellah mulled the question for a while. Probably *Scorpion*'s failure to establish contact was related to the foul weather. Storms as intense as the one causing the Chesapeake to boil would wreak havoc with radio transmissions. Still, it wouldn't hurt to make some inquiries.

Sometime after 1:00 P.M., Bellah phoned Atlantic Submarine Fleet Headquarters to see if it might have received a communication from *Scorpion*. No, he was informed. There hadn't been any word. It didn't seem a concern to anybody at HQ, though. They had no indication whatsoever of a problem with the submarine.

The women on Pier 22 figured that the storm must have delayed *Scorpion*'s arrival. The harbor was churning, the rain was punishing, and visibility was poor. A holdup was almost to be expected. Inevitably and by gradual degrees, though, doubts crept into some of the women's minds. Theresa Bishop, the COB's wife, was among those who'd grown ill at ease. She'd had an eerie, disturbing dream about Wally the night before. And when she had driven to the base earlier, she'd noticed that gale winds had toppled a tree not far from her home. As she stood on the rain-lashed dock with nothing to do but wait, her imagination turned along unwanted paths.

That wait had stretched on for quite a while when Theresa posed an idea to the rest of the women. If you went about four blocks from the pier to the main street, and then turned left, you would be a short distance down the road—about a third of a mile—from one of the naval station's entrance gates. There was a tavern just outside the gate that base personnel haunted in their free time, and it was bound to be packed that afternoon, with the inclement weather driving guys indoors for a beer and a bite to eat. Maybe somebody at the bar would have heard news about *Scorpion*.

"Let's walk over there and see if we can find out anything," Theresa said. Several of the women accompanied her to the bar. In the drenching torrent the bar seemed a long way off, and the women were soaked when they finally reached it.

But nobody in the place had any information for the wives. No wiser about what was going on than before, they were soon hiking back toward the pier through the wind and rain.

III

Sympathetic to the chilled, dripping-wet family members, Captain Bellah sent an aide to invite them onto *Orion*, where they could have some hot coffee and stay out of the wind and heavy rain.

Some took him up on his offer. Others lingered on the pier, or decided it was better to head home and wait. Sonarman Elrod stayed aboard the tender and did some busywork in one of its offices.

It wasn't until decades later that any of them learned a top secret search for *Scorpion* was already underway.

5. BRANDYWINE

"Forget about resolving these sad issues for the surviving
families."

—*Soviet Rear Admiral Viktor Dyaglo*

I

IN SEPTEMBER 1960, *SCORPION* WAS SOMEWHERE IN
European waters playing the hare to British hounds in hunter-
killer exercises with NATO and the U.S. Sixth Fleet. She hadn't
been originally slated to participate, but another fast-attack boat
broke down and *Scorpion* was chosen as a substitute. This would be
the sub's shakedown cruise, and cautious limits on speed, depth,
and area of operations were imposed on her.

Scorpion's first skipper, Commander Norman "Buzz" Bessac, felt
the restrictions were excessive, giving the submarine's British surface hunters unfair advantage—and a cocksure attitude that Bessac
found insupportable. It wasn't long before he'd had his fill of it.

Deciding to teach the Brits an object lesson in the evasive capabilities of a hot new Skipjack boat, Bessac broke with orders, took
the sub deep, and then went quiet. The ships that had been so successful tracking *Scorpion* to that point lost contact and were unable
to reacquire her. Soon the Brits became worried. No matter where

they looked, there was no sign of the sub. All at once it seemed the fun and games were over.

Later on, Commander Bessac had *Scorpion* rise to periscope depth to find the boat surrounded by empty ocean. While she'd been down, the British had left the area in an expanded and fruitless search.

Bessac must have taken great delight in having stymied his overconfident hunters. But what he hadn't known was that they'd become desperate when they couldn't find *Scorpion* and informed Royal Navy headquarters of her apparent loss—and that the British press had immediately latched on to the story. Soon the news was flashing across the Atlantic. Among the first American broadcasts to pick up on it was Paul Harvey's immensely popular *News and Comment* show on the ABC radio network. All around the country, the report shocked the relatives of *Scorpion*'s crewmen. One sailor's wife ran out to a neighbor's house in a sobbing panic, not knowing where else to turn. In an effort to calm her down, the neighbor advised that she should ignore whatever the Brits said. If anything had happened to *Scorpion*, didn't she trust the U.S. Navy to let her know?

As it turned out, the Navy had already heard from Bessac and been assured that all was well with *Scorpion*. Once it learned of the Paul Harvey report, it took hurried steps to quell the fears of the crewmen's relatives.

The parallels between this incident and *Scorpion*'s disappearance eight years later would be laced with darkest irony. In 1968, she would become a replacement for yet another boat that had been unexpectedly sent to the shipyard for major repairs. Also in 1968—as in the previous instance—family members got their initial information about the sub's apparent loss from the media.

But *Scorpion* would not return from that last deployment.

II

Fifty-six-year-old Admiral Thomas H. Moorer was an imposing figure in the U.S. military, a career naval officer whose World War II combat exploits began with the Japanese air attack on Pearl Harbor, and would continue throughout his subsequent assignment to the Pacific theater. In 1965, the sturdy, independent Moorer became the first U.S. naval officer to be given command of both the Pacific and Atlantic fleets. Two years later, President Johnson appointed him chief of naval operations.

Since June 1967, two months before he became CNO, Moorer had been haunted by an Israeli air and naval strike on a lightly armed American intelligence ship, the USS *Liberty*, that had made banner headlines around the world. Coming four days after the outbreak of the Six Day War, the surprise action left the Americans with scores of dead and wounded. The Israeli Defense Forces insisted it was a case of mistaken identity, but an incensed Moorer would never believe it. He was convinced the assault was initiated to prevent the United States from becoming aware of Israeli plans to seize the Golan Heights from the Syrians. The *Liberty* had been able to intercept the transmissions of all parties involved in the conflict, and Tel Aviv had known the Johnson administration was opposed to any attack on the Golan by Israeli forces. Moorer would go to his grave believing the assault was intended to blind the American military and, hence, blind President Johnson while Israel waged war on its own terms. Moorer believed Johnson and the Congress accepted the Israeli explanation for the attack on the ship for political reasons: Israel was the only U.S. ally in the Middle East, and exposing its actions as deliberate would have had serious ramifications at home and in the larger geopolitical arena.

On Thursday, May 23, 1968, days before the families of *Scorpion*'s crewmen would come out to Pier 22 in defiance of the storm, troubling information about the boat's status reached

Moorer's Norfolk office. Though he was far from a knee-jerk alarmist, the news must have instantly brought the *Liberty* debacle to mind. After radioing in that she had drawn near the Soviet ships, *Scorpion* had made no further position reports. She also hadn't responded to a series of three coded orders—sent out on May 23, 24, and 25—to contact Fleet Headquarters that Captain Wallace A. Greene, commander of Submarine Division 62, issued at the behest of Admiral Schade.

Absent other factors, *Scorpion*'s failure to answer Schade's messages would have been no cause for immediate anxiety. Whether or not he recalled the incident with the British in 1960, Moorer was aware of SUBLANT's Operational Order 2-67 requiring a submarine skipper to maintain strict radio silence when in waters where transmissions to base might compromise the safety of his boat. If the boat wasn't at risk, though, he was supposed to comply with a request to phone home. In other words, it was a judgment call. While on intelligence missions, the skipper would have latitude deciding whether it was all right to respond to a communication.

But even under benign conditions submarines didn't like staying near the surface very long. There was too much noise generated from the engines, and too much chance of having your antenna or periscope spotted, or broaching and getting painted by radar. The communications system was therefore designed to be fast.

The sub's quick transmits, or "flash messages," were ultra-high-frequency broadcasts of two or three seconds. These would originate from the radio shack on its starboard side, just aft of the yeoman's office, which was about the size of a telephone booth and among the few spaces on the boat even tighter than the radio shack. Like every fleet sub, *Scorpion* had the KW-7 Orestes cryptographic unit crammed in with her standard communications equipment. All incoming and outgoing broadcasts were sifted through this metal crypto box. You would code your messages,

It was the sinking of the Soviet Golf-class submarine K-129, shown here, that set in motion the events that would lead to the retaliatory sinking of *Scorpion*. (U.S. NAVY PHOTO)

The Soviets believed that the USS *Swordfish*, pictured here, was responsible for sinking K-129 in the waters off Hawaii. But *Swordfish* was more than 2,000 miles away, conducting a surveillance of Soviet naval activity in the Sea of Japan. (U.S. NAVY PHOTO)

The USS *Pueblo* was seized by North Korean forces on January 23, 1968. Confiscated from the spy ship and subsequently flown to Moscow was at least one KW-7 Orestes data encryption box. These units were used to process coded Teletype messages throughout the U.S. naval fleet. (U.S. NAVY PHOTO)

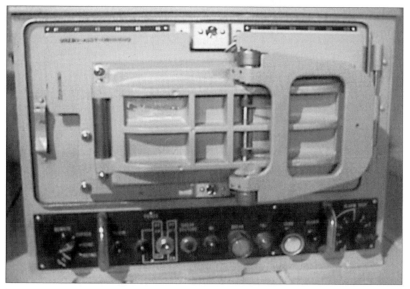

The front panel of a KW-7 cryptographic box circa the late 1960s. (COURTESY OF JERRY PROC VE3FAB)

In 1966, U.S. Navy communications expert John Anthony Walker, Jr., was recruited as a KGB spy. He would eventually lead the most damaging espionage ring in American history, providing the USSR with over one million classified military documents, including key codes that allowed the Soviets to decipher messages encrypted with the KW-7. (FBI ARCHIVES)

USS *Scorpion* at her launching on December 19, 1959. She was the eighth nuclear submarine built for the Navy by the Electric Boat Company. (U.S. NAVY PHOTO)

Thirty-seven-year-old Captain Francis Atwood Slattery was assigned to the USS *Scorpion* in December 1967. At the time, he was the youngest officer ever to command a nuclear submarine. (U.S. NAVY PHOTO)

Lost with *Scorpion*, Chief of the Boat Walter "Wally" Bishop was a member of the submarine's commissioning crew. He is remembered as a forceful and influential figure by the sailors who served under him. (U.S. NAVY PHOTO)

The son of Italian immigrants, Senior Chief Quartermaster Frank "Patsy" Mazzuchi joined the Navy during World War II. He was an avid history buff who would regale *Scorpion* crewmen with tales of the American Old West during late watches. (U.S. NAVY PHOTO)

In May 1967, Interior Communications Electrician Third Class Mark Vernon Foli transferred to the *Scorpion*. His wife, Barbara, remains angry over the Navy's handling of the sub's disappearance. (U.S. NAVY PHOTO)

Electrician's Mate Third Class Gerald Stanley Pospisil penned frequent letters home throughout *Scorpion*'s deployment to the Mediterranean. In his last correspondences to his wife, he would express concern about a possible delay in the sub's return to Norfolk. (U.S. NAVY PHOTO)

Scorpion sailors would hold "best beard" contests to relieve the tedium of extended deployments at sea. They are pictured here at ease in the crew's mess. (COURTESY OF DOUG KARIKER)

Scorpion, photographed from the tender *Tallahatchie County* while making her final port call in Naples, Italy. (U.S. NAVY PHOTO)

A stern view of *Scorpion* underway during training maneuvers in the Caribbean. The photo was taken about a year before the sub's disappearance. (COURTESY OF GREGG PENNINGTON)

Admiral of the Fleet Sergei Georgeyevich Gorshkov, commander in chief of the Soviet Navy. At the height of the Cold War, Gorshkov challenged U.S. sea power around the world, urging his ship captains to take an increasingly confrontational stance with their American counterparts. (SOVIET NAVAL ARCHIVES)

An airborne Kamov Ka-25 (NATO designation Hormone) antisubmarine warfare helicopter. Speaking out at risk of imprisonment or death in 2005, a former Soviet rear admiral revealed that an aircraft of this type was used to sink the USS *Scorpion* nearly four decades earlier. (SOVIET NAVAL ARCHIVES)

The mobile, highly adaptable Ka-25 featured state-of-the-art antisubmarine tracking equipment and weaponry. It could launch from a variety of Soviet naval platforms. (SOVIET NAVAL ARCHIVES)

Chief of Naval Operations Admiral Thomas H. Moorer authorized a quiet search for *Scorpion* four days before the submarine was
publicly declared missing. (U.S. NAVY PHOTO)

As the hunt for *Scorpion* commenced, the oceanographic research and submarine rescue ship USNS *Mizar* (T-AGOR-11) was dispatched to search for the sub in the mid-Atlantic. In late October 1968, after almost five months at sea, it located her wreckage about 400 miles southwest of the Azores archipelago. (U.S. NAVY PHOTO)

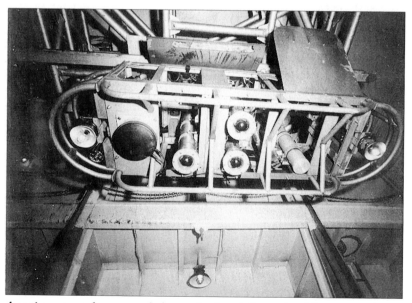

A unique towed camera sled was deployed from the *Mizar* to seek out *Scorpion*'s sunken remains. Here it rests on its bay doors between exploratory "sled runs," ready to be lowered thousands of feet beneath the ocean's surface. (U.S. NAVY PHOTO)

On July 20, 1969, the day Neil Armstrong and Buzz Aldrin landed on the moon, the deep submergence vehicle *Trieste II* became the first manned exploratory craft to descend 10,000 feet to *Scorpion's* abyssal grave. Officially dubbed a naval support ship, the destroyer pictured here observing the operation's surface activities bristled with signals intelligence and surveillance masts common to spy vessels. (COURTESY OF LORENZO HAGERTY)

In 1986, U.S. intelligence operative and self-styled undersea explorer Robert Ballard led a second series of classified dives to investigate *Scorpion's* wreckage, using *Trieste II's* successor, *Alvin*. Ballard's famed hunt for the sunken ocean liner RMS *Titanic* was a cover story that obscured his CIA mission. (PHOTO BY ROD CATANACH, WOODS HOLE OCEANO-GRAPHIC INSTITUTION)

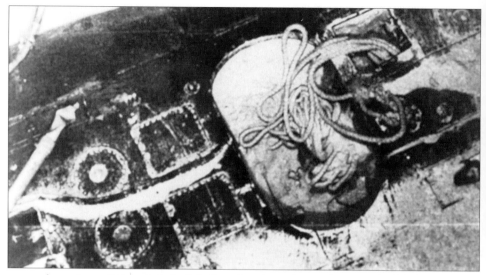

A section of *Scorpion*'s hull believed to have been photographed by the *Mizar*'s towed sled. (U.S. NAVY PHOTO)

Sail of *Scorpion* seen from USS *Tallahatchie County*, Naples, Italy. (U.S. NAVY PHOTO)

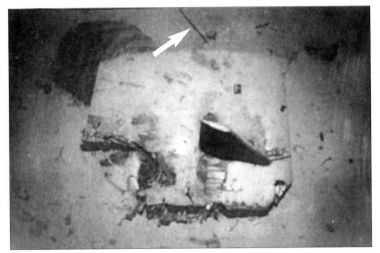

Sail of *Scorpion*, 1986, photographed from the deep submersible *Alvin*. High-ranking Navy officials have identified the "bite" visible in the sail's lower aft section as the point where a torpedo struck. The submarine's raised mast is barely visible at the top of the sail (see arrow), confirming she was at or near the surface at the moment of her catastrophic demise. (U.S. NAVY PHOTO)

Scorpion with her intelligence and radio communications masts extended. On patrol, these masts would have been extended only when she was near the surface, as when she was approaching her surveillance of the Soviet flotilla. (COURTESY OF GREGG PENNINGTON)

From left to right: Shannon Peterson (son of Chief Electrician's Mate Daniel P. Peterson), Joan Cowan (wife of Machinist's Mate First Class Robert J. Cowan), and Capt. MaryEtta Nolan (daughter of Chief of the Boat Walter Bishop) at a 2007 *Scorpion* memorial service in Norfolk, Virginia. The monument lists the names of all ninety-nine hands who went down with the boat. (COURTESY OF CAPT. MARYETTA NOLAN)

type them onto a tape that got punched with holes like a ticker tape, then come to the surface, run the tape through the KW-7 unit, and transmit at a fast rate.

Still, Commander Slattery probably would have chosen to avoid using his communications gear to transmit any messages during his sprint out toward the Canaries—and that was assuming his radiomen managed to break through the interference that had chewed up their signal to Nea Makri. Aware of the Soviet fleet concentrations that had prompted ASWFORLANT's operations in the area, Slattery would have leaned toward being cautious and observed radio silence. But checking the skid was a different story. During covert operations, you still downloaded it. You needed to know if a war was about to start, and unless raising the antenna might catch the eye of some Russian fisherman casting his line from a pier, or a Soviet fleet sailor leaning on the rail of his ship, you came up for the skid about once each watch. Radio silence or not, Admiral Schade knew Commander Slattery should have gotten the messages from Captain Greene. The question was, had they reached him in time?

Schade's concern could be traced back to earlier that day, when he'd received a tip from the National Security Agency that the Soviet vessels near the Canaries had produced atypically dense flurries of radio traffic between 0000 and 0303 hours on May 22. The NSA was the government's signals intelligence arm, which meant its essential purpose was monitoring global communications for possible security threats to the United States. Though its agents would have known of naval intelligence's interest in the Russian flotilla, and been apprised of plans to get a sub out for a recon, the timing and details of the mission wouldn't have required direct NSA participation or given NSA cause to tab the communications information as particularly urgent. Neither the agency nor the Navy had evidence that the grouping was an active, aggressive threat to U.S. civilian or military vessels.

Still, somebody in the intelligence chain had noticed that the Soviet radio bursts coincided with *Scorpion*'s broadcasts to Nea Makri. And that wasn't all.

For those who have heard of it at all, the cliff-rimmed island of Terceira in the Azores is known for its goat and cattle pastures, tobacco plantations, and rain. Few outside the military are aware it is also the site of America's largest regional air and naval base. In March 1968, the Navy's Lajes Field, named after its host city on the eastern part of the island, had gained a detachment of three Orion P-3B maritime patrol planes from Patrol Squadron 24 (VP-24) in Keflavik, Iceland. The Orions had been designed for antisubmarine warfare missions, and the growing number of Soviet subs in the transatlantic naval and shipping corridors near Portugal had necessitated their redeployment to Lajes.

Toward dusk on Wednesday, May 22, one of the P-3Bs was out tracking a Soviet Yankee SSBN known to be prowling the area. Speedier, quieter, and deadlier than their Hotel-class forerunners—they carried sixteen nuclear missiles that could be launched against land targets while the sub was underwater, a capability only U.S. ballistic missile subs had owned to that stage—the Yankee boats had been in service less than a year. For a new Yankee to be sniffed out so close to Western Europe signified a dangerous expansion of the USSR's strategic objectives, plain evidence of why the Orions had been dispatched to join the Lajes maritime patrols.

The P-3B had two principal tools for picking up submerged vessels: an ensemble of active and passive sonobuoys that would listen for the sounds a sub emitted, and a magnetic anomaly detector (MAD) that projected from a boom, or "stinger," at the rear of the plane and measured fluctuations in the earth's magnetic field produced by a submarine. In daylight, Orions flew at low altitudes—about two hundred feet above the water's surface—and were able to make MAD contacts of submerged vessels at depths of eight hundred feet. As the darkness of night spread over the ocean's surface, and the recommended patrol altitude increased for safety reasons, the MAD's detection range was reduced to depths of about five hundred feet.

Because of the MAD's limited capacity, the odds were slim that it would pick up a sub before an Orion crew had already gotten some sort of fix on its position from the sonobuoys. Their effective range varied with the type, or types, of buoys that were laid, but the average detection range was a two-thousand-yard circle— though it was possible for sounds traveling from hundreds, or even thousands of miles away to be picked up as background noise. On a surveillance and reconnaissance mission, a P-3B would drop multiple buoys at set depths and distances from one another, with each buoy's yield of noises transmitted to the plane over a dedicated channel. At the aircraft's acoustic sensor station, a pair of crewmen would monitor its readings on an AN/AQH-1 receiver for particular sonar signatures—say those of a Russian submarine—and then correlate them with the sound emissions detected by the other sonobuoys to lock on a target.

The aggregate of *un*sorted frequency emissions gathered by a buoy at any given second was known to Orion crewmen as a gram, and these would include not only the sounds of a possible target, but the typical underwater background noise that tested the skill and patience of every sonar technician.

As the P-3B flight out of Lajes was making its evening run, its buoys detected a sequence of noises that was anything but typical, rumbles originating from *somewhere* in the general area of the Azores. Because crewmen were trained to cue in on the unique aural signatures of whatever vessel they were tracking—at that particular time the Yankee-class—the extraordinary significance of these sounds may not have been immediately obvious to them. But the noises must have intrigued and baffled the analysts back at Lajes who reviewed the flight's daily mission data, carefully sifting through every tape-recorded gram of the sonobuoys' aural harvest.

Though assessing the precise location of their source was impossible given the limitations of the buoys—the noise was too far outside their tracking circle—the sounds were consistent with some sort of underwater explosion.

By May 23, this information would be passed on to Navy intelligence—and then communicated through channels to the commander of SUBLANT, Vice Admiral Schade, who was then preparing to leave for New London, Connecticut, to embark upon sea trials with the newly commissioned Sturgeon-class attack sub USS *Pargo* (SSN 650).

Whether or not Schade was the first to discern a pattern in the threads of the mystery that was fast wrapping itself around *Scorpion*, his suspicions were sufficiently aroused for him to have Commander Greene send out his coded messages on the skid. Nor was Greene the only recipient of urgent orders. By that time, hours had elapsed since *Scorpion* had made her aborted transmissions to Nea Makri, and nothing more had been heard from her. At Nea Makri's message center, the men who'd been on the ship-to-shore communications watch when the broadcast came in were instructed to dig through their burn bags for its coded printouts—and to decode them for a second time if they were found.

If the hope was that they'd gain some hitherto unnoticed clue to *Scorpion*'s condition and whereabouts in the messages, it was a desperate one. Before being deposited in burn bags and destroyed, classified printouts were almost always put through shredding machines. The chances that anything helpful would come from rummaging through the scraps of wastepaper in those bags were slim to none—and the Nea Makri search was unsurprisingly futile.

Schade was quick to apprise Moorer of the situation and request authorization to conduct a quiet hunt for the sub. With the *Liberty* incident still an open wound for him, the CNO was not about to take any chances. Moorer immediately gave his SUBLANT commander the go-ahead.

After laying out the parameters of the initial search, Schade went ahead with his plans to join the crew of the *Pargo* as an observer. It would in no way hinder his ability to manage the search for *Scorpion*, and might actually prove an advantage. *Pargo*'s exercises would not take her far off the East Coast and he could stay in regular communication with his administrative headquarters in Norfolk. And should a broader search become necessary, being aboard her would give him a jump on things. The speedy *Pargo* could reach the Virginia Capes in no time flat, allowing him to direct the operation from the sub.

III

As concern grew, the effort to find *Scorpion* commenced. COM-SUBLANT Schade ordered the Orions at Lajes back into the sky, and diverted surface vessels and submarines from their prescribed courses toward the sub's last reported position—and to the wide patch of ocean from which the unexplained acoustic event picked up by the P-3B's sonobuoys might have originated.

Because the secrecy of the hunt precluded its mention in deck and flight logs, its full scope may never be known. But anywhere between "a few ships and planes" to a dozen vessels with extensive air support are said to have been involved. According to one participant, the first vessel to reach the area was a fast-attack sub on which he served as an engineering officer. Traveling at flank bell— or maximum speed—from a nearby location, it used active sonar to conduct its solitary effort, and remained at it for the next five or six days.

Whatever its extent, the search proved fruitless, and Schade's and Moorer's apprehensions about *Scorpion* deepened as the week wore on. At SUBLANT headquarters, the two adjoining offices that comprised the message room hummed with monitoring activity. Communications streamed to and from the task force, but a general alarm wasn't sounded. The reason why remains a matter of conjecture. One explanation offered by officials was that the Navy was reluctant to distress the families of the *Scorpion*'s crew until they were absolutely positive something had gone wrong. As a prominent officer declared, "No observed changes in the pattern of operations of the Soviet ships, either before or after *Scorpion*'s loss . . . were evaluated as indicating involvement or interest in any way."

Rear Admiral Beshany would contradict this assertion after his retirement. "There was some communications analysis that the *Scorpion* had been detected by the group she had been shadowing and conceivably they had trailed her," he said. "There were some speculations that not only did they track her but attacked her."

The Navy had reasons for keeping a lid on things. Over the next few years these would stack up like weights atop the truth of what happened. Eventually *Scorpion*'s demise would be politically bound to the growing web of secrecy that surrounded another submarine's loss—this a Soviet ballistic missile boat that had gone down near the Hawaiian Islands a little over two months before. At its onset, however, the reasons behind the clampdown on information were probably more basic. The Navy was wary of having its submarine intelligence-gathering operations compromised, and a general alert would have raised unwanted questions from the crewmen's families and the media. But when *Scorpion* didn't show up at Norfolk on her due date, May 27, the clock was ticking on at least one secret: the sub's apparent loss would have to be officially acknowledged.

IV

On the USS *Bigelow*, word of the sub's disappearance spread in a hurry. There was no announcement over the shipboard public address system, and there didn't have to be. Men heard about it the

way they always would on Navy vessels—over card games, or picking up their rations during the midnight watch change, or just in
passing conversation while going about their routine business.

Years later, Ed Washburn would say he might have gotten wind
of the news from a radioman. One of them was his best friend on
the ship and they talked all the time. It could have been the radioman, since the guys in the radio shack were always first to know
things. *Bigelow* would have contacted Fleet Headquarters about
the transfer of material with *Scorpion*. Later, knowing it was the
last ship to see her, HQ would have contacted *Bigelow* for information on the sub. The radioman would have known something
was up.

Over the course of any given day, Washburn also had regular
dealings with the skipper and the executive officer. His administra-
trative duties in the ship's office required that reams of paperwork
pass across his desk. When a form or report had to be typed up,
the ninety words a minute he could clack out on a typewriter made
him the man to do it, and he'd see a steady parade of officers and
enlisteds who needed documents created or filed away. If there was
anyplace on the *Bigelow* where the swirl of scuttlebutt would ac-
crue force and momentum, it was the ship's office.

Wherever Washburn was when he first heard about the sinking, or whoever he got it from, he would distinctly remember the
same thing everyone else did. Within days after their exchange of
movies, reports reached their ship that *Scorpion* was missing and
presumed down. Beyond that it was just conjecture. There were
rumors the sub had run into a seamount. Whispers of something
more sinister involving the Russians. But what everybody on the
Bigelow knew was that the *Scorpion* had disappeared and a search
was underway in the Atlantic. Vessels were being called toward the
Azores, where the calamity was believed to have happened.

The news shook everybody up. Was *Bigelow* the last ship to
have had contact with *Scorpion*? Most guys on the destroyer fig-

ured the answer was yes. It was a sick, unsettling feeling that spread through the ship like a virus.

Bigelow couldn't join the search and rescue effort. It was too low on that damned JP-4 that the boilers were gobbling up by the minute. The destroyer had to get on to Gibraltar where it could re-fuel at the Royal Navy's port facility.

As *Bigelow* steamed on toward the Strait, the men decided watching some of the movies that had come over from *Scorpion* might lift their spirits. Lawrence Brooks was silent as he opened the 16mm cans and put up one of the films. So were the men gathered on the mess deck for the screening. The movie didn't help liven them up, though; it actually made them more somber. No-body laughed at the funny lines, or cheered at the exciting scenes, or clapped when the story was over. Nobody did or said much of anything. They couldn't forget that the sailors who'd last watched the movie were missing and probably dead. Thinking about it gave them the chills.

Ed Washburn had never experienced such quiet on the mess deck—all those men and you could have heard a pin drop. He wouldn't recall hearing it that quiet again.

V

By mid-afternoon on May 27 the Navy finally decided the time had come to shift gears. Four days of looking for *Scorpion* had passed without result. A nuclear sub had slipped into limbo with almost a hundred crewmen aboard. The limited search for her would have to be ramped up to a new level—one that could no longer be kept under wraps.

Aboard the *Pargo* in the waters off Narragansett Bay, Schade ordered the first search planes into the air at a little after one o'clock in the afternoon. Then, at 3:15 P.M., a Sub Missing alert radioed from Fleet Headquarters, broadcasting the message to vessels and air squadrons up and down the East Coast of the United States.

Schade then instructed the *Pargo*'s skipper, Commander Stephen A. White, to speed toward Virginia at a clip exceeding 20 knots. The sub would be followed closely by the 2,200-ton USS *Sunbird* (ASR-15), a submarine rescue vessel that was operating with her off Rhode Island and had participated in the search for the USS *Thresher* (SSN-593), a prototype nuclear boat that was accidentally lost on maneuvers in 1963.

VI

Responding promptly to Schade's orders, a massive naval search force began to launch out of bases ranging from Rhode Island and Massachusetts to Virginia and North Carolina, down to Florida and to Naval Station Lajes in the Azores. Within days, it would come to include 7,500 men and thirty-seven vessels—eighteen destroyers, twelve nuclear and diesel submarines, five submarine rescue ships, the oceanographic survey ship USS *Mizar*, and an oiler for replenishment of the vessels at sea. By the first week of June, a dozen surface ships and submarines already in the water—a French Requin-class diesel boat among them—would be summoned to boost the effort.

The initial search plan covered three general tracks. One was off coastal Virginia in the relatively shallow water along the edge of the continental shelf, where *Scorpion* would have made her approach to base. Another was the vicinity of Hyères Bank and Cruiser Seamount, neighboring volcanic structures in a chain of underwater peaks and ridges from which the unexplained rumbles detected by the P-3B subchaser on May 22 were thought to have emanated. The third and broadest track retraced a path running twenty-five miles north and south of the two-thousand-plus mile route *Scorpion* was believed to have taken on her homeward journey.

As the vessels were manned and deployed, squadrons of long-range maritime patrol aircraft rumbled off the tarmac in airfields up and down the U.S. coastline—and as far away as Lajes—to aid in the search. Soon the skies over wide expanses of the Atlantic buzzed with Orions, older Neptune P2Vs, and large Air Force and Coast Guard Hercules C-130s tricked out for search-and-rescue efforts. At the peak of the hunt, twenty-seven flights would take to the air each day.

On Monday, May 27, Orion pilot Lieutenant Edward M. Brittingham, an instructor with the training squadron VP-30 in Jacksonville, was in Norfolk for a training conference when he and a student crew were hurriedly briefed on the type of buoy markers and flares *Scorpion* had been carrying, and then ordered into the air to look for her. By 5:45 P.M. Brittingham and his trainees were streaking over the open sea.

The Orion would run what was known as a ladder search, flying parallel to the likely route of the sub for a short distance, then cutting across it for a longer, perpendicular leg to the north or south, then flying the same pattern in reverse. As with the naval flotilla, their goal was to cover both sides of the route.

The sortie would take the Orion two hundred miles east of Norfolk through turbulent skies. Bad weather would be a severe problem into the night, not only for the aircraft, but for the entire search-and-rescue effort. The P-3's array of electronic equipment was of no use in seeking a downed submarine in waters that, just fifty or sixty miles away from shore, would have reached abyssal depths of thousands of fathoms. If *Scorpion* had sunk, she would have plunged to the bottom in minutes, and come to rest far beyond the range of sonobuoys and magnetic anomaly detectors. That left an Orion's crew to conduct visual searches from behind large bubble windows located on the aircraft's port and starboard sides, and on the underbelly aft of the cabin. Throughout their searches, the airmen would take turns sticking their heads into the bowl-like spaces behind the thick, concave glass panes, craning them this way and that as they sought debris or oil slicks the nuke may have left behind on the surface.

At one point, Brittingham and his men spotted a group of buoys tumbling on the waves below, but whatever glimmer of optimism that gave them was quashed when they realized their sightings didn't match anything that would have been aboard *Scorpion*. Back over the Atlantic the next day, they went out beyond the previous day's distance and found some more floating "junk." Again, though, the flotsam wasn't associated with the sub, and they returned to base discouraged.

About the time Lieutenant Brittingham's first run over the ocean concluded that night, the submarine rescue vessel USS *Petrel* (ASR-14) was getting set to depart Naval Station Charleston, South Carolina. Aboard by nine o'clock was Rear Admiral Lawrence Bernard, the commander of Submarine Flotilla 6, who had been named senior officer of the search force. The *Petrel* would haul for the Virginia Capes carrying Bernard and a covey of subordinate officers, but communications problems would force them to transfer to the guided missile frigate USS *William H. Standley* (DLG-32) in the early morning hours of May 29. The *Standley* would then become the search's command ship, leading a line of four other surface ships and five submarines spaced between five and ten miles apart on a speedy 2,200-mile voyage to the Azores, with the submarine element following the skimmers by 135 miles to ensure that at least one of the elements would be covering *Scorpion*'s assumed track in daylight at all times.

On the *Pargo*, meanwhile, Schade was roving the continental ridge with a group of nine other submarines and nineteen surface ships—and struggling with the storm that had ripped into the Virginia coast. Though it had tapered off inland, it was still creating tempestuous offshore conditions on the night of May 27, stirring up high winds and fifteen- to twenty-two-foot wave crests that tossed one submarine, the USS *Shark* (SSN-591), into 22 degree rolls.

While *Sunbird* nevertheless continued to work closely with *Pargo,* a rescue attempt probably would not have been doable until the storm abated, even if *Scorpion* were found at a shallow depth. The *Sunbird* carried an assortment of SCUBA and deep-sea diving gear, equipment designed to control fire and flooding, a fantail-mounted towing apparatus, and a crew trained to deal with every dangerous contingency that might arise during search-and-rescue operations. But its main piece of personnel rescue equipment, a McCann submarine rescue chamber designated SRC-19, was a steel diving bell that had been little improved from the original version developed in the 1930s. Divided into two pressurized crew compartments and a water ballast tank, the SRC was designed to be lowered over the sub's escape hatch from aboard the *Sunbird* and to lift its two operators and seven of the sub's crewmen to the surface with each return trip.

On the evening of May 27, Admiral Moorer conducted the first in a string of Washington news conferences. Volleyed with questions about the SRC rescue chamber, Moorer told reporters that the rescue bell could be effective at depths of "several hundred feet." An aide to the admiral then expanded on his statement, saying it could be used to retrieve survivors trapped as deep as 650 feet beneath the surface.

They were being less than completely straightforward. Yes, the SRC could withstand the underwater stresses of 650-foot descents and ascents. But the problem would be putting it where the rescuers wanted it. Out on the continental shelf, where Schade's in-close search was concentrated, the Beaufort scale readings approached Force 10 going into the darkness of night. For the *Sunbird* to attempt an evacuation it would have to be moored and stable on the surface above the submarine, a tough assignment in calm waters, and close to impossible on those heavy, pitch-black seas. The manager of the Navy's Deep Submergence Systems Project, Captain William J. Nicholson, conceded as much in an interview after Moorer's press conference, when he admitted the tempestuous weather would make it "difficult" to use the bell "effectively" below three hundred feet.

Asked about the chances of retrieving survivors from the deep sea, Moorer frankly admitted there would be no way it could be done. So perhaps the admiral was clinging to some tenuous shred of optimism that *Scorpion* had made it as far as the fifty-fathom curve when he spoke of the Navy's available rescue procedures—at that stage, the sounds picked up by the P-3B sonobuoys near the Azores were the closest thing that existed to hard evidence the sub had gone down, but they could not be definitively linked to *Scorpion* absent other still ungathered data. Given his knowledge of her intelligence mission, and of her failure to respond to three successive radio communiqués from SUBLANT, it is more probable that Moorer realized it was, at best, a long shot that the sub was anywhere near Norfolk, and hesitated to publicly reveal what must have been a leaden resignation among his staff about the fate of the submarine and her crew.

VII

Storm or no storm, delayed homecoming or not, somebody had to feed the kids.

Theresa Bishop might have known the day would be a bumpy one from the way it started out. There had been the large, uprooted tree she'd seen as she left home that morning. At the pier, she had shivered through the long, unavailing wait out in the gale for her husband, Walter, to return aboard *Scorpion*. She had also convinced some of the other wives to hike over to the tavern near the gate with her, and see if anybody there had heard an explanation for the sub's lateness. When that, too, proved fruitless, she'd returned to the pier and waited some more. Finally, Captain Bellah's man had told everyone it might be best to head back home. If word came about the sub, they would be contacted.

That advice had made sense to most of the wives, Theresa among them. The oldest of her three children, John, was only nine. She needed to put dinner on the table for him, Mike, and Mary Etta. Nothing would be accomplished by standing around in the cold and rain. Most likely the sub wouldn't come in till the storm-tossed waters outside the harbor settled anyway.

Slightly before six o'clock, Theresa was at the kitchen sink washing dishes when John shot in from the living room, where the television was tuned to the local news. His words were clear over the rattle of dirty plates and bowls under the tap.

"There's something on TV about the *Scorpion* missing," he said.

Theresa went numb, her dirty dishes forgotten. Her sole focus now was the news bulletin. But other than to say a search was on for the sub, the story didn't give any details. Still, it was clear that this situation was very different from that scare back in 1960. Walter Bishop had been aboard back then. He was a plank owner, and had been with *Scorpion* from the beginning. That time the Navy had immediately dismissed the British reports. Now it was making no denials.

Within a short while the Bishop residence was filling with worried visitors—friends, and the wives and children of Walter's shipmates. Wally was a chief and a lifer, and the others were hopeful the Bishops' phone might ring sooner than some others'. Nobody spoke, the silence in the place was thick with trepidation. They just waited for the phone to ring.

It did, around seven-thirty. The caller was a Navy official, but he had little to add to the televised report. His intention had been to confirm that the story was essentially accurate. A search for

Scorpion had commenced, and the crewmen's families would be informed of continuing developments.

In the tense quiet of the Bishop home, a long wait was about to get painfully longer.

VIII

Barbara Foli was another of the sailors' wives who took Captain Bellah's advice and finally decided to wait for updates about *Scorpion* at home. A next-door neighbor had offered to baby-sit for her daughter when she left for the pier that morning, and Barbara had accepted. But it had gotten to be late in the afternoon, and she'd been reluctant to unduly impose on the neighbor's kindness.

At around the same time Vice Admiral Schade's Sub Missing alert, or SUBMISS, was going out on official Navy frequencies, Barbara was back in the dryness of her apartment tucking Holli in for a nap. With the baby in her crib, she peeled off her soggy clothes and climbed into bed. Between hustling out of the apartment early, standing in the rain for hours, and worrying about Vernon, she felt dejected and exhausted.

Barbara dozed off as soon as her head hit the pillow, only to be awakened by a rapping on her front door. Startled and a little out of sorts, she thought for sure it was Vernon, jumped excitedly out from under her covers, and hurried through the living room to answer the knock.

When she opened the door, Barbara instantly registered two things: the storm clouds had broken to reveal wide patches of blue, sunny sky, and the person standing in front of her wasn't Vernie after all. Rather, it was her neighbor, the same woman who'd watched Holli.

Barbara invited her inside, but she didn't budge from the doorway.

"Bill wants you and Holli to come to our house," the woman said. Bill, her husband, served on another boat.

Barbara looked out at her and noticed she was standing very stiffly. It gave her a nervous feeling. Then she saw the concern in the woman's eyes.

"What's happening?" she asked.

The woman just repeated that Bill wanted her to wake the baby and bring her to their house. Now Barbara's nervousness inched toward a more ominous feeling. It was the woman's tone. And the way she just stood there with that terrible, grim look in her eyes.

Barbara pressed the woman to tell her more. Something was wrong, she was sure of it. She didn't intend to go anywhere until she found out what it was.

At last the woman relented. She and Bill had been watching television when a report came on the evening news. A sub had been declared missing and it was *Scorpion*.

Everything that followed was a confused whirl for Barbara. She knew that her neighbor Bill was a chief, a lifer. That meant he earned enough to afford a telephone. Because of his status, Barbara hoped it also might mean he'd have better luck than she would in getting more information about the boat.

Her heart slamming in her chest, struggling with her composure, she rushed to snatch Holli into her arms and went next door. As the evening wore on, and no further news arrived, Barbara's neighbors urged her not to go home. They had an extra bedroom, and she and the baby were welcome to stay the night.

Barbara accepted their offer. She needed to be around someone, if not for her own sake, then for Holli's. Earlier in the week, right around when *Scorpion* was originally due in, Barbara had suffered from insomnia and numbness in her face and arm. It had gotten so bad that she'd kept going over to the mirror to inspect herself. But each time Barbara looked there'd be nothing visibly wrong with her, and she would figure she was okay, rub her arm to get its circulation flowing, and go back to bed trying to forget it. Then the numbness, that strange sensation on one side of her face, would return. She'd never experienced anything like it, and it scared her out of her wits. What if she was having some kind of seizure? Being stuck without a phone in her apartment had given her a helpless feeling. Say she passed out—or worse—and nobody knew? What would happen to the baby?

Barbara hadn't really believed anything might be wrong with Vernie. But tonight was different. Tonight she didn't want to sit staring at her television set alone.

Soon after she got to her neighbors' place, Barbara asked to use their phone to call Illinois. She needed to tell her family about the submarine. But when her mother picked up at her end, Barbara discovered they already knew. Her mom blurted that she'd been sitting around the kitchen table with a couple of friends while Barbara's sister watched television in the next room. Then there had been a news flash about an overdue boat, and her sister had suddenly called out for her mom to come listen.

"My God," she'd said, distraught. "Isn't that *Vernie's* sub?"

Moments later they knew it was, and her mom's friends were scraping together any money they had in their purses to help her pay for an airline ticket to Norfolk. Barbara's sister wanted to keep her company, so her mom ran out to borrow another $300, enough for both of them to fly out first thing in the morning.

That night there would be no sleep at all for Barbara. Closing her eyes was impossible. There were only her thoughts of Vernie and the sub playing out against the relentless blare of emergency sirens from the Norfolk docks. On past midnight they sounded as shore leaves were abruptly curtailed, crewmen were summoned to waiting vessels, and one ship after another departed to join the search.

Sitting up in bed, staring into the darkness with the wail of the sirens in her ears, Barbara pinched her arm harder and harder to see if she'd wake up from what she prayed would turn out to be nothing more than a horrific dream.

IX

Bordered on one side by a swamp, and along the others by large fields of scrub trees and rampant grass, the Camp Allen naval prison humped up conspicuously in an undeveloped section of the Marine Corps' family housing complex about a mile from Hampton Boulevard in Norfolk. The night the SUBMISS was declared, Bob Davis, the sailor who'd arrived too late at the dock to board *Scorpion*, was serving his thirty-day sentence behind Camp Allen's razor wire fences and iron bars. The clank of his cell door opening roused him from his bunk. Standing outside the cell was a Marine guard who had come to tell Davis a duty officer wanted to see him.

From behind his desk a short while later, the officer informed Davis of *Scorpion*'s disappearance, and suggested he give his parents in Florida a ring to let them know he was okay. It was an act of decency. Davis was a likable guy, and the officer was aware he'd been ashamed to tell his father, a state cop, that he'd gotten tossed behind bars for missing his boat's departure. As far as his family was concerned, Bob was aboard *Scorpion*.

Though shaken by the news of the boat, Davis took the officer up on his offer, called his parents, and discovered that they'd also heard about *Scorpion* and were sick with worry. As he put their fears over his well-being to rest, Davis offered an explanation of why he'd been left behind, admitting that he'd gotten into a situation that landed him in the brig. But he would rarely share the full story with anyone. He cooked up a modified version that was substantially more palatable than the truth—to him no less than those to whom he passed it off.

Davis remained in the Navy for years after his release from confinement, though it would be an inconsistent career that saw him bumped up and down in rate. He'd always feel charmed by fate, and people would find the rakish, devil-may-care attitude he'd gained from his experience kind of disarming.

But Bob Davis wasn't as carefree as he seemed. A charmed life may come with a high cost, and Davis would never be satisfied that he'd paid anything close to what he really owed.

X

Like so many connected to *Scorpion*, Bill Elrod got the bad news on his television set.

After hanging around *Orion* all day waiting for word of *Scorpion*, he called it quits at the squadron office around 5:00 P.M. and drove home to join his wife for dinner. Still traumatized from the loss of her unborn child, Julie had been concerned about the lateness of Bill's shipmates and close friends aboard the sub, men their personal tragedy had forced him to leave behind in Rota.

When she asked whether there had been any sign of the *Scorpion*, Bill told her nothing had been seen or heard from it, and gave what he still wanted to believe was the probable explanation—stormy weather. As they were getting ready to eat, however, a breaking story on the *CBS Evening News* destroyed any confidence the Elrods might have had of that being the truth.

Scorpion was officially missing. Faced with this cold reality, learning it along with millions of other viewers who'd never even heard of the sub, they were stunned.

It was a reaction mirrored in households all across Hampton Roads as the sirens of departing search vessels tore the night to shreds, and reporters from every major news outlet in the nation converged upon the town.

XI

Interior Communications Electrician Jerry Pratt's tour on *Scorpion* began in May 1964, and came to an end three years later, on his birthday. With his first stint in the Navy completed, he'd reenlisted and gotten transferred off the boat while it was in Portsmouth, Virginia, for its final yard period. He'd loved the *Scorpion,* but his new wife had a baby on the way, and he'd elected for refresher school so that he could be with her when it came and then spend a little time learning the ropes of parenthood before getting attached to another submarine.

In late May 1968, Pratt graduated from training school and received orders to report to the USS *Puffer* (SSN-652), the second of the new Sturgeon-class ballistic subs to enter the nuclear fleet. The program he'd taken at the Great Lakes Naval Training School on Lake Michigan, and some additional classes in New London, had brought Pratt up to snuff on the systems aboard the modern boat, which was homeported in Pascagoula, Mississippi.

After graduating at New London, Pratt found himself with a few extra days on his hands before he had to be in Pascagoula. Though it had been almost a year since he'd left *Scorpion,* he still knew most of the crewmen and had a lot of close friends among them, married and single. Having kept in touch with the guys and their spouses, he'd gotten wind that she was due back from the Med on May 24, and decided to stop in Norfolk to meet her while driving down from Connecticut with his wife and newborn son. Pratt not only wanted to see his old shipmates, but figured he would be traveling almost 1,400 miles in a car that had seen its best days and didn't want to push his luck. Not with the baby along for the trip.

Pratt and his family got to Norfolk on the 23rd and stayed overnight at a friend's place. Even though *Scorpion* didn't show up the next day, it didn't occur to him that she might be in trouble. In fact, Pratt had allowed for some leeway insofar as the timetable for his drive to Mississippi and didn't absolutely need to get right back on the road. That made him hopeful he could wait for her arrival.

Pratt stuck around Norfolk for yet another full day, but the boat never showed up in port. Now he'd have to hit the road or risk being late for his assignment on the *Puffer*. He wasn't worried because he knew from personal experience that it would be a mistake holding the sub to a strict return date. If *Scorpion* had been delayed because of some last-second orders, this wouldn't be the first time. Also, the Ship Arrivals line had never officially confirmed the May 24 ETA her crewmen wrote about in their letters home. That, coupled with the fact that the Navy had given no suggestion that anything was wrong, hinted SUBLANT might have had some prior expectation that the boat might be off schedule.

On May 25, Pratt and his wife finally said their goodbyes to their friends, got the baby settled in the car, and started on their way again. But the vehicle was soon showing signs of crankiness—not a good development with almost a thousand miles remaining on their trip. Plagued with engine trouble, Pratt somehow managed to steer his family along nine hundred of those miles before he turned into the parking lot of a Holiday Inn in Mobile, Alabama. Despite being just an hour's drive or so outside Pascagoula, he was bushed. With sundown approaching, he thought it would be wise to check into the motel and start out fresh and alert in the morning.

It was now Memorial Day, May 27.

By six o'clock, Pratt had peeled off the clothes he'd worn all day and gotten into the shower for a quick scrub. Outside in the bedroom, his wife turned on the television, but he couldn't hear it over the sound of spraying water around him.

Then, suddenly, someone was knocking—no, *pounding*—on the bathroom door. The noise was so loud it startled Pratt.

"What is it?" he asked from under the hissing showerhead.

"Get in here, Jerry!" his wife cried. "Now!"

Alarmed, Pratt shut the tap, jumped out of the shower, and snapped a towel off the rack. Still dripping, he gaped at the TV in dumbstruck silence. Walter Cronkite was reporting that *Scorpion* was missing in action. As of about three o'clock that afternoon, the Navy had initiated a search.

Pratt stood frozen in place. He could scarcely believe what he'd heard. But a SUBMISS wouldn't have been called unless the Navy had been concerned about the sub for a while. Why had the families been misled into thinking everything was okay?

Pratt stared at the television, his mind grappling with the news, trying to make sense of it—a struggle that only worsened with the passage of time. In bed later on, between bouts of sleeplessness, he would be tormented by unbearable dreams about *Scorpion*. If asked, he might have found it hard to say which was worse: tossing sweatily in his dreams or staring up into the empty, implacable darkness.

Pratt would have time to decide. The insomnia and dreams would be a problem for the rest of his life.

XII

When the all-hands call went out at 8:45 P.M. on May 27, most of the crewmen from the USS *William H. Standley* were on shore leave or liberty. They had just returned to Mayport Naval Station in Florida after exercises with the USS *Intrepid*, leaving a skeleton crew aboard on the night watch.

At one bar after another near the base, Navy shore patrolmen went pushing through crowds to round up *Standley* sailors who had just settled in over their drinks. They were to return to their ship immediately. A U.S. submarine was in trouble and they had to embark on a search-and-rescue mission.

Sailors would generally exchange choice remarks about the SP guys when they blew in shouting orders, but not this time. This time their loud conversation and laughter died down to a sober hush as they hurriedly paid their tabs. The frigate's crewmen would only learn the name of the missing submarine—USS *Scor-*

pion, a Skipjack nuke out of Norfolk—after they had gotten underway, but it wasn't really important what boat it was, or where it was homeported. Their fellow sailors were in peril and they needed, and *wanted,* to help.

It was almost one o'clock in the morning on May 28 before the *Standley* was ready to make way. As he'd gone to his work area, nineteen-year-old Radarman Third Class Richard Shafer had estimated a third of the crew was still off the ship as they left port. With so many men on liberty, he guessed there hadn't been time to wait for all of them to return.

Shafer would soon find himself surrounded by high-ranking officers, though. They had originally been on the *Petrel,* but problems with some of the equipment aboard the submarine rescue vessel had forced a transfer right around sunrise on May 29, a day after the *Standley* reached the Virginia Capes.

The collection of brass overwhelmed Shafer. His work area was in the Combat Information Center, or CIC—a room lined with electronic display consoles in which sonar, radar, radio, and meteorological information was gathered and integrated with data coming in from other fleet vessels. For the rescue effort, his job would be to man a wireless underwater telephone station at the Naval Tactical Data System in the CIC's commodore's command area. Once, as the *Standley* made its transatlantic crossing to the Azores in what many crewmen later swore was record-breaking time, he looked around from his console and saw no fewer than eight top officers conferring within a few feet of him—Rear Admiral Bernard, two vice admirals, three captains, and two commanders. Shafer wished he could have eavesdropped on them, but he was wearing a full-ear-coverage headset that muffled the sound of their voices. Everybody on the boat was wondering what had happened to *Scorpion.* He'd heard rumors that it had gotten into an accidental collision with a seamount or a Russian submarine, rumors of sabotage—all kinds of stories were circulating on the ship. If Shafer could have made out what the brass were saying, he would have been the most popular guy onboard.

As it was, he stuck to his duty. With the *Standley* steaming ahead on its search track, Shafer would broadcast the hail, "Brandywine, Brandywine. This is Steamer, Steamer, over!" on the sonar unit about every ten minutes. Brandywine was *Scorpion*'s radio call sign, and Steamer was *Standley*'s.

Shafer remained at the console for the better portion of the next nine days. Pressing the transmit/receive switch, hailing, taking his thumb off the switch, waiting for a reply. And then starting his hail again.

"Brandywine, Brandywine. This is Steamer, Steamer, over!"

To Shafer's lasting sorrow, the hail was never answered.

XIII

The power plant on a nuclear sub uses large amounts of water for cooling and generating steam for its turbines. But water naturally contains charged trace minerals that have a corrosive effect on machinery, so it must be filtered before it becomes nuclear process water. If you are running an atomic reactor on a submarine, you do not want radioactive liquids streaming from leaky pipes.

To create process water for its reactor, a nuclear submarine is equipped with a mixed-bed deionization system constituted of a tank, or bed, filled with two types of polymer resin beads. Smaller than pinheads, the porous, hollow beads have thousands of microscopic, spurlike projections inside them that are either positively or negatively charged. As water flows through the beads, the ionized particles attach themselves to the projections—positives to negatives, and negatives to positives—and leave the tank as deionized process water.

Like any filtration system, a resin bed needs to be periodically replaced, and as its expiration date approaches a sub's nuclear engineers will ready it for disposal. In 1968, the expired resin, which had the potential to be radioactive, would be flushed into the ocean at a predesignated distance from land. Though environmental concerns would later put an end to the practice, it was routine in those days of lesser ecological enlightenment and regulatory control.

Bound for a resin-dumping area in the Atlantic, the nuclear attack submarine USS *Skate* had been out of New London about a day when it received orders to abandon its activities and proceed at flank bell to a location off the Virginia Capes. A U.S. sub was believed to have gone down while returning to Norfolk from deployment, and the *Skate* was to join up with a search element preparing to retrace the route from its homeport to the coordinates of its final situation report somewhere out near the Azores.

Machinist's Mate Third Class Bob McDaniel had been a member of *Skate*'s crew for just under two months, having reported to her a few weeks after she returned from a northern run. Still a young sailor working on his submarine qualifications, he was distressed to hear that another Navy sub had in all probability sunk without survivors. But he noticed that some of the older hands were taking the news especially hard, and had paled when they heard the boat was the *Scorpion*.

As the *Skate* raced out to meet the other vessels bound for the Mid-Atlantic, he talked to some of the guys and learned why—there were personal links between the crews of the two subs. Back in late 1967, they had both been in the shipyard at Portsmouth, and were tied up alongside each other for quite a while. The crews and their families had gotten acquainted, and many had socialized. Some of them had kids who'd played together.

McDaniel would recall few pleasant moments during his trip to the Azores. With the exception of the *Pargo* back off Norfolk, all the subs were instructed to remain on the surface so they could intercept any radio signals that a disabled *Scorpion*, or her message buoys, might be transmitting. But the round-bottomed *Skate* had been designed for submerged travel, and in the early going she rolled violently on the storm-tossed waters. Soon almost everyone aboard was seasick, and the captain went down to periscope depth to try to give them some relief.

Unfortunately, it was short-lived. No sooner had McDaniel's stomach stopped turning than a radio dispatch from SUBLANT ordered *Skate* back up to ride the heaped, crashing waves. With no other ships within miles of the sub, McDaniel wondered how headquarters found out she had gone down to periscope depth. It was only years later that he concluded the SOSUS hydrophones must have detected her.

At last the waters around the *Skate* calmed, and her crew started feeling better—physically, at any rate. The dark mood of the long-timers was pervasive, their personal loss something that came to be felt even by guys who had gotten assigned to the sub after her Portsmouth yard period. As they combed the ocean with heavy hearts, there would be no shortage of volunteers up on the sail for lookout duty.

Bob McDaniel was one of them. His first turn came several days into the trip and, emerging topside, he was surprised to find himself blinking into the glare of a hot, blazing sun. Yes, he'd supposed the weather had improved—that much was evident from the steadier seas beneath the *Skate*'s keel. But the total absence of clouds was a surprise. The water around him glittered with brightness, and the men who had preceded him on lookout duty were lobster red on their faces and arms. They had traded seasickness for horrendous cases of sunburn.

McDaniel would spend many long hours on the bridge—in fact, it was during the search that he got in his lookout time for his qualifications. As *Skate* pushed inexorably toward the Azores, the young sailor observed many things new to his experience. There were the inquisitive right whales swimming in groups along the sub's course, their huge black bodies occasionally breaching the water. There were also the wooden barrels, debris, and oil slicks that McDaniel thought might be signs of *Scorpion* until the veteran lookouts told him otherwise, pointing out that they were close to the commercial shipping lanes, where flotsam, jetsam, and spills of various sorts were commonplace.

In the end, the *Skate*'s search would be marked with futility, leaving McDaniel to share in the disappointment felt by all those who crossed the Atlantic with Admiral Bernard. Though the task force would spend over a week at sea, and receive support and assistance from patrol aircraft and a dozen other vessels, it would not come across a single fresh clue to the lost sub's whereabouts.

XIV

A daily memo of record from the Lyndon Johnson presidential archives dated May 28, 1968, and submitted by Rear Admiral Tidwell Shepard, Jr., director of operations (National Military Command Center), read in part:

> Atlantic fleet air, surface and submarine units are continuing to search for the USS *Scorpion* on an eastward tract from the Virginia Capes. *Scorpion* was due at Norfolk Naval Base at 1300EDT 27 May from extended Mediterranean deployment with the Sixth Fleet. The submarine with a complement of 99 officers and men failed to arrive. *Scorpion* was last heard from at 212001 EDT at a position 400 nautical miles south of the Azores. The submarine carried two Mk 45 nuclear torpedoes.

Shepard's terse, dry language on behalf of the NMCC—the command and control center for the entire military—was accurate as far as it went. But his memo did not at all suggest the desperate urgency of the search. Nor did it mention that the Navy's main civilian troubleshooter had been pulled into the search with utmost haste.

His name was Dr. John Piña Craven, and he was literally and figuratively bound for mysterious waters.

It would not be his first time entering them.

XV

On Wednesday, May 29, Vice Admiral Schade returned to shore after nearly forty-eight hours of plumbing Virginia's coastal waters aboard *Pargo*. Together with the submarine rescue vessel *Sunbird*, the sub had located five sizable objects of interest, two of which were identified as the husks of sunken merchant ships, and a third that was determined to be a barge. Another appeared large enough to be a submarine on the sub's sonar readings, and *Sunbird*'s divers lost no time going down for a close-up look. They soon found themselves staring wide-eyed through their masks at what a May 31 newsmagazine account would describe as "a relic of World War II."

This was accurate as far as it went, for they had chanced upon the decaying wreck of a German U-boat. Over two decades earlier, the enemy sub had been lost on a foray into waters near one of America's largest naval installations. What her mission might have been was something no one but those who'd ordered it—and those who perished aboard the sub—would ever know.

As May tilted toward June, Schade would continue to direct *Sunbird* and the rest of the close-in search force from his administrative office at SUBLANT headquarters, while providing remote logistical support to Admiral Bernard's operations in the Azores.

But on both sides of the Atlantic, hope was rapidly fading. Thus far, nothing had been found except old, rusted metal corpses, and whatever unspeaking ghosts might haunt their watery graves.

6. LOST

"When the waves of death surrounded me. The floods of ungodliness made me afraid."

—*2 Samuel 22:5*

" 'Wouldst thou,' so the helmsman answered,
'Know the secret of the sea?'
Only those who brave its dangers,
Comprehend its mystery.' "

—*"The Secret of the Sea," Henry Wadsworth Longfellow,
quoted in Rear Admiral James W. Kelly's memorial
meditation for the* Scorpion *crewmen, June 6, 1968*

"Walker was the greatest case in KGB history. We deciphered millions of your messages. If there had been a war, we would have won it."

—*KGB officer Vitaly Yurchenko*

I

AS TOP SCIENTIST FOR THE NAVY'S OBSCURE SPECIAL Projects Office, John Craven was the country's leading pioneer in the area of undersea technology and leader of its submarine intelligence program. He was also the boss of the Navy's ultrasecret Deep

Submergence Systems Project, under whose mandate he had spear-headed the evolution of the deepwater submersible vehicles that would become indispensable tools of modern oceanic exploration.

Late on the afternoon of May 27, 1968, Craven was driving home to Virginia after an exhausting day at his Washington office, when he heard about *Scorpion* being overdue over his dashboard radio. At the time he was up to his ears overseeing a clandestine hunt for the lost Soviet submarine K-129, which U.S. intelligence had made one of its foremost priorities. But the bulletin that a search had been launched for the missing U.S. submarine convinced him he'd better swing his car back around toward the capital.

Craven was soon inside the frantic Pentagon War Room, where he was given the assignment of finding *Scorpion* and determining what sank her—if that proved to have been her fate. Though usually permitted great latitude while going about his work, Dr. Craven would, in this instance, receive blunt instructions to rule out hostile actions as the cause of *Scorpion*'s loss.

It is striking to this day that he'd be held to such constraints. Fears of a Russian attack were prevalent among Navy officials, including Rear Admiral Beshany, the deputy chief of submarine warfare operations who'd been one of the officers responsible for *Scorpion*'s spy mission to the Canaries.

"There was some communications analysis that the *Scorpion* had been detected by the group she had been shadowing and conceivably they had trailed her . . . some speculations that not only did they track her but attacked her," he admitted in a newspaper interview after his retirement.

At any rate, Craven, spurred by his thoughts of the sub's ninety-nine missing crewmen, jumped at the task regardless of how much he disliked having his hands tied. A half decade before, four of his researchers and over a hundred sailors had perished during the trial run of the USS *Thresher* in the Gulf of Maine. The tragedy would be etched in his mind and heart forever.

While looking for K-129, Dr. Craven and his scientific team had begun to use vanguard techniques that combined mathematical probability studies with the analysis of acoustical data from the SOSUS system. Now Craven would be quick to suggest that they apply identical methods to the *Scorpion* hunt—and was just as quickly hit with some disappointing news.

A man named Captain Joseph Kelly was one of Dr. Craven's most trusted colleagues in the Navy and its best SOSUS expert. As Craven later recalled, Kelly or his envoy was at the Pentagon huddle that evening and learned that there *wasn't* any SOSUS information. With five days having elapsed since *Scorpion's* disappearance, it was a near certainty that the event had occurred in an area of weak SOSUS coverage: a blind—or more properly *deaf*—spot in the network.

Craven considered that. No, it was not good news at all. But he knew it wasn't disastrous. Other clues to the sub's whereabouts existed, and he must have been apprised of them at the meeting. One would have been the coincident timing of the NSA radio intercepts with *Scorpion's* situation report to Nea Makri. Another, the noises picked up near Lajes by the *Orion's* sonobuoy lines. They had been registered at approximately 18:59 Greenwich Mean Time on May 22. If they'd emanated from *Scorpion*, those sounds would not only fix the time of her sinking, but provide some idea of her location. It would be a *very* general idea, true, nothing that could compare with SOSUS by even the most generously optimistic reckoning. But Craven would have other sources in addition to SOSUS from which to draw information.

There was, he knew, more than one set of ears listening beneath the sea.

II

In the opening minutes of Thursday, May 30, a Neptune P2V patrol plane and six Navy vessels engaged in the close-in search for

Scorpion picked up an apparent distress call from the waters off Norfolk: "Any station this net, this is Brandywine."

As the fliers informed their commanders of the SOS, radio technicians aboard the Sturgeon-class fast-attack sub USS *Lapon* (SSN-661) obtained a generalized reading on its point of origin. Atlantic Fleet Headquarters, meanwhile, met the news with extreme caution. The Navy was sitting on ample intelligence that *Scorpion* had gone down a week earlier near the Azores, thousands of miles from Virginia's coastal shoals. Also, a similar intercept by the diesel submarine USS *Chopper* on the first night of the official search had proven inside an hour's time to be a false alarm. Because this latest broadcast had not conformed to typical hailing protocols, expectations were low that it was any more genuine.

Regrettably for the crewmen's families, the news reporters who'd migrated to Norfolk over the last seventy-two hours shared none of SUBLANT's restraint. Whether they had heard the SOS while scanning maritime radio bands or gotten it leaked to them from a Navy source, they hurried to file reports of the transmission before its authenticity could be verified. It did not take long for their stories to air on radio and television outlets around the nation.

In Norfolk, a community desperate for the least shred of hope couldn't contain its optimism. Glued to the television with her mother and sister, Barbara Foli listened to one television announcer speculate that the submarine might arrive within a day. Soon a commotion erupted outside her windows, with jubilant cries coming from everywhere around her. Rushing from her apartment, she saw that men and women who didn't even have loved ones on *Scorpion* had spilled onto the street and were cheering and literally jumping for joy.

"It was like balloons going off into a dark night sky," she said later, trying to describe the elation of the moment.

But that burst of hope wouldn't last. She had returned to her apartment to watch for additional televised updates when her neighbor, the chief's wife, came for a sobering visit. The Navy had acknowledged having intercepted the "Brandywine" transmission, but was unconvinced it was an actual distress call.

Sometime in the next twenty-four hours, naval officials would issue a terse declaration that there was a "ninety-nine percent chance" it had not come from the missing submarine. Their belief was that it was either the result of honest human error on a search ship, a transmission from one of several private boats in the area named Brandywine, or a sick hoax.

Across Norfolk, the somber mood settled heavily back in.

III

Had anyone asked the students working at Columbia University's Lamont Geological Laboratory oceanographic research station on the Canary Island of La Palma, off the West African coast, whether the station monitored the sounds of aquatic life—the a cappella symphonics of migratory whales, for example—the staffers who worked there could have honestly replied that, yes, of course, that's exactly what they did. In fact, a sign outside the complex welcomed locals and beachgoing tourists in for a listen.

The La Palma facility recorded the natural music of the sea. That was the truth—but just not the *whole* truth. Under its manager, former U.S. Air Force officer Peter Green, the La Palma outpost also, and mainly, thanks to the funding contracts it had accepted from the Office of Naval Research, tracked the sounds of missiles fired from ballistic submarines in the Navy's marine testing grounds in the Atlantic. The missiles would launch into the air, and radar towers would track them. Then the missiles would fall into the water, and La Palma's deep-sound channel hydrophonic arrays—electronic ears set at a depth where sound waves travel vast distances—would register the resultant sounds that went bouncing off an undersea rock face aligned with their sensors. Between the

two modes of detection, technicians could map out the weapons'
flight paths from beginning to end. As might be expected, the military had an acronym for the tracking system—MILS, which was
shorthand for the Missile Impact Location System.

On the morning of May 28, La Palma was radioed by Gordon
Hamilton, a scientist who ran another civilian-slash-MILS outpost in Bermuda and had set up the La Palma station as one of its
subsidiaries. Hamilton had gotten a phone call from Craven early
in the morning. Years before, they had worked jointly using
SOSUS and Hamilton's hydrophones to triangulate the position of
Thresher after its sinking. Now Craven had briefed Hamilton
about *Scorpion*'s disappearance and asked if his listening outpost
had picked up any peculiar sounds that might be associated with
it. When Hamilton heard that the submarine was believed to have
gone down somewhere near the Azores, he told Craven that would
probably put it outside the range of his hydrophones in Bermuda,
but that his La Palma station was at a perfect location for such
readings. He'd check with it and get back to him.

And so, Hamilton radioed La Palma and asked one of the technicians to review his recordings for the past several days starting
with May 22. This was a high-priority affair—a submarine was
missing—and Hamilton needed to know if there was anything
anomalous on those tapes that could help find the missing sub.

It took the tech only a short while to examine the audiotapes.
There were indeed some hydrographic "trains" that appeared of interest, along with corresponding seismographic data on printouts—part of the lab's civilian underwater research was, after all,
geological. Hamilton was excited. Thanks, he said. Now I need
you to fly everything you've got to Washington. When? Try the
next flight out.

When Craven and Kelly examined the recordings in Washington, they were encouraged. There were acoustic sequences that
could possibly be linked to the submarine in five stretches of the

Atlantic that ran broadly along her course. But mustering the resources to scour all of them for sunken wreckage or floating debris fields would be impossible. They needed, somehow, to narrow the search.

Kelly thought he might have the solution. Just as the Navy had MILS labs, the Air Force's Technical Applications Center had hydrographic stations of its own eavesdropping on Soviet nuclear arms tests. It was possible they'd detected something that would allow for a triangulation, and closer study, of the five events on the La Palma recordings and charts, and thereby isolate the most promising one.

Kelly's brainstorm paid off. An AFTAC underwater microphone array off Newfoundland yielded recordings that seemed to match up with the information obtained from the MILS outpost. Like the La Palma material, they were hastily flown to Washington.

Craven and Kelly turned everything they had over to the Naval Research Laboratory's chief acoustical scientist, Wilton Hardy, for analysis.

Within days, he'd recommend a wide but theoretically manageable search area to them.

It would be designated Point Oscar.

IV

For the first week or two after *Scorpion*'s loss, the viability of the Navy's methods for sustaining and saving the lives of crewmen aboard a submerged and disabled submarine—or recovering the boat itself—would be a theme that permeated countless lines of newsprint. On May 28, an Associated Press wire article quoted Admiral Moorer and Captain Nicholson on the practical use of the McCann rescue chamber, and went on to describe the procedures by which *Scorpion* crewmen would enter it and make their ascent. It also mentioned an emergency escape technique that would involve the "donning of inflated vests which carry men to the surface." A United Press International wire service article published on Tuesday, June 4—eight days after the sub was confirmed overdue—began with a paragraph stating that the Navy had flown "sophisticated underwater gear to salvage ships near the Azores Monday as the search for the *Scorpion* began its second week with diminishing hope of finding the 99-man crew alive."

But diminished hope or not, reporters continued asking questions about the chances of men surviving on some emergency reserve of oxygen or air pocket aboard the sub, even as the Navy did everything it could to tamp down such unreasonable speculation. A June 8 article attributed to UPI cited unnamed Navy sources as explaining that "the vessel—if still intact—likely has exhausted its oxygen supply," adding that *Scorpion* "carried bottled oxygen and self-contained units for clearing carbon dioxide from the air . . . but this would keep the men alive only about five days, depending upon the number of crewmen using it."

The ongoing search effort, and the absence of any wreckage, made it understandable that journalists would push on with hypotheticals. Nuclear submarines did not go down every day. Their missions and operations were secret by design, and many reporters had a poor grasp of the physical forces weighing against a potential miracle rescue of a sub's crew after so long a period. But if the press had kept a tighter focus on Norfolk, its members would have understood that, on June 6, Admiral Moorer and his subordinates had already given the families of the *Scorpion* sailors the clearest and most unambiguous acknowledgment possible that their men were dead—a memorial service.

V

Since his arrival in Norfolk, things had turned around in dramatic fashion for John Walker. He had once cringed to see his bills in the mailbox, and hesitated to answer his phone for fear a creditor was on the line. Now he could buy anything he wanted without a second thought. And then at the end of May 1968, and heading into June, the tragedy that befell Norfolk's naval community ironically contributed to his gains.

As a storm of urgent communications about *Scorpion*'s disappearance blew through SUBLANT headquarters, Walker was perfectly positioned to reap the intelligence dividends at its epicenter. The top secret documents he'd acquired detailed everything the Navy knew or suspected about the submarine's loss, every phase of the search, every attempt to gather information from SOSUS and correlate it with the underwater noises detected by the Lajes patrol flight. Though SOSUS hadn't yielded much early on, the Russians had found what the hydrophonic data *didn't* reveal to be as significant as what it did, since it pointed to exploitable gaps in the network coverage.

Walker's cash take from sharing *Scorpion*-related messages with the Soviets matched, or possibly surpassed, the windfall he'd earned after delivering the Orestes key lists months ago—and those messages were so easy to snatch, he didn't even bother using the Minox camera. It was always a little dangerous to photocopy the keys, since he would have to offer some plausible excuse if he was caught doing it. But naval communications were normally reproduced in multiple and then filed for routing to different channels, which made handling them around a Xerox machine consistent with Walker's duties as watch officer. Had anyone seen him with copies of the messages, it would have seemed completely routine.

Yes, Walker had fared well. The Russians considered the *Scorpion* documents he'd provided a major intelligence score. They had not only rewarded him accordingly, but expressed their appreciation and desire for more in a note at a recent dead drop. Whatever had happened to *Scorpion*, Walker was convinced it wasn't his fault. In his estimation, the Cold War was just another level of the game he was playing, a magnification of it. He believed the notion that Russia and the United States would ever go to war was ludicrous. Why would the Soviets want to provoke an atomic shooting match with the United States by bringing down one of its subs? And even if the information he'd sold the Russians had been used in staging an attack—he still wouldn't be responsible. As he had explained to his wife, the instant a man joined the Navy he took the chance of putting himself in harm's way. Those sailors on *Scorpion* had known that when they enlisted or took the entry exam for Annapolis. They had recited their oaths and accepted the risks.

Walker hadn't dwelled on the loss of the sub's crew. Barbara and the other women around the base could sit around spilling tears over it. Those sailors were gone, and whatever suffering they'd experienced would not be worsened or lessened if he took advantage of every opportunity the disaster presented. One of the best had come up days after it happened, and astonishingly it bore a connection to the eye-opening SIOP blueprint he'd stumbled across on the *Simon Bolivar.*

On watch at the message center when the order came in, Walker and another man were to decrypt and relay a command from the highest levels of the Navy to the Polaris submarine fleet in the Atlantic, initiating a series of ballistic missile strikes against the USSR.

Back when he'd served on the *Bolivar,* Walker had been involved in weapons system readiness tests that measured the competency of a Polaris submarine crew in the event a nuclear strike was ordered. As a radioman, his job was to decode the launch command from the NAVCOM and hand it to the captain and executive officer as they raced into the radio shack. Only the sub's top officers—probably the very two men Walker would provide with the decoded launch command—would know it was all a simulation.

At SUBLANT, Walker had been at the transmitting rather than the receiving end of the launch command. Just as in his radioman days, he hadn't known the whole thing was a test until it was almost over. The drill had been that realistic—and this time it had thrown the entire ballistic submarine force into near-strike mode. With the Pentagon brass looking at evidence it believed might implicate Russia in *Scorpion's* loss, and theorizing that an attack on the sub might be the first move in a larger outbreak of hostilities, it had wanted to test the preparedness of the systems and personnel that would set off full-scale U.S. retaliation.

Afterward, Walker would marvel at finding himself with a pivotal role in the implementation of the SIOP. The one-megaton thermonuclear warhead of a single A3 Polaris missile was a hundred times more powerful than the atomic bombs that leveled Hiroshima and Nagasaki in World War II. A boat like the *Simon Bolivar* carried sixteen A3s, each with a range of 2,500 nautical miles. For that reason, America's SSBN fleet was the forward element of its nuclear defense strategy, the greatest edge it had over the Soviets.

John Anthony Walker was stunned to realize that a single act—or failure to act—on his part would completely wipe out that advantage. The longer he pondered his own importance, the more it intoxicated him. And inevitably his thoughts turned to how he might profit from the situation. What might the Russians pay him for a guarantee to delay or withhold transmission of the Polaris launch orders in a real wartime scenario, and in so doing cut out the very heart of America's strategic defense plan?

Walker decided on a dollar figure, wrote his proposition on a sheet of notepaper, and then inserted the note into the dead drop package he'd brought from Norfolk to yet another remote location. A million dollars seemed a fair amount. No, he did not believe an atomic war was imminent, but it would be quite an insurance policy if one did break out. In a world of nuclear devastation where people were scampering like insects to survive, a million dollars would carry a man a long way.

Walker felt certain the KGB would jump at his offer. How could it not? This time he'd acquired a prize eclipsing all the secret codes, manuals, and dispatches he'd sold them in the past. This time, his hand held the key that would put Russia on the winning side of nuclear Armageddon.

VI

Built as an icebreaking Arctic cargo ship in the late 1950s, the 266-foot USNS *Mizar* had undergone a major conversion in 1963 and 1964, reentering service as an oceanographic research platform attached to the Naval Research Laboratory. Though its unloaded displacement was 1,850 tons, the specialized scientific gear it carried added another two thousand tons, and then some, to the chunky diesel-electric vessel's weight. Amidships, inside a large, rectangular bay that resembled an aircraft hangar, a pair of hydraulic doors on the deck would open to allow the lowering of exploratory submersible gear into the ocean. Forward of the enclosed well deck was a higher and even bulkier structure that contained the vessel's laboratories and operational areas. Among the most interesting pieces of equipment on *Mizar* were towed metal sleds outfitted with powerful strobes, cameras, sonars, and a magnetometer not unlike those on the magnetic anomaly detectors projecting from the tail of Orion antisubmarine warfare planes. These sleds each weighed a couple of thousand pounds, were housed in the mid-deck bays, and would be deployed from the well—or moon pool, as the sailors aboard referred to it—with electrohydraulic deep-sea winches able to reel it down into the abyss on three miles of cable.

As chance would have it, when the SUBMISS for *Scorpion* went out on May 27, *Mizar* was en route to Norfolk for repairs.

Back in 1963, *Mizar* had been an integral part of the search for *Thresher*, and Dr. Craven and his team now decided to divert her to the hunt for the American sub, sending her to the Point Oscar area they'd targeted based on the hydrographic and seismological readings obtained from La Palma and Newfoundland.

Working in close coordination with the NRL and SUBLANT, Craven arranged for the vessel to be hastily dressed up with additional communications and cryptographic equipment before her civilian skipper, Chester "Bucky" Buchanan, took her out of Norfolk on the second day of June.

Mizar had joined the armada of vessels speeding toward the Azores.

VII

Barbara Foli would receive three messages from the Navy in the week or so after *Scorpion*'s disappearance.

The first and briefest came on Tuesday, May 28, and stated what was already obvious: the submarine was overdue. The second message reached her on May 30 and used language that designated the boat and her crew as missing—a status that would enable the spouses of the crewmen to collect their monthly pay, though Barbara did not immediately understand what it signified about the Navy's assessment of Vernon's prospects for survival. In this message, too, was a reassurance that an all-out search-and-rescue effort for the submarine would continue.

The next message arrived on June 5 and was the most devastating.

The instant she answered the door, Barbara knew that it would be different from the previous statements. Those messages had arrived as regular telegrams, but this third was being hand-delivered by a pair of official-looking Navy representatives. One of them wore a blue service dress uniform. The other was a chaplain.

Standing in front of her, the man in the dress uniform quietly introduced himself and his companion and then asked if they could speak with her in private.

Barbara widened the door to let them through. By this time her sister had had to fly back home, but her mother had remained in Norfolk to help prop her up and take care of Holli. Now they waited for the men to say what already must have been dreadfully apparent from their expressions.

Moments later Barbara's worst fears were confirmed. The pair of Navy representatives had brought official notification that *Scorpion* had been presumed lost. Vernon Foli and all aboard the sub were dead.

The declaration was flat and final in the silence of the room. As a casualty assistance call officer, or CACO, the man in the blue dress uniform was trained to avoid using a gentler but perhaps vaguer euphemism. There could be no ambiguity, no confusion, no failure by the next-of-kin to accept the reason for the visit. They had to face the irrevocable reality of their loss and begin at once to prepare for its ramifications.

Vernon was dead.

Dead.

The CACO was respectfully courteous expressing his regrets on behalf of the secretary of the navy. If his delivery had a scripted tone, it was because he was required to follow certain rules of military conduct. The objective was to be helpful and considerate but keep an emotional remove, a neutral demeanor that would encourage the bereaved to stay composed and understand the information to be relayed. He explained that he would answer any questions Barbara might have about funeral arrangements and her benefit entitlements, gave her his card, and told her that he would call as more details about the loss of *Scorpion* became known. She didn't bother to mention that calling wouldn't be possible because she had no telephone.

Before leaving, the CACO and his companion invited Barbara to a memorial service for the men of *Scorpion* to be held at the base chapel the next day. This information would be given to all the wives and family members of the sailors who'd perished on the submarine.

The Navy's chief of chaplains, Rear Admiral James W. Kelly, conducted the service and delivered a lengthy meditation to the stunned mourners. He spoke eloquently of courage and honor and sacrifice, of pride and service, of the mystery of death and the eternal promise of resurrection. On behalf of the Navy, he pledged to help the families absorb the impact of their losses.

"May I say this one last personal word," Admiral Kelly said as the service concluded. "We, the shipmates and friends of your loved ones lost at sea, offer you such strength as we may have in this hour of need. Chaplains and other representatives of the Navy have communicated our concern and support already. I feel the need only to confirm what they have said so well. We offer you each condolence and comfort as we are capable of giving. And we pledge to you that, in partnership with God, who will provide for your loved ones' fulfillment in another world and another life, we here will continue the search for truth, their concern for human liberty, their desire for growing usefulness, and will carry on the selfless service which they set for us. You will remain in our prayers. We pray that God will grant you understanding and peace and the blessing of limitless new resources with which to build a satisfying future."

Just two days after the memorial observance, a moving truck rolled to a stop in front of the rental property the Folis occupied behind Ocean Beach Boulevard. It was a big orange Bekins semi. Barbara had not requested the movers. She did not remember anyone connected with the Navy asking her if or when she wanted to leave Norfolk. Had they done so, she would have told them she preferred to stay on for a while as the search continued. She and the other wives who weren't from the Norfolk area were simply notified that arrangements with moving companies and airlines had been made for them. Barbara wasn't given a date for the truck's arrival; she had thought she'd have some time to prepare. But suddenly, here it was.

Barbara's mother was incredulous, and expressed her feelings to the driver. He acknowledged his discomfort with the awkward circumstances.

"This," he said, "is terrible."

But terrible or not, he had a job to do. Barbara felt irrelevant, pushed aside by the Navy whose promises of support were still fresh in her mind. Not until later would she realize how many other *Scorpion* wives had the same thoughts and emotions.

The movers went to work boxing her possessions. They were fast and methodical filling one carton after another, packing up every last item exactly as it had been set in the house. They took the "Happy Homecoming" ribbons and paper chains Barbara had put up around the living room. They took Vernon's razor and shaving cream from atop the vanity. They cleared the canned green beans, soups, and seasonings arranged in neat rows on the kitchen shelf. Though it had already been opened, they packed the canned ham Barbara had meant to serve Vernon after *Scorpion*'s return. The Folis hadn't accumulated much furniture, but whatever there was got carried out to the semi.

Barbara's feeling of emptiness was beyond description. It was as if a sucking vacuum had opened inside her. Just two years before, she and Vernon had left small-town Illinois on what had seemed like a great adventure. They would see places far from those they knew. They would share different kinds of experiences. Together they had created their new life. Together they had started a family. Together they were supposed to eventually enjoy the return home.

But now Barbara Foli was leaving without her husband. Leaving in a hurry, and not by choice. For her it was all a rush: Bang,

bang, bang. Into the boxes, onto the truck, here's your air ticket, goodbye.

But she wasn't yet ready to go. Not until she said the only good-bye that mattered to her. On her own terms, and in her own chosen time and place.

VIII

In Kincaid, Illinois, it was eleven o'clock at night on June 5 when the cab arrived at the home of Vernon Foli's parents, its headlights glancing over the lawn as it slowed to a halt. The vehicle's rear passenger door opened, and a man in a naval officer's dress uniform got out. His face sober, he strode up to the front door in the darkness.

On the other side of the door, the Folis braced for the worst— as did their daughter Carol, who had come to stay with them. Over a week ago, they had learned of the SUBMISS from Walter Cronkite on the *CBS Evening News*. Vernon's mother had phoned Carol at home to tell her, but Carol had tried to settle her down, assuring her it was probably a mistake. Then Carol's oldest brother, Richard, called and told her she'd better go take care of their mother. Richard was also in the Navy, stationed near Da Nang, in Vietnam.

Carol had packed some clothes into a bag. Richard's phone call had turned her world on its head—right until she'd heard his voice at the other end of the line, he was the brother in the military she'd always worried about. In Carol's mind, Richard was the one in serious jeopardy. Vernon had been safe, or as safe as a serviceman could be. Now the realization that there were no safe places had come barreling over her.

Carol sped out to Kincaid to join her parents, a thousand thoughts flashing through her mind. She and Vernon were the youngest of the family's six children, born eighteen months apart.

Like any brother and sister they had had their fights, but with only the two of them still at home as they entered their late teens, they'd grown close. Vernon was caring and gentle with her, a favorite uncle to his nephews and nieces, the kind of guy you would instinctively turn to for help. He had a knack for being able to repair things around the house, especially if they ran on electricity. If a radio conked out, he would open it up, study its parts, find out what was wrong, fix it, and put it back together. And he'd done a lot of rewiring around the house—not only for their mother, but for Barb's grandmother. With all the electrical contraptions that were becoming available, and so few outlets in the older homes they occupied, there had been extension cords everywhere, and blown fuses when too many things were running at once. Vernon had rerouted the cords to distribute their power loads and cut down on the short circuits.

People could depend on Vernon, and that wasn't just true of his relatives. There was the man in town who had a little shop with a gasoline pump out front. He would let you charge your gas and pay up once a month. But before he joined the Navy, Vernon had gotten laid off from his job at the equipment company in Springfield, and was unable to pay his tab. So he went and talked to the owner of the shop, and they came up with a plan. Vernon worked there without a salary to make good on his debt, and the owner of the place couldn't have been more appreciative. Dependable, yes. The word summed up Vernon as well as any other.

Now nine days had passed since Carol got that original call from her mother about *Scorpion*. Nine days since Cronkite, and not the military, told America that the sub was overdue. And she and her parents immediately knew in their hearts why the officer at the door was there to see them.

It was eleven o'clock. In Kincaid the streets were still and quiet and the windows of its few thousand homes mostly dark behind their drawn shades and curtains. Men in officer's garb did not show up in cabs with good news at that time of night. Not in small town like this, and probably not anywhere.

Answering their door, the Folis admitted the CACO into their living room.

And he told them what they had most feared hearing.

IX

In the waning days of May 1968, and for months afterward, the Russians had their hands full with the intelligence jackpot gained from the *Scorpion* affair.

From the time the submarine disappeared, Oleg Kalugin and Boris Solomatin had been swamped with information relevant to the Navy's efforts to contact and locate her. Walker would have given them the three urgent, unanswered dispatches from COM-SUBLANT to *Scorpion*. He would have furnished copies of all the messages that either passed through or originated from the Norfolk message center relating to the secret hunt for the sub and the scramble to correlate the acoustic data from the Orion P-3B sonobuoys with anything SOSUS might have picked up. From May 27 onward, he would have copied them on the orders that started the official search and the particulars of its makeup, scope, methods, and findings as it progressed. In slightly over two weeks, Walker had opened a broad window of insight into America's reaction to the loss of one of its nuclear submarines, and the fears about Soviet culpability that were boldly and drastically under-scored by the Polaris launch drill.

But for Solomatin, Kalugin, and their superiors at KGB head-quarters, it was imperative that the Americans never learn that Walker had given them an advance tip about his assignment to SUBLANT. If U.S. intelligence *did* find out he'd been in a position to provide the Soviets with KW-7 keylists and tech manuals by

January 1968, there was a distinct possibility that they would begin to discern the Russian fingerprints that were all over the *Pueblo* operation.

The leathery Solomatin had seen it all. An infantryman in the Great Patriotic War, he was subsequently versed in the art of espionage at the Moscow State Institute of International Relations, a training school for the KGB elite. What he hadn't learned about spying at the institute, veteran experience had taught him. He had long appreciated that the Walker case was a "once in a lifetime" intelligence opportunity and, as it applied to his personal fortunes, an unrivaled avenue of career advancement. But even so, Solomatin must have been astounded to learn of the nuclear missile drill that Walker described in his dead drop note, and of his offer to sabotage an actual naval launch command for a million dollars.

Kalugin had surely brought the American's note to Solomatin's desk with appropriate haste, and expected that it would hook deeply into his thoughts. But it wasn't within Solomatin's discretion to accept or reject such a proposal. Solomatin might have drawn upon instinct and experience to formulate his recommendations to his superiors. He would have wasted no time letting them know about the proposal, however.

As a professional KGB man, Solomatin was quick to discern the value of the information in which he dealt, and this was not the sort of thing one could sit on.

X

Before *Scorpion* crewman Doug Kariker checked out of the Navy in 1967, his best friend on the boat was Interior Communications Technician Ronald Lee Byers. Ronnie, who was from upstate New York, had been on the sub two years when Kariker reported to her. Both were single at the time, and they quickly found they shared similar interests. Whenever they could swing it, they took liberty together. Ronnie was Doug's running buddy, and it was while they were out pounding Virginia Beach one day that Ronnie met a young woman named Linda Taylor. She would marry him after Doug left the service.

As far as sports and athletics, Ronnie's skills ran the gamut. A physically strong kid, he liked to compete. Back at Palmyra Macedon Central High, he'd played on the football and bowling teams, and set pole vault and high jump records that would remain for years to come. He also showed flair with a pool cue, though that talent wasn't the sort that would have made for a notation in his student file. Probably it was one he'd perfected—if not altogether gained—after his graduation from Pal-Mac.

On weekend liberties during *Scorpion*'s homeport stays, Byers and Kariker had liked to hit downtown Norfolk, drinking and shooting pool at bars Kariker would have never stepped into on his own. Ronnie would hustle guys for beers, then for money—small amounts of money to start the night. When his opponents got frustrated over their losses, he'd raise the stakes. Doug couldn't have begun to count the times they would have to hotfoot it out of some watering hole after taking guys' cash at the pool table, Ronnie's angry targets cursing and making threatening remarks as they chased the sailors down the street. Once, Kariker fell down a flight of steps trying to get away from some really bad guys Ronnie had hustled. "If I was sober, I would've broken my neck," he recalled with a laugh.

In late February or early March of 1967, Kariker received his honorable discharge from the Navy. Shortly before that, *Scorpion*'s executive officer, Lieutenant Fountain, tried to talk him into reenlisting. He offered Kariker a guaranteed billet on the sub, promised him entry into nuke school, and whatever else he could to persuade him to return.

"Here's the thing," Fountain said. "We're going into an overhaul, and then we're making a Med trip. Have you ever been to the
Mediterranean?"

No, Kariker told him. *Scorpion's* patrols throughout his service
period were in the Atlantic. He was from a working-class family, a
twenty-year-old Louisiana boy who'd enlisted in the Naval Reserve while still a high school junior, and then done a couple of se-
mesters of college before starting active duty. When would he have
gotten the chance to make such a voyage?

Fountain continued to dangle incentives. "Well, the Med offers
the greatest liberty ports in the world. You could stay onboard
Scorpion for the yard period, then go on the trip with her. See
places like Spain and Italy. In the meantime you can start all the
prework for nuclear power school, take the correspondence
courses. And when you get back, you'll be enrolled."

Fountain's final carrot was to remind Kariker of the Navy's
reenlistment bonus of $10,000.

"Hey, it would buy you a nice sports car," he'd added.

Kariker was almost won over. It wasn't just the draw of the
bonus and exotic foreign lands. Nor was it really Fountain's assur-
ances of an open door into nuke school, which would lead to better
naval pay and a highly sought-after civilian career. The plain and
simple truth was that Kariker loved submarines. His fascination
with them had started when he was about eleven, and he'd seen
the underwater combat drama *Run Silent, Run Deep* in the theater.
And it meant everything that he got along with his shipmates, felt
ultimate trust in their abilities, and considered *Scorpion* a tremendous boat. He could not recall her having had a major operational
problem. In fact, it was while Kariker was aboard that she was
awarded the coveted Battle Efficiency "E" hash mark, a citation he
would always remain convinced was well earned.

Still, Kariker had realized he would need to re-up for six years
to get into nuke school, and that seemed an awful lot of commit-

ment. As it was, he owed the Navy four years of reserve duty, three of which would be on active status. That meant he would have to spend one weekend a month on drills, and two weeks a year on active duty to fulfill his obligation.

After considerable soul-searching, he declined Fountain's offer. Sorely tempting as he'd found it, Kariker missed New Orleans, where he was born and raised, and had a burning desire to return to college before it was too far behind him.

In late spring of 1968, Kariker was due for his first active reserve duty since his return to civilian life. Having won his dolphins on *Scorpion,* and figuring he wasn't that up-to-date as far as the systems on diesel boats, he'd wanted to take his duty aboard a nuclear sub. But he was informed that he couldn't get two weeks on a nuke, and so instead put down for the USS *Argonaut,* a World War II conversion submarine that none too coincidentally was homeported in Norfolk. Kariker figured he would do his active in early June, right about when *Scorpion* was supposed to get back from deployment, and hook up with some of his former shipmates. He was especially keen on getting together with Ronnie Byers. Going to Ronnie's house, spending time with him and his new bride—that sounded like a blast.

It was never to be. Kariker heard the unbelievable news that *Scorpion* was overdue right around the time he was leaving for Norfolk. When he got there, and discovered *Argonaut* was already out at sea searching for her, it felt like he'd tumbled headfirst into a nightmare.

As Bill Elrod had done aboard the *Orion* just days before, Kariker spent a week of his active duty shuffling papers on *Argonaut's* tender, using it as excuse to keep busy while awaiting word of his former shipmates. Then, on Wednesday, June 5—the same day all of America awakened to learn of Robert F. Kennedy's assassination—Admiral Moorer made the official pronouncement that *Scorpion* was "presumed lost," an artful phrase meaning the

Navy had determined that the boat and its crew had gone down.

Reading to reporters at his press conference, he said, "With these harsh, unbending facts, I can only ask that you join me in paying tribute to the men of the *Scorpion,* to their families, and to their service. Their families, the wives and children of *Scorpion*'s men, have shared acceptance of the sea's challenge with their husbands and fathers just as we in the Navy, and indeed all Americans, now share so deeply the loss these families have sustained."

The chief of naval operations then had a written statement passed around to the press corps. This spoke to the unsuccessful results of the search in harder detail:

Now, because of the lack of any evidence of *Scorpion*'s presence on the surface or in waters which would permit rescue, we must conclude that she was lost in the depths of the Atlantic. This conclusion is based on the fact that we have had no signals in the form of sonar or radio transmissions, flares or messenger buoys, nor have we observed any debris specifically identifiable with *Scorpion.* These facts compel us to conclude that she is not in a location where recovery of the crew could be effected or salvage conducted.

No place in the country hung under a darker, heavier pall of gloom following the news than Norfolk, where national and personal tragedies had intermingled and overlapped. Doug Kariker was long-faced and somber the day he had to return home. There would be no reunion with his shipmates, no good times with Ronnie and Linda Byers. Ronnie and all the others on *Scorpion* were gone.

Leaving for Louisiana, Kariker would travel the same southbound roads recently taken by another former *Scorpion* crewman who'd planned to be around for the sub's homecoming. He and Jerry Pratt were old buddies. They had served together on the boat, and shared the night watch on the steering and diving station for several months. There were always three men on that watch. A man at the bow plane controls at the helm, another at the stern planes, and a rotator who usually fetched coffee when he wasn't sitting in one of the two chairs. Once Kariker went into his discipline, which was interior communications, he would be assigned the auxiliary electrician forward watch—a roving watch that separated him from working closely with Pratt. But he'd spent many hours with the feisty little guy nicknamed Seabag, and gotten to know him well. If the men had known they had missed connecting with each other, both would have regretted it.

As it was, Kariker's thoughts were solely with *Scorpion*. Like everyone back in Norfolk, he'd grasped at a lingering, vaporous hope that the sub would show up. Then, even as that hope dissipated, he had prayed for a miracle. But now he'd admitted to himself that there wouldn't be one.

Perhaps, however, some part of him realized that wasn't entirely true. He knew he would have been aboard the boat if he'd reenlisted—would have perished with the others if he'd taken up Lieutenant Fountain's offer. And he'd come close to it, very close. Pondering that, Kariker came to feel blessed, as if God had been looking over his shoulder when he made his decision.

It may not have comforted him at the time. But as he got older, and wed, and was able to watch his children and grandkids grow tall, it helped.

XI

She wasn't yet ready to go. Not until she said the only goodbye that mattered to her. On her own terms, and in her own chosen time and place.

The orange Bekins truck had rumbled off toward the highway. A plane bound for Illinois would soon be waiting at the airport, a seat on it reserved for her and the baby.

Everything she owned was on its way to the Midwest, but Barbara Foli wasn't ready to join it.

A short while before she was supposed to leave Norfolk, Barbara gathered her year-old daughter into her arms, stepped out her front door, and turned down toward the tidal inlet at the end of her street. Slowly, she walked by the other houses lined up on the way to the dead end. About five of them stood in a row, their windows facing the street. Barbara did not notice if anyone was at the windows. It wasn't important to her that somebody might be watching. She passed the houses one by one, carrying Holli against her, looking straight ahead as she walked onto the thick grass, and then across it to the low, flat bank at the water's edge.

Barbara paused there on the damp ground. She set her daughter down, crouched to take off her shoes, and rolled up her pants and sleeves. Then she rolled up Holli's pants, hoisted the baby back into her arms, and waded out.

When she was a little less than knee-deep in water, Barbara stopped again. She stood with Holli, staring out at the mouth of the inlet, holding her as the current washed around her slender ankles and calves. Gently, she took hold of her daughter's hand, leaned over, and guided it into the water. Holli's hand was small and warm in her own. The cool water flowed over them. They swished their fingers around in it, mother and daughter, together.

Barbara felt a comfort knowing her husband was in that same body of water. The sea in which the Navy said he rested was bathing over her. Whether he was alive or dead, it was the only place she could find him.

She stood there for a long time, talking to Vernon. The mild ebb and flow of the current somehow brought him to her and the child they had conceived in their love, and carried some part of them away to him. It was as if they were touching, joined across whatever measureless gulf lay between them.

Barbara found it hard to leave the water that day. When she finally did, she knew she would be able to leave for home, too. The time for her parting with Norfolk, Virginia, had come.

It was much later that a Chicago newspaper published the report: Outside Norfolk, days after the loss of the nuclear submarine USS *Scorpion,* the widow of one of its crewmen had entered the water with her child in a possible suicide attempt.

That was not the reason. If anything, she had come to make a lasting pledge of the heart, and find the reassurance that not all that was gone was truly lost—and that it was okay to look ahead, and move on as best she could, and live.

XII

On June 8, 1968, after a funeral service at Saint Patrick's Cathedral, the body of assassinated New York senator and presidential candidate Robert F. Kennedy and a large group of mourners rode a train to Arlington National Cemetery for RFK's burial.

On August 20, the Soviet Union sent 200,000 mechanized infantry troops to invade Czechoslovakia, crushing the government of President Alexander Dubček, who had introduced liberal reforms into the independent nation's Communist system.

On August 28, the city of Chicago was rocked with a bloody confrontation between police and thousands of demonstrators who'd gathered at the scene of the Democratic National Convention to protest the Vietnam War.

By October 30, the total number of American armed servicemen killed, wounded, or missing in action over the course of the war was approximately 100,000. By year's end, this terrible figure would be up 37,650 from the previous year's total.

Also on October 30, in a lonely swath of ocean some four hundred miles from the Azores, the USNS *Mizar* was getting ready to make her seventy-sixth run towing a deep-sea sled across a *Scorpion* search box that had been refined by Craven and Hamilton using innovative mathematical probability studies. By now *Mizar* was the sole remaining vessel from the massive fleet that had been assembled to find *Scorpion* five months ago. SUBLANT had been eager to bring *Mizar* in for a refit for weeks. There had been problems with the sled's sonar. The sled itself had been damaged when it hit an undersea bluff. Fixing these problems cost money, as did keeping the ship out at sea, and the frowns of the Navy's budget people were growing longer with each successive run. *Mizar*'s efforts hadn't brought results. In Washington, Craven was badgering, inveigling, and pleading with the naval brass to hang in there a little longer. *Mizar* was closing in on *Scorpion*, he insisted. There had been tantalizing photographs of debris that was believed to be from the sub. A breakthrough was coming. Give it another week, another day, and his calibrations would be proven out.

Aboard *Mizar*, Bucky Buchanan was nearing the end of his leash. If he didn't find *Scorpion* soon, there wouldn't be many more sled runs.

As that thirtieth day of October prepared to dawn, in a darkroom aboard ship, photographer John Zambon's eyes widened as he was inspecting photos from sled run 75. With him in the room was the ship's operational commander, Captain James T. Traylor.

Buchanan and the rest of the crew would soon be ecstatic. They had found what they were convinced were portions of *Scorpion*'s hull.

The next four sled runs would locate other large sections of the submarine, and on the last day of October, Admiral Thomas Moorer would declare to a press busy chasing other headlines that the USS *Scorpion* had been found.

"It is hoped this new evidence will enable the Navy to ascertain the cause of the loss," he announced.

But the Navy already possessed every piece of evidence it needed to know the cause, and had determined to keep it secret from the public.

XIII

The United States government has never offered an official explanation for the sinking of the USS *Scorpion*.

A U.S. Navy Court of Inquiry is a formal investigative board with origins dating back to the eighteenth century. Normally consisting of senior naval officers, legal advisers, and technical experts, it is a nonjudgmental body charged with investigating incidents that involve substantial loss of life, legal consequences, or that may present international ramifications. Once its hearings conclude, the Court offers its deliberations and recommendations to the naval command in a report of findings of fact.

Convened from June to December 1968, an eight-man U.S. Navy Court of Inquiry panel assembled to look into *Scorpion*'s loss would leak a series of speculative causes to the press. Based on testimony from a group of witnesses that began with Admiral Schade, and went on to include Craven and a long parade of officers, engineers, and sailors familiar with nuclear submarines, the explanations would range from a main battery explosion to undetermined mechanical failure, to the accidental detonation of one of the sub's Mk 37 torpedoes, to possible failure of the trash disposal unit and/or the propeller shaft.

Craven was—and remains—convinced that the acoustic evidence proved a torpedo explosion was in fact responsible. The late Admiral Bernard Clarey, who in 1968 was the second-highest-ranked officer in the United States Navy and would later command the Pacific Fleet, agreed.

Several American submariners who were operating within sonar range of *Scorpion* when she sank have provided firsthand observations that support Craven's forensic conclusions. They remain anonymous because the oaths of secrecy they took on entering the submarine service are still in effect.

"We were in the area when the *Scorpion* went down," said one of them. "Our sonar picked up an explosion about the same time *Scorpion* went down. It was an underwater explosion . . . sounded like a torpedo explosion. At the time we didn't give it a lot of attention, it was a ways off. But when we heard about the *Scorpion*, we knew immediately what had happened." The sailor would add, "Before we returned to port, we were warned to keep quiet. And there was no doubt, they [Navy debriefers] were very serious."

For Craven, a key question while studying his SOSUS data was whether the blast was generated internally or externally—which is to say, whether it occurred within one of *Scorpion*'s torpedo tubes, or came from a warhead hitting the sub's hull from outside. He is on record as stating that the first explosion recorded was external and consistent in magnitude with a torpedo detonation.

Navy officials were quick to reject that contention and pursue alternative explanations.

In July of 1969, half a year after the investigative board's inconclusive findings, the Navy authorized Craven to lead a top secret expedition that would use the bathyscaphe *Trieste*—an aquatic mini-dirigible designed by the Swiss explorer Auguste Piccard and purchased by the U.S. Navy in 1958—to dive almost eleven thousand feet beneath the Atlantic for a close survey of *Scorpion*'s hull and debris field.

The records of *Trieste*'s nine dives were mostly classified, and produced no definitive answers despite a wealth of photographic and eyewitness data. But the Navy's position that mechanical failure was the likeliest cause of the disaster was subsequently reversed as the torpedo malfunction theory began to take firmer hold.

In the "Opinions" section of the Navy Court of Inquiry's official findings of fact—obtained by the press in 1993 under the Freedom of Information Act—the "most probable" explanation given for *Scorpion*'s sinking was that one of the Mk 37s went into a hot run, a situation in which the weapon's motor is inadvertently activated while inside its tube. As conjectured by the panel, Commander

Slattery then had the torpedo jettisoned into the surrounding ocean and ordered a rapid course change, conducting a 180 degree turn meant to trigger a safety device that would shut down the weapon before it could strike the sub. To support the Navy's latest preferred hypothesis, data was released suggesting that *Scorpion* did indeed reverse direction in the moments before her destruction. But forensic analysis of the wreckage provides no evidence to back up that notion.

The Navy also neglected to point out that the Mk 37 torpedo carried by *Scorpion* had a top speed of only 24 knots per hour—and that, according to the Navy's own estimate, its ability to sink a nuclear attack sub was approximately 10 percent or less. *Scorpion*'s maximum speed was about 45 knots. If the submarine had launched the weapon, she could have easily accelerated to a safe distance.

Only an improbable series of human and mechanical failures occurring at once—Murphy's Law taken to an absurd nth degree—could lead to the torpedo actually striking the sub.

It is crucial to note that U.S. submariners have themselves dismissed the errant torpedo scenario as pure gossamer. According to Captain Zeb Alford (Ret.), the former skipper of *Scorpion*'s sister ship USS *Shark* (SSN-591), releasing an armed torpedo was entirely contrary to standard procedure.

"If you did have a hot run, what you would do was let the torpedo's battery power run down and then remove it from the torpedo tube and disarm it," he said.

Alford's statement is supported by numerous interviews with torpedomen who served aboard Skipjack-class nuclear attack boats—including some who had once served on the *Scorpion* herself.

An alternative theory that the Mk 37 detonated inside its tube is no less specious. Analysis of the photographic evidence of *Scorpion*'s largely intact torpedo room shows not a single telltale sign of an interior explosion. In fact, the evidence suggests the contrary.

Lieutenant Commander Ross Saxon, a former submarine skipper who participated in the six-month search expedition and inspected *Scorpion*'s wreckage from aboard the deep-diving *Trieste*, made yet another challenge to the prevalent hot-running torpedo theory. Though Saxon would dispute the contention that the submarine had been struck by a torpedo, it was a view based primarily on his observation that the torpedo doors on *Scorpion*'s bow were tightly shuttered, indicating that no armed torpedo had been fired from them before the submarine was destroyed.

Saxon's comments do not address the possibility that the war shot might have come from a hostile—specifically a Soviet—submarine or aircraft.

XIV

In the years since the Navy Court of Inquiry released its uncertain findings, many theories regarding the loss of the *Scorpion* have been advanced. Often these are based on some previous event involving a ship or submarine and seem plausible at first blush. When closely scrutinized, however, significant flaws emerge, and the theories unravel.

A high-level intelligence source involved in the Navy's search for *Scorpion* would say this under strict condition of anonymity: "Our orders were very clear. Find the submarine and find out what happened. But keep in mind, it was not hostile action and hostile action is not to be given any consideration." The intent, he went on to explain, was to keep the public from learning the facts behind the sinking of the USS *Scorpion*. "In this business you have to keep secrets. I've been taught how to hide the truth. To hide the truth, you create a cover story, a plausible story, one that is believable. If you keep telling it enough times, people will believe it."

And so, any evidence implicating the Soviet Union in the attack on an American fast-attack submarine would have to be suppressed. Anyone who challenged its concealment was told that he or she would be out of a job, or even criminally prosecuted.

Does the Navy know what happened to *Scorpion* on May 22, 1968? Yes. Have the families of *Scorpion*'s crew ever been given an honest accounting of the incident? No. But take away the impossible—and the highly improbable—and all that remains is the one creditable explanation.

In other words, the truth.

7. TRAPPED AND KILLED

"Captain, you are very young and inexperienced, but you will learn that there are some things that both sides have agreed not to address, and one is that event [the sinking of the USS *Scorpion*] and our K-129, lost for similar reasons."

—From a conversation between Rear Admiral Pitr Navoytsev, First Deputy Chief for Operations of the Soviet Navy, and Captain Peter Huchthausen, U.S. Naval Attaché, Moscow

"When you have eliminated the impossible, whatever remains, however improbable, must be the truth."

—Sir Arthur Conan Doyle

I

"WE ARE ABOUT TO BEGIN OUR SURVEILLANCE OF THE Soviets."

On the night of May 22, 1968, in the middle of the Atlantic, *Scorpion* rose in the heaving seas for what turned out to be her final radio transmission to SUBLANT. Standard procedure had called for her to maintain her distance from hostile vessels, and the boat's skipper had taken all required precautions, giving him reason to feel confident his message went undetected. But this had not been the case.

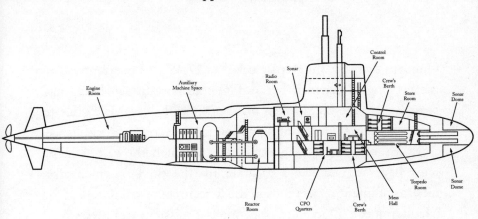

In the radio room on one of the Russian ships loitering near the Canaries, a team of KGB communications experts had intercepted *Scorpion*'s broadcast. Within moments, key information from the communiqué was routed to the helicopter-bearing destroyers that had left Algiers on or about May 18, following the approximate course of their quarry past the monolithic Rock of Gibraltar, and then southward across the Mid-Atlantic.

Shortly after *Scorpion* slipped back into the depths, National Security Agency monitors detected a frenzy of radio traffic from Russian warships in the area. The brief interval between *Scorpion*'s transmission and the Soviet radio bursts, combined with the close proximity of their ships to *Scorpion*, would send up a red flag to Admiral Schade when he was notified of it the next day.

By then, however, it was too late. The Soviets' eavesdropping had given them the sub's exact position and ETA for her mission objective. The Orestes KW-7 crypto box and manuals removed from *Pueblo* in January, coupled with the modification instructions and weekly key lists John Walker provided after the ship's seizure, had enabled the Soviets to read all coded transmissions sent between U.S. submarines and Fleet Headquarters.

The Americans had been duly baited, and were entering the wide-open jaws of their trap.

II

Onboard *Scorpion,* the ship's clock read 17:45, or a quarter to six in the evening Greenwich Mean Time. Almost fifteen hours had passed since she had broken off contact with Nea Makri due to electrical interference, continuing toward her target of surveillance.

In a sense, the open ocean voyage through the vast Atlantic must have seemed like a vacation for the tired crewmen after months of intense operations in the fiercely contested waters of the Mediterranean. One more stop, one last mission, and they would be homeward bound to the real world of family, friends, sunshine, and long hot showers. If their voyage resembled those that preceded it, the men had stood their watches, performed needed maintenance, worked on their qualifications, washed their clothes, read, slept, played cards—anything to help pass the time. In more serious moments, they would have also thought about what lay more immediately ahead. Few operational secrets are kept on a submarine. It hadn't taken long for word to spread that *Scorpion* had a new mission, and that its arrival at Norfolk was again to be delayed. There would have been some obligatory grumbling at the news, but as *Scorpion* closed the distance on the enemy ships, that would have diminished. Though they didn't talk about it much, and some probably couldn't have articulated it if they had tried, the crewmen were aware they were the tip of America's military sword, their country's first line of defense against the Soviet Union. They took great pride in their ship and in their abilities as sailors and submariners. They were professionals and they acted like professionals. They shared a sense of higher purpose.

Right now, however, they were still a fair distance from their destination, and most activities aboard ship were firmly rooted in the mundane. It was almost six o'clock, and the scents wafting through the ventilation system from the galley had every conscious man thinking about one thing and only one thing—dinner.

The crew of *Scorpion* ate family-style, their food and dishes already on the tables, and the crowded mess would have been alive with noise at that hour, the racket of good-natured banter punctuated by the clinking of silverware against plates.

Men assigned to the upcoming watch were allowed to eat first—as one finished eating, another crewman would take his place. The line started in the torpedo room and headed aft through the watertight door into the mess area. Cooks wearing stained T-shirts and white aprons splattered with a sampling of the evening's cuisine carried platters of hot food to the tables and retrieved the empties. Pitchers of milk and the sugary flavored drink they called bug juice—or Kool-Aid, as unwary civilians called it back on terra firma—were passed around while guys talked about home and cars, wives and girlfriends, and how many days they had left before their hitches were up. Some of the repartee inevitably would be directed toward the short-timer, the man nearing the end of his enlistment:

Hey short-timer, how many days left?

Thirty-six and a wake-up! How about you?

Five sixty-three and a wake-up!

Holy shit, if I had that much time I'd fucking kill myself!

Yeah, tell me about it!

On any given night, though, the really hot topic was the scheduled flick. *Scorpion*'s highline transfer with the destroyer *Bigelow* had replenished the sub's well-viewed movie stock, and the conversation about the films that had come aboard would have been livelier than it had been in a while. It was hard to say much about a movie everybody had watched so often they could recite the lines before they left the actors' mouths. But here was some new entertainment—relatively speaking. Since the Navy's stock of approved—and sometimes decades-old—movies was a far cry from the blockbusters shown in theaters back home, it always seemed that at least one guy in the audience had already seen the film, and couldn't resist the urge to play movie critic.

When permission was granted by the officer of the deck to burn the flick, the sailors would have crowded into the tiny mess deck. Every seat would have been taken, with the overflow standing in the back or lining the passageways. Maybe a five-gallon container of ice cream was brought out; maybe a plate of hot cookies and milk; maybe some coveted and delectable oven-fresh sticky buns. It was a surreal scene: men packed into a small space, shoulder to shoulder, eating snacks and watching movies hundreds of feet beneath the surface of the Atlantic while en route to spy on a group of enemy ships. Strange, yes, but to the men of the USS *Scorpion* and thousands of other submariners during the Cold War years, it would have been a typical evening at sea.

III

One level above the mess in *Scorpion*'s darkened control room, the voices would have been hard to make out beneath the continual hum of the ventilation fans.

Very well, I have the watch.

I stand relieved.

With those words the last of the watch standers were relieved, the sailors on duty giving their reports to the men taking over their stations. There is an invariable ceremoniousness to the changing of the watch; it is a moment at which the centuries of naval tradition underlying the relaxed relationships among submarine crewmen become most visible. The watch is a transfer of serious responsibility. The watch is where your response to a sudden crisis might mean life or death for everyone on the boat. The watch is all business.

It was different for the men who'd been relieved.

Free of their duties, the hungry sailors would have flown down the ladder to the crew's mess, calling out a warning to those below: *Down ladder!* In a hurry to reach the source of the food smells filtering throughout the sub, some men would have slid down, hands holding the rails, feet held high. Each would have hit the deck, swung around, and headed toward the watertight hatch and bulkhead that separated the operations compartment from the most forward compartment of the submarine, the torpedo room.

Hey, you lucky bastard!

Lucky Bastard would have turned to the men behind him and grinned. Standing there in the hatchway, he knew he would get the next available seat in the mess. The chow line extended from this point well into the torpedo room. As the new arrivals headed for the end of the line, they would strain to see past the first man and get an idea of how long it really was. They always hoped it was short, but almost always that wasn't the case, and they would have no recourse except to mutter small prayers that the line would start to move, especially if the cooks were serving something choice like cheeseburgers or pizza—and on a boat where Frank Patsy Mazzuchi was a veteran chief, you could count on pizza being a staple.

Racked to either side of the men as they waited in the narrow passage, so familiar as to be unnoticed, were some of the most efficient and lethal weapons in the Navy's arsenal. There were stubby wire-guided Mk 37s, the latest in antisubmarine technology. There were also the huge Mk 14 Mod 5 torpedoes, modified since their introduction a quarter century earlier, and capable of delivering their massive 643-pound HBX warheads to targets nine thousand yards away at speeds of 46 knots—which meant they could take out virtually any surface warship that ventured within range. Farther back, *Scorpion*'s two Mk 45 ASTOR torpedoes, each equipped with a W34 nuclear warhead, rested in the outer slots of the racks. Designed for killing Russia's best nuclear submarines, each of these supremely dangerous fish could swim fast, go deep, and detonate with an explosive punch equal to ten thousand tons of TNT.

Please God, let there be some food left by the time I get to sit down.

IV

It had been full daylight when the Soviet Kamov helicopter rose from the deck of the battleship on what was logged as a late afternoon training exercise, its twin rotors spinning on their shafts to whip a strong downwash of air over the helipad below. In the cockpit of the chopper, his hands on its control levers, a KGB Special Forces pilot had peered out at the restless Atlantic and swung off on his secret assignment.

Designed for antisubmarine warfare, and ideally suited to shipboard operation, the new Ka-25 helicopter was equipped with dipping sonar for sub detection, and housed a pair of AT-2 acoustic homing torpedoes in its weapons bay.

Though its outer performance range with a typical armament load was around 250 miles—probably sufficient for its mission—that distance could be increased with auxiliary fuel tanks mounted on each side of the cabin and connected to its main fuel system.

Shooting along at its maximum speed of 119 knots, the Kamov took an intercept course for the U.S. submarine. The Soviets knew its depth and its speed, and assumed it would be traveling a straight route to its destination. To detect it in the water, the pilot only had to travel to a point along its track, deploy a line or two of passive sonobuoys, and wait.

But detecting it would not be enough. Although manufactured as an advanced antisubmarine torpedo, the AT-2 was a short-range weapon. If the helicopter fired it while the submarine was at depth, the probability was high that the fast-moving sub would conduct a successful evasion. The first shot had to count, then, for there might be no second chance. That meant luring the submarine up to periscope depth.

Reaching his station in advance of the submarine, the pilot settled into a hover and released his passive buoys. Once the sub was detected, the copter would drop an active dipping sonar array from its canister on the fuselage. Its pinging would draw the sub's attention and allow for a pinpoint lock on her position.

It was now late afternoon, the eastern horizon beginning to dim. The Kamov's shadow on the ocean's surface matched its stationary hover. In its cockpit, the weapons officer had already warmed the AT-2's analog tracking circuits—Soviet torpedoes utilized vacuum tube technology in 1968—and readied the weapon for launch.

Moments after the passive buoys registered his target, the chopper pilot reached for a switch on his instrument panel and dropped an active array into the ocean.

V

The control room on *Scorpion*'s upper level would have been a quiet contrast to the suppertime mess as her officer of the deck stood at his watch station. The layout of the control room's stations roughly corresponded to the points of a clock, and the OOD occupied a raised platform in the center of the room, the submarine's two periscopes to his rear. Forward and to his left was the ship's control panel. Facing it at a station that bore an unmistakable resemblance to the cockpit of a passenger plane—with good reason—were two seats occupied by the submarine's planesman and helmsman, the sailors who controlled the motion of the submarine, flying it through the sea.

The diving officer, who was responsible for keeping the submarine at the depth ordered by the OOD, sat behind them on a small locker covered with a green cushion. Near him was the lee helmsman, usually just called the control room annunciator or messenger, a seaman who had the job of transmitting speed and directional orders to the engine room. The chief of the watch manned the ballast control panel farther back on the port side, at the OOD's nine o'clock position. At his one o'clock position on the starboard side, the quartermaster sat at a plotter's table covered with nautical charts. Besides updating the ship's track and keeping an eye on ocean depth and topography, his many duties included recording each order and navigational change in his log and notebook. At three o'clock were the submarine's fire control panels and the station for the fire control technician. Behind them at five o'clock was the sonar shack. Inside the cold, dark shack, noise picked up by the submarine's sensors was converted to optical lines monitored on display consoles. Here the sonarmen stood watch. Without them, *Scorpion* would have been blind and helpless.

It must have seemed that the watch had just begun when the OOD heard a voice crackle out of the 8MC—the sonar room to conning tower intercom: *Conn, sonar. We have active sonar.*

Active sonar. The directional bearing the sonar supervisor gave next would indicate that the source of the acoustic pulse his crew had detected was coming from above them, and resembled what one would expect from a Russian surface vessel—but with a much lower range and intensity.

At their stations in the sub's control room, the men knew two things for certain: *Scorpion* had company, and that company was probing the water. Moments before, she had been alone. Now her crew was facing a potential hostile, and a lot of questions needed to be answered. The situation typified life on a submarine, where long hours of boredom were punctuated by sudden moments of high alert. If anyone's composure altered, the outward signs would have been subtle. A tilt of a head, perhaps. Small adjustments in posture. The planesman and helmsman would have sat more upright in their seats, anticipating orders to change the submarine's depth, speed, and course. The chief of the watch, diving officer, and quartermaster would have swiveled their chairs a bit to watch the OOD.

They would have been poised and attentive. Their training and qualifications had prepared them for situations like this one. But they weren't in the Med, where it seemed the water around them was always infested with Russian subs and skimmers. They were in

the open Atlantic. Here contacts were few and far apart. And even
then they were mostly plodding commercial freighters that did not
use active sonar. Active sonar meant there was a military entity
above them.

The officer of the deck would have asked Sonar to verify that
there were no other contacts in the area, and they would have assured him their other readings were negative—there was just the
single active source overhead.

For the OOD, Sonar's confirmation that *Scorpion* didn't have
another sub on her tail might have warranted a small exhalation of
relief. But there were still too many questions. Was the airborne
contact a plane? A helicopter? Obviously, one or the other. His
standing orders were to summon the captain in the event something unusual occurred, or if the boat was in any possible danger.
And while the ship might not have been at immediate risk, the situation fell neatly into the unusual category.

Now the OOD would have called the skipper to the control
room, briefed him on what was happening after he'd raced up the
steps to the conning tower, and then announced: *The captain has
the conn, I retain the deck.* At that point, Commander Slattery officially took over the conn and would order *Scorpion* up to periscope
depth—forty feet below the chop. If the sub and her contact were
close, he might have put a few thousand yards between them to
play it safe.

The decision to rise to periscope depth would have been different in time of war. Even before Slattery reached the conn, his
OOD would have immediately changed course and gone deep,
minimizing the sub's acoustic profile. But at Slattery's last check
with SUBLANT, the Great Bear had not been close to pouncing.
There was nothing in the last batch of messages from SUBLANT
to suggest that East and West were shooting at each other. *Scorpion* was traveling in international waters, and the Russian ships
she was assigned to investigate were well over the horizon. Except

for their original contact, her sonar was clear—she was alone in the water. Slattery's orders were to investigate Soviet activity in this part of the Atlantic, and whoever was pinging would bear closer examination. If he was connected to the group of ships *Scorpion* was assigned to investigate, his presence might provide a clue to why the Russians had ventured so far from home, to this remote spot in the Atlantic.

As the submarine began her ascent, countless hours of repetitive drills and exercises translated into instant reactions in the control room. The quartermaster would have stood at his plotting table making hurried entries into the ship's log. The helmsman would have acknowledged the skipper's order to reduce speed—*Helm ahead, one-third*—with a clear, automatic, *All ahead one-third, aye sir.* He would have reached toward the panel in front of him where the engine-order telegraph was mounted, and turned the knob counterclockwise to the one-third position.

In the small maneuvering compartment on the starboard side of the engine room, the throttle man would have been alerted by a clanging bell and looked up to see that one of two needles on the engineering telegraph had shifted to ahead one-third. He would have called out the order to his fellow crew members—the engineering officer, the reactor operator, and the electrical operator. He would have reached a hand out to his dial and moved it to the one-third setting. With his other hand, he would start to spin the large stainless steel throttle wheel to its closed position, restricting the flow of steam to the engines.

Back in the control room, the lee helmsman would have watched his telegraph, waiting for an answer from Maneuvering. It would come quickly, the machine's second needle jumping to match the first, the bell once more ringing out. In a loud voice he would call to the skipper:

Maneuvering answers ahead one-third, sir.

Very well.

As the lee helmsman announced *Scorpion*'s arrival at periscope depth, her speed decreased to 5 knots. Close to the surface, the swells of the Atlantic gently rocked the sub from side to side. One level below in the mess and elsewhere throughout the ship, crewmen would sense the slowing of the boat, a shift in inertia causing them to sway ever so slightly. The deck tilted a little, and they leaned the opposite way in unison, compensating for the new angle. If you had hit the rack to take five, you might have slid one way or another on the mattress. If you were doing pushups on your fingers and toes, you might have done a minor flop. Glasses and dishes might have wobbled on mess tables, and checkers slid off game boards. A few men might have glanced at their wristwatches—*Humph, not time to download the skid*—but then quickly dismissed the change in attitude and gotten back to whatever they were doing. There were always a dozen good reasons for the OOD to head up to periscope depth. *Scorpion* was a fast-attack sub, a hunter-killer, not a missile boat on deep patrol. Darting around the ocean and checking things out was her job.

Up in the control room, it was a different story. The mood must have now in fact gotten very serious as Slattery ordered the raising of *Scorpion*'s AN/BRA-9 helical antenna and football-shaped VLF loop antennas, and then reached up for the ring that controlled the extension and lowering of the periscope.

His announcement to the control room crew: *Raising Number One Scope.*

The quartermaster would have made a log entry.

To compensate for the change in the boat's trim at her shallow depth, meanwhile, the diving officer would have given her a little more negative buoyancy than normal to reduce the chance of broaching. Her slower speed also offered the benefit of cutting down on the noise of her machinery and water flowing across her hull. While making her less visible to enemy radar, this increased the effectiveness of her sonar. With the background racket muted, the sonar's reception would have been clearer, making the precise bearing of the acoustic pulse easier to nail down.

In the sonar shack, the crew would recheck their findings, their supervisor snatching up his handset to confirm them.

The contact was definitely Russian, and very probably a helicopter.

VI

As *Scorpion*'s periscope broke the surface, Commander Slattery pressed his face to its eyepiece and swept the horizon.

He would have recognized exactly what confronted him almost at once, rendering the latest update from Sonar moot. The Kamov helicopter was at a hover, its blades churning the water beneath it into a white froth. Slattery would see a cable stretching from its fuselage down to the ocean's choppy surface and know it was attached to an active sonar dome.

Within seconds, the helicopter would have pulled in the ball, dipped its nose, and shot in *Scorpion*'s direction. Slattery must have been momentarily puzzled. He'd risen to periscope depth a cautious distance away, and his boat was still hidden underwater. But the helicopter's rapid oncoming course as its transducer was reeled in meant it knew her precise location. Unaware of the lines of passive buoys that would have allowed the pilot to vector in on *Scorpion*, Slattery might have guessed they had gotten a visual or radar fix on her periscope. Though he could not have known it, they may well have done that to augment their passive sonar readings.

Slattery would not have concerned himself with the helicopter's method of acquisition for very long. The chopper was moving fast and would reach his boat in seconds. In so many ways, this must have been reminiscent of the NATO war games he'd played in the Mediterranean for the past three months. *Scorpion* had now been cast in the unenviable role of the real-life hunted.

Despite the helicopter's aggressive posture, the skipper must have believed its aerial charge was probably more bluff than anything. Again, he might have thought of the Med, and his encounters with the Russians there. But his standoff with their warship back at the conclusion of Dawn Patrol had nearly escalated into a serious clash. The vessel had seemed to be genuinely intent on ramming or even firing on *Scorpion,* and might have done so if the American fighters hadn't arrived to escort his submarine from the area. Slattery may have thought—or preferred to think—he was looking at a bluff, but he still couldn't have been sure what the chopper was up to. His priority would have turned from investigation and surveillance to evasion. He would have wanted to shake the helicopter, and then sort out whether to take another look at it later on, or resume his course toward the flotilla.

But first things would have come first. Near the surface, *Scorpion* was vulnerable. With the helicopter closing on the sub, he'd need to get her back into her element. The chopper's sonar was limited in range and accuracy. Slattery had to take his sub down, where she had the advantage.

Slattery's emergency dive command would prompt instant responses from the planesman, helmsman, diving officer, and chief of the watch. They would start to take the sub to a depth of 150 feet, which was standard operating procedure. Once there, they would have awaited further orders.

Slattery would have known what to do next. In oceanographic terms, thermoclines are layers of water where temperatures change abruptly with depth. The sea's warmth comes from the sun, and most of it is absorbed in the layer reaching from the surface down to about two hundred feet. Weather and even time of day can affect the depth of the surface layer. But two hundred feet is a reliable average. Below that, in the main thermal zone, the plunges in temperature are steep. The deeper one gets, the colder and more densely packed water molecules become. And the denser and heavier the water, the greater the likelihood that sound waves traveling through it will bend away from the sub.

Because active sonar utilizes a series of targeted sound pulses, the deeper thermals wreak havoc with its effectiveness. Noises in dense water are distorted and deflected. They bounce around.

Slattery was a young skipper. His résumé of command went back less than a year. But he had been a submarine officer for over a decade. He'd made the first deterrent patrol on *Tunny* in a period of international crisis, and earned his quals on *Nautilus* while she slipped in and out of Soviet waters. Smart, resourceful, the quickest of studies, Slattery had been in similar predicaments before and knew how to elude the chopper—lower his scope, find a thermal to hide under, sprint off, and then come up behind it. But while faster than most ships and any other submarine of her era, *Scorpion* was still bound by Newton's first law of motion. She weighed in at over 7.5 million pounds and had been cruising at five knots. It would take several minutes to overcome her inertia, drop below a thermal, and accelerate from periscope depth. And at its low altitude over the surface, the lighter, quicker Kamov was already darting toward her like a dragonfly across a pond.

It would only take seconds for the chopper to close within five hundred yards of its target and put her within torpedo range.

At around 18:59 Greenwich Mean Time on May 22, 1968, the USS *Scorpion* simply ran out of time. On command, the weapons officer aboard the Kamov released its torpedo. As the weapon met the water its tracking sonar went active and acquired the sub almost at once, its speed increasing to 40 knots.

Aboard *Scorpion*, the sonar crew would have identified the distinctive, high-pitched whine of the torpedo's propellers even as it became audible to the naked ear through the boat's two-inch-thick hull. Then, over the 8MC, an excited voice from the sonar shack would have notified the control room of the torpedo's speed and bearings.

Launched from a distance of about 500 yards, the submerged
torpedo needed only thirty seconds to reach its target. Commander Slattery would have shouted out a series of desperate orders to
get the boat up to speed at flank bell and call the men to General
Quarters—in other words, their battle stations.

It is doubtful they had a chance to react. *Scorpion* had just
begun her dive when the torpedo blew.

VII

"1859:35—Torpedo warhead explosion on port side of middle of sub causes rapid flooding of control room and other
areas amidships."

—*Supplementary Record of Proceedings of Court of Inquiry by
Commander-in-Chief, U.S. Atlantic Fleet*

The Soviet AT-2 antisubmarine torpedo carried a mechanism
called an acoustic noncontact exploder. This detonated the explosive charge in the weapon's 330-pound warhead an instant before
it struck its target, generating a hydrostatic shockwave that raced
down the side of the pressure hull to slam it with tremendous
force. The torpedo fired at *Scorpion* went off close-in to port,
where the trailing edge of the sail joined with the hull. In addition
to the shockwave that rocked the hull, kicking it sideways to starboard, some of the force vented upward and sent a white geyser of
seawater high into the air. The rest of the brunt hit the operations
compartment, blowing a two-foot hole in the steel pressure hull
outside the control room. In a very real sense that was the equivalent of a head shot.

Inside Control, the destruction was immediate and chaotic.
Crewmen were thrown off their feet and out of their seats. Instrument panels, switchboards, and other pieces of equipment were
torn free of their mounts to expose hydraulic lines and electrical

wiring. Dislodged ladders rocketed through the air or went skidding across the deck. Readout screens and dial coverings shattered. Men and equipment collided with pulverizing force in the tiny sonar shack. In the storage room aft of the shack, cabinets filled with printouts and microfiche toppled and slammed together. Desks and chairs tumbled helter-skelter in the ship's office.

Besides Commander Slattery, there would have been between twelve and fourteen watchstanders in Control. Most of them, flung like rag dolls against hard steel surfaces and edges, would have died or been instantly rendered insensible as the compartment buckled inward and opened to let in the sea.

As the ocean roared through the gaping tear in the hull at over 150 pounds of water per square inch—triple the pressure of the stream from a fire hose—the air inside Control gained density, turning the spray into a thick foglike mist. The same compression effect makes the human body feel as though giant stone hands have clapped down on it, front and back. It would have dimmed the crewmen's sight and caused sudden losses of hearing and balance that were partly physiological reactions to the tremendous pressure on their eyes and ears, and partly caused by the cloud of vapor around them. For the men who briefly clung to life and consciousness, it must have seemed as if a dark gray shroud had fallen over their vision, bringing on terrible confusion and disorientation.

The cramped control room flooded in less than half a minute. Hydraulic systems failed, electrical systems shorted out, and the space went dark. Communications to the rest of the boat would have ceased. Voltage sizzled through the blackness in arcing, blue-white flashes as highly conductive saltwater poured over straggling live cables and wires. The surge of ocean through the operations compartment would sweep men and equipment down the ladder to the lower decks as it overflowed into midlevel staterooms, bunkrooms, and wardrooms, went washing through the mess, and then cascaded down into the main battery compartment on the deck below.

At the rear of the sub, the nuclear reactor scrammed—an automatic shutdown triggered by the disruption of the boat's electrical systems—and key equipment tripped offline. *Scorpion*'s propulsion system was dead.

In sections forward and aft of the control room, crewmen recovering from the shock of the blasts would have done everything they could to save their vessel. Amid torrents of icy saltwater, engineers would wrestle with the diving planes and blow the ballast tanks in an attempt to surface. Other hands would slam shut the watertight hatches on the interior bulkheads. Save the boat would have been their first reaction, what their training told them to do. *Save the boat*. But with the control room flooded, and the rest of Operations heavy with rising seawater, the submarine's descent could not be halted. The streamlined teardrop hull that gave the Skipjacks their great aerodynamic speed came with a sacrifice of internal space, reducing the size and capacity of the ballast tanks. Blowing them couldn't have generated enough positive buoyancy to offset the inrush of seawater through the gaping wound *Scorpion* had sustained. She was heading down.

Death would come by drowning for the sailors who'd held out inside these sections. With the sub already at a depth of about three hundred feet, the ocean's subfreezing temperature would offer a small mercy. In waters hovering around 32 degrees, the human dive reflex is triggered: The heart rate slows, the blood flow to the limbs decreases, and an involuntary contraction of the throat muscles closes the airways. Sailors gasped for breath for only a moment before blacking out.

Behind the torpedo room bulkhead in the most forward section of the boat, one man pulled a life preserver from a storage locker and struggled into it. But even while still at a shallow depth, no man or group of men could have dislodged the hatch against the massive opposing water resistance. When the hatch finally did blow open, it was because of an upward, high-pressure water spike from the impact of *Scorpion* hitting bottom.

Months later, submersible pilots investigating the wreckage would spot the body of the crewman in a life vest still securely fastened around his chest.

VIII

18:59:56

Twenty-six seconds after the torpedo's detonation, a second catastrophic explosion tore through *Scorpion's* operations compartment as the saltwater inundating its lower deck reacted with acids spilled from ruptured battery cells. The violent blast produced a cloud of noxious chlorine gas that filled the compartment, supplanting whatever air was left in the space to kill anyone alive inside it.

Aft of the torpedo room, the invading sea went on seeking points of lesser resistance, rushing through the access tunnel into the reactor and auxiliary machinery room. As the floor of the tunnel gave way under the water's weight, the reactor compartment one level beneath it was flooded.

Her midsection swamped with water, the damage from the torpedo explosion increasing the drag on her port side, *Scorpion* was now descending in a wide spiral.

IX

"1901:06–03—Torpedo compartment bulkhead collapses causing rapid flooding."

—*Supplementary Record of Proceedings of Court of Inquiry by Commander-in-Chief, U.S. Atlantic Fleet*

Soon after the battery explosion, *Scorpion* was wracked with yet a third inner convulsion. Though her pressure hull's operational depth was rated at seven hundred feet, the U.S. Navy had a safety factor requirement of 1.5 for its submarine fleet, which meant the depth at which a sub's hull would succumb to water pressure and collapse—or its crush depth—was calculated by multiplying its operational depth by a factor of one and a half. This gave *Scorpion* a crush depth of 1,050 feet and perhaps better, since there was some latitude built into the rating system.

But safety factors were guidelines for *normal* submerged operations. They were not meant to account for a cataclysmic event such as a direct torpedo hit. When a submarine was dealt that sort of blow, safety factors became irrelevant.

In Skipjack-class boats, the bulkheads separating the internal compartments were rated for between three hundred and five hundred feet. They did not need to be stronger. Any circumstance in which they were exposed to the full, raging pressure of the sea at such depths meant the sub was already crippled beyond recovery.

Its hatch dogged, the watertight bulkhead between Operations and the torpedo room would have almost certainly withstood the battery explosion in Operations. But as *Scorpion* continued her dive, the implacable pressure of the water that had completely immersed Operations would warp the metal bulkhead inward until its integrity started to fail. Just before it yielded, its individual plates split apart at the seams, allowing the ocean into the torpedo room in jets that measured about 600 psi. A person standing in front of the bulkhead would have been cut in half by such concentrated spurts. When the bulkhead finally relented altogether, the wall of seawater that entered the torpedo room flattened men, gear, and weapons against the sides of the boat with crushing force. For the sailors trapped in the room, loss of consciousness occurred in microseconds as a rapid increase in hydrostatic pressure closed off the blood flow to their hearts and brains and collapsed their lungs.

Her bow flooded, *Scorpion* had taken on a steep downward

angle and picked up speed. With only her engine room still intact, the submarine went into a nosedive for the abyssal darkness.

X

"1901:10—Engine room bulkhead collapses aft into engine room, causing 85-foot stern section of submarine to telescope forward into auxiliary machinery and reactor compartment."

—*Supplementary Record of Proceedings of Court of Inquiry by Commander-in-Chief, U.S. Atlantic Fleet*

Ninety-one seconds after the attack, the last of *Scorpion*'s internal bulkheads gave way. With all her compartments breached, and the weight of the water she'd taken on more evenly distributed throughout them, *Scorpion* was no longer nose-heavy and had assumed an almost level attitude in the water. But she was still gathering momentum, debris spewing from the mortal wound in the side of Operations as she continued her plunge to the sea bottom. One piece of metal would slide aft along the hull to strike the windmilling propeller and leave a sizable gash in a blade.

Scorpion had acquired a speed of something between 30 and 40 knots—almost fifty miles an hour—when she slammed into the ocean floor on her belly, throwing up a great cloud of sediment. On impact, the water in her operations compartment was compressed into a hydrostatic shockwave of inestimable magnitude, almost obliterating the compartment. The boat's hull had a weak spot near the section known as frame 67, where the conical interior walls of the ballast tank joined the tapered outer hull of the engine room more than midway down her length. Under unimaginable stress, the two structures bent in different directions. When their welds finally snapped, the pressure exerted by the ocean collapsed the stern of the boat forward into the mangled hull of her operations compartment like a segment of a telescope. The incredible force of this thrust flipped whatever was left of Operations onto its starboard side.

Breaking away from Operations, the torpedo room at the bow shot forward to score a deep trench in the soft abyssal muck. The final impact spat the sub's propeller and its attached shaft eighty yards from the ruined submarine's major structural components. Wrenched from the operations compartment, the sail came to rest on its port side, a section missing from the lower aft, where the torpedo exploded. In photographs, this notch resembles a vicious bite mark.

Three miles beneath the surface of the Atlantic, broken in two, *Scorpion* had come to her final rest on the gentle slope of a volcanic crater near 35° north and 35° west. Her bow facing north-northwest, her aft section pointed to the east, she was in a rough line with America, and the Norfolk homeport she would never see again.

XI

With the sub's death registered on their sonar, the Ka-25's mission crew messaged the destroyer's surveillance room to confirm their target had been acquired and destroyed. Then they darted from the scene.

The Kamov did not return to the ship from which it had taken off, but instead landed on its companion, reducing the chance that anyone outside the Special Operations unit would notice it had returned one torpedo short of its original payload.

Two months after he'd set a U.S. submarine in the sights of his gun, Admiral Sergei Gorshkov, commander in chief of the Soviet Navy, had shot and killed one in the name of misguided vengeance.

The victim's government would ignore the weapon's smoke, quietly letting it dissipate.

8. BOAT'S WAKE

"Fathoms down, fathoms down, how I'll dream fast asleep."
—*Herman Melville*, Billy Budd

I

FROM THE TIME THEY WERE MARRIED, WILLIAM AND Doris Slattery had been diligent about mailing Christmas cards to their many friends and relatives. In western Maine, where winter falls like a hammer, the holiday season is a treasured reprieve from the cheerless dark mornings, darker nights, and all-too-brief intervals of limp, cold daylight in between.

In May 1968, the Slatterys were devastated by the death of their only son aboard *Scorpion*. So, too, were the rest of West Paris's thousand or so citizens. Francis had always been a born leader to the people who knew him. When he graduated from Annapolis, and later gained command of a nuclear submarine, he became the pride of the town, a local hero.

That December, Bill and Doris did not send out their customary holiday greetings. Instead, Doris sat at her desk penning letters of condolence to the families of every man that died serving under Frank out in some forsaken part of the sea. Ninety-eight letters of condolence.

Doris would set up a memorial to her son in his old room, adorning a table with photographs of Frank in his officer's uniform, along with many of the commendations he'd earned. When she and her husband passed away within months of each other in 2003, their neighbor, the town librarian, purchased the table at an estate sale. It remains one of her most cherished possessions, a reminder of the times she had spent with Doris pointing out testaments to her son's gleaming but tragically foreshortened naval career.

II

On December 23, 1968, Captain Lloyd M. Bucher and the crew of the USS *Pueblo* were placed aboard a convoy of buses by their North Korean captors, driven toward the South Korean border, and marched across the bridge at Panmunjom—known as the Bridge of No Return—into American hands. Brought to the foot of the bridge on an ambulance were the remains of Fireman Duane Hodges, the sailor who had been killed in the explosion when the ship was attacked. Minutes before Bucher's release, a North Korean officer ordered him to make formal identification of the sailor's body, which was shrouded in gauze inside a plain wooden coffin. The same officer would then give Bucher and his fellow prisoners reading copies of the U.S. government's official apology to North Korea for *Pueblo*'s "crimes" against its people, provided to North Korea as negotiated terms for her crew's release.

It was eleven months to the day after *Pueblo* had been seized. Her crewmen had suffered unspeakably brutal tortures and conditions of relentless, abject deprivation during their imprisonment.

Recalling his first night of captivity in a barracks-like structure in Wonsan, *Pueblo*'s chief communications technician, James F. Kell, would later tell how he and many of the other sailors had quickly become resigned to imminent death. They had expected "a flash of light and a mushroom cloud," Kell's euphemism for a massive U.S. retaliation against the Communists for their unprovoked assault. They would have welcomed that response that night, and wished for it with even greater fervor as their misery wore on. According to Kell, they were disappointed when it never came.

In early 1969, a Navy Court of Inquiry convened to determine the facts of the *Pueblo* incident. Their eventual findings recommended that Commander Bucher be tried by general court-martial for failing to adequately resist capture by the Koreans and destroy classified materials, among other offenses. Secretary of the Navy John Chaffee rejected the recommendation with a statement that the men of *Pueblo* had "suffered enough."

It might have done more for Commander Bucher's pride and reputation, as well as better served the cause of justice, had the secretary acknowledged that, facing an aggressive force with vastly overwhelming armed superiority, Bucher had done everything within his power to protect his ship, crew, and the intelligence materials and equipment they had aboard. After months of sadistic treatment at the hands of the North Koreans, another outrage had been committed against Bucher, this time by his own government.

Despite feeling that his honor had been tainted, Lloyd Bucher, a loyal patriot, would remain active in the Navy until 1973. A year or two prior to his retirement, a chief petty officer aboard a ballistic missile submarine would make Bucher's acquaintance at a chiefs club and come to know him fairly well. The club, he said, was Bucher's hideaway. The embittered former *Pueblo* captain would shun the officers club and do very little socializing with commissioned officers, feeling few of them had adequately defended his honor after the naval commission's findings.

"The chiefs don't judge me," he confided to the submariner one night. It was his belief that more of them knew what it was like to come under enemy fire than the men at the "O Club."

In 1989, twenty years after their nightmare in North Korea had ended, the men of the *Pueblo* were issued POW medals at the behest of Congress. This honor followed the Pentagon's prolonged initial objection on grounds that, since a state of declared war had not existed between North Korea and the United States when they were made captives, they were technically to be considered detainees.

After Lloyd Bucher's death in a nursing home in 2004, Stu Russell, the president of the USS *Pueblo* Veteran's Association and one of Bucher's fellow hostages in the North Korean prison camp, would say this about his former commander: "The man was a giant. I don't know where he got the strength and courage to go through what he did."

He was not referring to Bucher's experiences in North Korea.

III

In the early morning hours of May 20, 1985, after almost twenty years of spying on his country, John Anthony Walker Jr. stepped outside a motel room in rural Maryland and was arrested by two FBI agents who had tailed him from a dead drop. His activities had been under investigation for months. Barbara Walker, whose troubled marriage to John had dissolved in 1976, had informed on him, having become angered by his failure to make his alimony payments while continuing to live an excessive lifestyle—and date beautiful women.

Soon after John was taken into custody, his brother, Arthur, son, Michael, and friend Jerry Whitworth were brought in and charged as Walker's accomplices. Within eighteen months, all were tried and convicted of treason and espionage. John, Arthur, and Whitworth were sentenced to life in prison. Michael received lesser concurrent sentences and was eventually paroled.

John Walker spent the next two decades being transferred between high-security prison facilities. Around 2000, he was shifted to the Allenwood Federal Correctional Complex in Pennsylvania at the foothills of the northern Allegheny Mountains. Surrounded by gentle rolling countryside, Allenwood looks as though it belongs on a college campus. The main entrance is located on Pennsylvania Highway 15 just across from Clyde Peeling's Reptileland and Subway sandwich shop, an accredited roadside zoo that doubles as a popular lunch spot. Except for an inconspicuous sign, a traveler would never suspect Allenwood of being a prison that houses some of America's most notorious mobsters, murderers, terrorists, and spies.

Gaunt, sunken-eyed, and diabetic at sixty-nine years of age, a sparse fringe of gray the only remnant of his once full head of dark hair, Walker spent nearly six years at Allenwood before he was moved to the U.S. Medical Center for Federal Prisoners in Springfield, Missouri. By then his deteriorating health had left him almost blind and suffering from leg problems that forced him to walk with a cane. At Allenwood, Walker was described as gloomy and moody, but still arrogant and self-absorbed. He was permitted restricted visitation from close relatives and friends but few showed up. He interacted little with other inmates but was surprisingly talkative to prison workers. He never mentioned submarines, his work as a Navy communications technician, or his time in the Navy at all. He did, however, like to speak about flying and his sailboat. He had no access to the Internet but spent many hours listening to National Public Radio over a headset, and typed out at least two unpublished political and autobiographical manuscripts in which he would express no remorse, but rather seek vindication, for his felonies.

Walker's writings modify his frequently asserted beliefs that the United States and Soviet Union would have never allowed the Cold War to escalate into an atomic conflagration. In his revised view of the era—a departure from earlier statements that he'd spied only for financial gain—he assumes a central, heroic role in keeping the peace, and justifies his treason as an act of conscience that saved the world from near-certain nuclear holocaust. In providing the Soviets with a means to eavesdrop on U.S. communications and analyze its military movements, Walker claims to have reduced their fears of falling victim to a surprise attack. He insists his offer to compromise a possible SIOP launch was met with unexpected indifference by Boris Solomatin's KGB superiors and points to this as evidence that the Russians never considered open aggression against the United States. When, in the mid-1980s, journalist Peter Earley presented him with an alternate explanation, suggesting they might have simply mistrusted a spy and traitor with so critical a responsibility, Walker was dismissive. He also refuses to entertain the notion that his pilfered intelligence would have given Russia a decisive military advantage had the two superpowers actually engaged in combat.

Walker would occasionally give his prison guards at Allenwood copies of one of the manuscripts to read. When challenged about the motives for his crimes, he would shut down to them for two- or three-week stretches, not speaking to them at all.

While Walker was at the facility, each inmate had a job for which he got paid between 12 and 43 cents an hour. A favorite motto among them was, "We pretend to work and they pretend to pay us." This was almost identical to a common joke among proletariat workers in the former Soviet Union.

If and when Walker becomes well enough to leave the Medical Center for Federal Prisoners in Missouri—it is said there is no better than a 50 percent chance of that—he will return to the Allenwood facility to serve out his sentence. He is eligible for parole because federal legislation mandates that life convictions handed down before 1987 are paroleable. An inmate can apply after doing a third of his time. Walker has not yet made application, and it is unlikely a board would be receptive. However, prison workers have said that precedent usually translates a life sentence into thirty years, or about two-thirds of one's sentence absent behavioral problems, of which Walker has had none.

This would set his projected release date at May 15, 2015.

IV

Back when the *Scorpion* tragedy occurred, Electronics Technician Jerry Shire was on covert patrol aboard the ballistic submarine USS *George Washington Carver* (SSBN-656) somewhere in the North Atlantic. He and his shipmates didn't hear of the sinking until they returned from deployment, and the married guys' wives told them they were briefly scared to death that the lost submarine might have been the *GW Carver*. None of the wives ever had more than the vaguest idea where their husbands were under the deep blue sea, and when the television news reported a missing nuclear sub, the Navy had been slow to substantiate it and to verify the boat's identity.

Other than that, and his natural sadness over the loss of an American submarine and her crew, Shire hadn't had any personal experiences tying him to *Scorpion* until a couple of years later.

Shire finished his hitch in the Navy aboard the rustbucket submarine tender USS *Orion* at Destroyer and Submarine Pier 22 in Norfolk, Virginia. From January through October 1970, his duty station was its Electronic Repair—or R-4—Division, where he was in charge of the antenna repair shop. Also in the division were a few sonar technicians working in a different shop on another deck of the tender. One of the techs was a fellow named Bob Davis.

Davis was a sonarman second class, though Shire had heard he had been bumping up and down in rate and pay grade. Once, and maybe more than once, he'd cycled from a first class rating to lowly seaman status—for every promotion he won, it seemed he found a way to get a demotion. Usually, a guy with slides that extreme had disciplinary problems, but all Shire knew was that

Davis was easy to like. They hit it off from the start of Shire's tour, and enjoyed many long nights at the base's Windjammer Club, or the Acey Deucy as guys called it, since that was where the first class petty officers—or "Aces"—and second class petty officers—or "Deuces"—went to escape the anarchy of the shoddier enlisted men's club. At the Acey Deucy the food was good, the music was live, and there were pretty local girls to dance with.

Though Davis spent a whole lot of time mopping the deck, everybody in R-4 Div treated him with a sort of deference not often granted to an ordinary swab jockey. The word was that he'd served on the USS *Scorpion* for quite a while, and was a shipmate of the guys aboard the nuke when she went down. For a sailor, and especially a bubblehead, something like that was comparable to losing almost a hundred brothers.

Davis never spoke of the men who were gone, but wore the *Scorpion* shoulder patch on his jumper's right shoulder seam, and had sewn various other *Scorpion* emblems onto his work jacket. It absolutely went against regs to wear another vessel's patches on the ship you were stationed aboard, and the *Orion*'s master-at-arms, whose job was to maintain general order, had constantly barked at him to get rid of them. But Davis always ignored him, which probably hadn't helped his rating status one bit. Still, about all the MAA could really do to punish Davis for his infraction was shove a mop handle at him, and point to a bucket of sudsy water. It was Davis's *Scorpion* connection—you had to feel for him.

In the nine or ten months Shire served on *Orion*, he and Bob Davis had done plenty of long-distance driving together. Shire and his wife had a place in Baltimore, where they planned to settle down after his discharge, and he would commute there to be with her on weekends. Meanwhile, it happened that Davis was dating a girl who lived west of North Charles Street around Johns Hopkins University, on University Boulevard, Shire thought. Davis would make the trip up with Shire on Fridays, and help pay for gas. In those days the roads weren't all interstates, and the ride could take maybe six or seven hours, and Shire appreciated having him for company.

On the one hand, Shire got to know Davis pretty well during those long rides. But there was always a part of Davis nobody knew. Shire sensed that part might be too far away for anyone to get close to, that it might have gone down in ten thousand feet of water with the crew of his old boat. He could never quite bring himself to ask Davis how he avoided losing his life in the tragedy. Most of the guys on *Orion* who did broach the subject with him were answered with silence. How was it Davis knew all the hands onboard *Scorpion*, and yet wasn't on the boat himself? Shire couldn't help but wonder about it during those late nights at the Acey Deucy, and cruising around with Davis in his Chevy Nova six-banger.

Still, some of the guys on *Orion* must have caught Davis at the right moment to pry the story out of him. And eventually, Jerry Shire got it from them.

As Davis told it, he and another sailor had fallen into some legal trouble—Shire thought it stemmed from an unpaid debt—back in the States before leaving aboard *Scorpion* on her Mediterranean deployment. Davis said he'd sort of forgotten about his problems with the law during the patrol, figuring he would straighten things out when it was over. But when *Scorpion* moored at Rota, Spain, just before her transit home to Norfolk, the military police caught up with him and the other sailor, yanked them off the boat, and flew them off to Norfolk for court-martial. The day he and his buddy were put in the air, said Davis, *Scorpion* left Rota and was never seen again. Davis insisted that if he hadn't gotten dragged into custody, he would have been on the boat when she went down with the rest of his shipmates. If you wanted to thank or blame anyone for his being alive, it was the MPs, he said.

In all the time they knew each other, Jerry Shire had no reason to be skeptical about Davis's account of how he'd missed going down with his ship. Shire was unaware that *Scorpion* did not moor at Naval Station Rota on her return voyage, or get closer than the breakwater out beyond its harbor, or spend more than an hour there before making her departure. Shire did not know that Davis still lived and breathed because he had missed the boat.

Davis may have conceived of his falsehood the night *Scorpion* was revealed to be missing, when a compassionate duty officer at the Camp Allen brig had him roused from his cell to phone his parents and tell them he was okay. He was the son of a highway patrolman. If it was MPs that took him off the submarine, Davis could have done nothing to stay aboard with his shipmates. But being late for the boat's departure from Norfolk because of a spat with his girlfriend? That was something else. It might be that Davis worried about the questions that would be asked of him—perhaps by his father, perhaps by his fellow Navy men, possibly by all. Had his girlfriend really been struck with a premonition of disaster? Hidden his car keys? Was there even a lovers' quarrel between them that morning? Or had he just dallied too long after spending a romantic Valentine's night with her?

The answers aren't known. But what is certain is that Bob Davis's presence on *Scorpion* on May 22, 1968, wouldn't have prevented her from being lured into a Soviet trap. Instead, it would only have added his name to the list of ninety-nine sailors who plunged down into the abyss with the boat.

V

Barbara Foli remembers her late husband, Vernon, as someone she could depend on to stand by her side. In a room filled with people, he would intuitively understand when she felt ill at ease, or vulnerable and in need of a little support. When he moved close to her, and took hold of her hand, it made her feel special and strong.

Barbara remarried some years after Vernon's death aboard *Scor-*

pion, but would divorce in 1990. When her second marriage failed, she learned that she was no longer eligible for the widow's benefits that a U.S. Veterans Administration representative had told her would be her entitlement. Had Barbara been informed of certain deadlines regarding her divorce filings, she would not have forfeited those benefits. Instead, she was cut off. Vernon's reassuring hand must have been a keen absence to her at that time.

It would be eight years before new legislation restored some of the benefits Barbara had been promised as the wife of a serviceman who had died on active duty. With her long personal struggles as impetus, she would become involved with an organization of military survivors called Gold Star Wives of America. Formed at the conclusion of World War II, the organization is dedicated to educating the spouses of members of the U.S. armed forces killed or disabled in the line of duty about their rights and entitlements, as well as aiding them in other ways. In its six decades of existence, Gold Star Wives has received frequent acknowledgment from military and congressional leaders for its diligence in assisting widows and widowers of deceased service members.

For Barbara Foli, finding ways to help widows and widowers avoid, or at least negotiate, the hardships she faced after Vernon's death has become a driving passion. She hasn't forgotten those difficulties, as she has never forgotten the dark, rainswept day in Norfolk that forever changed her life.

At a USS *Scorpion* memorial gathering held over thirty years after the boat went down, she and Holli Foli were joined by more than twenty other members of Vernon's family. In attendance were all three of his sisters, one brother, five nieces, their spouses, and some of their children. When the nieces were little girls, Vernon had often played with them and lifted them into his arms.

Decades after his loss, Barbara Foli, and so many of Vernon's loved ones, had come to hold out their hands in support of him, as they continue to do until this day.

VI

On the evening of Tuesday, March 13, 2007, the Los Angeles–class nuclear powered submarine USS *San Juan* (SSN-751) fell out of radio contact with a carrier strike group during a joint training exercise off the Florida coast.

A submarine missing alert was issued within hours. It was the first since *Scorpion*'s loss almost four decades before, when the Navy waited five days to send out a SUBMISS.

Immediately asked to help with the search-and-rescue effort was the International Submarine Escape and Rescue Liaison Office in Norfolk, an Internet-based support group that draws on experts and resources from dozens of nations around the world —including Russia—to assist in submarine rescue emergencies. ISERLO was a four-year-old organization established in response to the accidental sinking of the Russian nuclear submarine *Kursk*, after it was determined that more than forty crew members might have been saved had a fast, coordinated international rescue effort been implemented.

At around four o'clock on the morning of March 14, in the *San Juan*'s homeport of Groton, Connecticut, the Navy began notifying crewmen's family members of the situation through a prearranged system of military and personal contacts called a phone tree. Fortunately the submarine reported in safe at 6:00 A.M., before many relatives could be located. Three hours later, naval officials at the Groton submarine base held a special briefing to allay whatever remaining fears the sailors' families might have held.

The cause of the *San Juan*'s apparent disappearance was soon declared to have been a communications problem.

In Norfolk, Virginia, Captain Mary Etta Nolan, U.S. Navy, had felt her heart sink when she'd heard news of the missing sub. Nolan's father was Walter Bishop, *Scorpion*'s Chief of the Boat when the sub went down with all hands. Her family still lived with the terrible memory of being kept out of the Navy's information loop when *Scorpion* vanished, still suffered the pain and uncertainty born of decades of continued secrecy surrounding the submarine's fate.

Mary Etta cried with relief when she heard the *San Juan* had shown up. The crewmen's loved ones had gone through hell, but they'd been kept abreast of the situation as it developed, and everything had turned out okay for them in the end.

Afterward, Mary Etta had briefly wondered if word of the sub's communication lapse ought to have been withheld from the families until it was clear whether something was wrong, sparing them the agonizing, uncertain wait they endured before they heard their men were safe. But then she remembered the Navy's long silence to the *Scorpion* families and the devastation they felt upon discovering that the submarine had been gone for five days before they were informed.

Perhaps the Navy had learned something from *Scorpion*, she thought.

It was always better to know.

EPILOGUE

"Ninety-nine men aren't worth the destruction of civilization. Other reasons had to be found for the loss."

—*A highly placed U.S. intelligence source involved in the Navy's official* Scorpion *investigation*

"The families of the K-129 [crewmen] know how they died. *Scorpion* families should also know. The Cold War was a real war. It should never happen again. Maybe the truth will keep it from repeating in the future."

—*A former Rear Admiral of the Soviet submarine force*

BETWEEN 1985 AND 1986, MARINE SCIENTIST AND SELF-professed deep-sea hunter Bob Ballard bookended his celebrated discovery of the shipwrecked RMS *Titanic* in the North Atlantic with at least two separate—and secret—expeditions to inspect *Scorpion*'s wreckage.

Ballard would later divulge that he'd been a commissioned U.S. naval intelligence operative for over thirty years. Descending aboard the Woods Hole Oceanographic Institution's deep-submersible vehicle *Alvin*, he would have the stated mission of learning "why it sank and, if possible, to salvage its nuclear torpedoes."

The Navy had hoped Ballard's *Scorpion* dives would conclusively determine the reasons for her sinking and disprove the theory—by then gradually becoming eschewed in favor of vague assertions of possible mechanical failure—that a torpedo hit was responsible. To do this, *Alvin*'s robotic camera, Jason Jr., would be sent out to remotely enter the submarine and transmit images from its forward torpedo rooms.

Aside from the few photos and edited videos released of *Scorpion*'s exterior hull sections, the findings of that expedition remain classified to this day. Ballard will not comment on the reasons why, but he has since claimed that the camera was unable to make its way into the forward compartments—a mission for which he admits Jason was specifically designed.

Weeks later, however, the robot would succeed in entering the *Titanic*'s badly deteriorated hull and navigating a rusty labyrinth of passages and stairs to its grand ballroom. The videos it recorded have since become famous the world over.

There have since been multiple top secret, deepwater dives to the site of *Scorpion*'s wreckage. And whatever Ballard's dives may or may not have revealed, no fewer than four former Soviet captains or submarine officers interviewed for this book contend that the USS *Scorpion* was sunk in retaliation for the loss of K-129.

In October 2005, a retired U.S. admiral with direct knowledge of the *Scorpion* incident and subsequent expedition to find her confirmed the true facts about *Scorpion*'s sinking.

And so we arrive at the final question: Why did the U.S. government keep the Soviet killing of *Scorpion* and her ninety-nine crewmen a secret?

As is most often the case in affairs of state, the reasons are complex and overlapping. In 1968, President Lyndon Johnson was mired in the Vietnam War, and trying to cope with the social turmoil that was a consequence of its unpopularity. He had come under sharp criticism from political opponents for not launching a retaliatory strike against North Korea after the *Pueblo* seizure—a decision he claimed to have made in order to prevent the execution of its hostage crew. Whether his stated reasons were right or wrong, or even entirely truthful, is a discussion for another time and forum. But coming on the heels of *Pueblo,* Johnson knew that revelations of an unprovoked Communist attack on a second American warship—this time with loss of all hands aboard— would leave him with little recourse but to engage in a military response. This one, however, would have to be against the USSR, a global superpower, and the principal threat to America's national security.

As a major Cold War intelligence figure told us, "Ninety-nine men aren't worth the destruction of civilization. Other reasons had to be found for the loss."

These *other reasons* continued to be offered even after Johnson left office and his successor, Richard M. Nixon, moved cautiously toward his first détente initiatives. As Rear Admiral Pitr Navoystev, first deputy chief for operations of the Soviet Navy, would later advise an American interviewer, "You will learn that there are some things both sides have agreed not to address, and one is that event [*Scorpion*] and our K-129, for similar reasons."

Speaking with the same interviewer—a retired American naval officer—Soviet Vice Admiral B. M. Kamarov would be even more direct about the matter, explaining, "A secret agreement had been reached between the U.S. and the Soviet Union in which both sides agreed not to press the other government on the loss of their submarines in 1968 [K-129 and *Scorpion*], in order to preserve the thaw in superpower relations. A full accounting of either submarine's loss might create new tensions."

The truth of what happened to *Scorpion* was concealed, then, first for reasons linked to the Johnson administration's myriad political struggles, and then to Secretary of State Henry Kissinger's nuclear disarmament negotiations with his Moscow counterparts—backdoor parleys that would eventually lay the groundwork for the Strategic Arms Limitation Talks. In the overall political scheme of things, mutual U.S. and Soviet silence about the death of two submarines became a bargaining tool for peaceful coexistence. Overshadowed by larger global events and foreign policy imperatives, the deaths of the twelve officers and eighty-seven enlisted men of the USS *Scorpion* have been largely forgotten—except by their parents and widows, and the children who would grow up without their fathers.

AUTHORS' NOTE

It was for the American people, who deserve to know why the men of *Scorpion* were sent into harm's way and how they died, that we originally began writing this book. But as our work progressed it became equally important for us to reveal the truth to their surviving relatives. In a very real way, the families have remained standing in the rain, as they were that bleak day in Norfolk almost forty years ago.

Precisely how much effect did the ultimate sacrifice of *Scorpion*'s crewmen have on the course of history?

Still just a couple of decades removed from the fall of the Soviet Union, we may lack the overarching perspective to know. But that they bravely *contributed* is certain. Today an untold number of East Europeans and Russians are free of Soviet domination because the brave men who served aboard *Scorpion*—and others like them—were willing to sail into harm's way in the name of freedom. Today our own nation's children live in a better, safer world despite the many new threats that have emerged to jeopardize that freedom.

Scorpion's crewmen were killed while defending themselves against a blatant act of war, and we all share in owing them a debt of gratitude. An honest recounting of their final days, hours, and minutes is our attempt at repaying some small portion of that debt.

—*Ken Sewell and Jerome Preisler, December 2007*

ACKNOWLEDGMENTS

Writing a narrative of historical events that took place four decades in the past is always difficult. The challenge is compounded when many factual links needed to tell the story remain hidden by multiple levels of government classification. This book would not have been possible were it not for literally dozens of people who came forward to share their time, information, and recollections of the national tragedy that occurred in May 1968

We are most indebted to the wives, children, and former shipmates of the ninety-nine men lost with the USS *Scorpion*, many of whom opened themselves to reliving deeply painful memories so we could render a faithful and accurate picture of their experiences. Our particular heartfelt thanks go to Barbara Foli Lake, Carol Foli, Ruthann Crowley, Richard Hogeland, Tim Pospisil, Judy Rehm, Capt. MaryEtta Nolan, NC, USN (RC), Joe Perham, Vance Bacon, Eleanore P. Inman, Doug Kariker, Gregg Pennington, Jerry Pratt, Bob McClain, John "Mac" McClaren, William Lee, Bill Hyler, and Capt. Sanford N. Levey, USN (Ret.).

We extend profound gratitude to our Russian sources, who must remain anonymous but spoke out about the attack on the USS *Scorpion* at risk of life imprisonment or death. Without our researcher and follow-up interviewer in Russia, Svetlana Stepanova [pseudo.], we might never have unlocked the final mystery. Thanks also to Eugene Soukharnikov for his work with Russian materials, and to David Hughes for his impeccable translations.

Others whose memories were invaluable in allowing us to reconstruct the days and weeks surrounding the submarine's disappearance include Richard Shafer, Mike Werry, Ed Washburn, Lawrence Brooks, Terry R. McCue, Phil Pagnoni, Bob McDaniel, Jerry Shire, Dennis Solheim, Gary Cox, and Peter A. Smith. A special thank you goes to former Skipjack-class submarine crewmen Todd "Pitt" Slater, Gene Lee, John Kinard, Wes Jones, and Joe Verse for their contributions.

For helping to inform various aspects of this manuscript, our appreciation goes to Dr. John P. Craven, Cmdr. Will Longman USN (Ret.), Cmdr. Paul Grandinetti USN (Ret.), George G. Ellis, Bill Ramey, Clint Richmond, Captain Third Rank Igor Kolosov (Ret.), Capt. Edward M. Brittingham USN (Ret.), Captain James Brantley Bryant USN (Ret.), Ralph Lewis, Lt. Cdr. Marty Diller USN (Ret.), and Capt. Robert J. Anderson USN (Ret.).

We are grateful to Patricia Makley, the wonderful librarian at the West Paris Public Library, for opening the doors to Cmdr. Francs A. Slattery's past to us, and to her son William for his digital scans.

Thanks to Edward L. Blanton YNC USN (Ret.) for his assistance in poring through naval archives, and also to Frank Parker for his research.

Jerome's lifelong friend, Lee Kabilyo of Giannini-Kabilyo Design in Rhode Island, came through on short notice with a superb interior diagram of USS *Scorpion*.

The usual debts are owed, and well overdue, to Suzanne Preisler. Nor will Joney and Mickey be forgotten.

This book would never have seen the light of day without the encouragement and commitment of John Talbot of the Talbot Fortune Agency, Inc., our friend and agent of many years.

Last but not least, sincere appreciation goes to our editor, Bob Bender, for his confidence in us, and his receptivity and diligence in helping us shape this manuscript into its best and final form. Thanks also go to his assistant, Johanna Li.

NOTES

PROLOGUE: ABYSS

While conducting our research for this book, we drew a wealth of information about *Scorpion*'s final weeks and days from declassified portions of the "Findings of Fact from the Record of Proceedings of a Court of Inquiry Convened by Commander in Chief U.S. Atlantic Fleet at Headquarters Commander in Chief U.S. Atlantic Fleet, Norfolk, Virginia, to Inquire into the Loss of USS *Scorpion* (SSN-589) Which Occurred on or about 27 May 1968, Ordered on 4 June 1968."

The coordinates of *Scorpion*'s final resting place in the Mid-Atlantic come directly from copies of *Trieste* II logs shared with the authors by a participant in some of the bathyscaphe's early descents to photograph the wreckage site, conducted under the direction of Dr. John P. Craven between June and July of 1969.

Deep-sea hunter Robert D. Ballard's top-secret *Alvin* dives to explore *Scorpion*'s ruins followed Craven's dives by about seventeen years, occurring while Ballard was a CIA operative. Technologically superior to the slow and somewhat ungainly bathyscaphe, *Alvin* was fully able to maneuver about the wreckage and capture videotaped images of *Scorpion*'s damaged compartments. These remain largely classified.

Our reconstruction of *Alvin*'s pre-dive and dive routines, knowledge of her technology and operation, and understanding of the deepwater environment's effect on the human body and psyche, owes much to several lengthy conversations with George G. Ellis, a former deepwater submersible pilot who, for over a decade, conducted numerous scientific and classified government missions aboard both *Alvin* and *Trieste*. Conducted between the latter part of 2005 and early February 2006, our interviews were followed by several e-mail exchanges that helped expand upon, clarify, and illuminate certain points.

Additional information on *Alvin,* including the now-declassified dates of its *Scorpion* dives, was obtained from the Woods Hole Oceanographic Institution's Web site, www.whoi.edu.

Ballard claims to have resigned his secret commission as intelligence operative around 2002. He has admitted that his expedition to discover the sunken remains of RMS *Titanic* was a deliberate cover story for his investigative team's multiple trips down to *Scorpion*'s watery grave. Both he and Former Secretary of the Navy John Lehman (1981–1987) have recently stated that the robotic Jason Jr., famed for gaining access to *Titanic*'s grand ballroom, was the product of then-classified military technology developed for entering *Scorpion*'s forward compartments.

While much of what we learned about Ballard's *Scorpion* missions comes from confidential sources, it was supplemented by statements Ballard made to Ron Berker in his July 2004 article "Deep Secrets" for *Men's Journal.* Additional information about Bob Ballard was obtained from the article "Famous Explorer Returns to UCSB" on www.dailynexus .com, and the unedited transcript of a February 1991 interview with Ballard that may be read at the Academy of Achievement Web site, www .achievement.org.

Sherry Sontag and Christopher Drew's book *Blind Man's Bluff: The Untold Story of American Submarine Espionage* (New York: Public Affairs, 1998) was also helpful.

CHAPTER 1: GORSHKOV'S GUN

I

A former Navy intelligence officer informed much of what we know of the Soviet Union's role in the seizing of the USS *Pueblo,* and the KGB's acquisition of at least one KW-7 Orestes cryptographic unit and operational documents from the vessel while it was in North Korean hands. Speaking under condition of anonymity, several cryptographic experts who worked on the development of the KW-7 box gave us details about its function and durability.

"An Analysis of the Systemic Security Weaknesses of the U.S. Navy Fleet Broadcasting System 1967–1974, as Exploited by CWO John Walker," a master's thesis by Laura J. Heath, Major, U.S. Army Command and General Staff College, Fort Leavenworth, Kansas, added insight and texture to our narrative of the *Pueblo* incident and later segments in the book concerning John Walker.

There are numerous published works about the *Pueblo* seizure, many derived in whole or in part from the firsthand accounts of the ship's crewmen. These contain minor discrepancies relating to the sequence of events immediately before, during, and after the North Korean attack on the vessel. Most of the apparent contradictions are explained by the psychological and physiological effects of combat situations on human perception. The sources we relied upon for insight include, but are not limited to:

"The Psychological Effects of Combat," an entry by D. Grossman and B. K. Siddle in *The Encyclopedia of Violence, Peace and Conflict* (New York: Academic Press, 2000), and "Behavioral Psychology" by K. A. Murray, D. Grossman, and R. W. Kentridge from the same publication.

Also informative was Grossman and Siddle's article "Critical Incident Amnesia: The Physiological Basis and Implications of Memory Loss During Extreme Survival Situations" from *The Firearms Instructor: The Official Journal of the International Association of Law Enforcement Firearms Instructors,* Issue 31, August 2001.

We've used our best judgment to present the most logical and consistent narrative of the *Pueblo* takeover based on the major known facts of the incident, information shared with us by members of the naval intelligence community, and the public accounts of American sailors involved in the attack and subsequent hostage ordeal. Some of the books we used for background and source material were:

Richard A. Mobley's *Flash Point North Korea: The Pueblo and EC-212 Crisis* (Annapolis: Naval Institute Press, 2003).

Cdr. Lloyd M. Bucher, USN, and Mark Rascovich's *Bucher: My Story* (New York: Doubleday, 1970).

Robert A. Liston's *The Pueblo Surrender* (New York: Evans, 1988).

Additional insights and perspectives were provided to us by T. Michael

Bircumshaw, a former Skipjack-class sailor and the current editor of *American Submariner Magazine*; Michael Hyman, a radioman second class (ret.) and former assistant editor of *American Submariner Magazine*; Joseph W. Moser, former leading yeoman aboard the USS *Lipan* (ATF-85); and Darrell Rushing, former Mediterranean department representative (MedDepRep) on the USS *John Adams* (SSBN-620).

Sponsored by the USS Pueblo Veteran's Association, the Web site www.usspueblo.org proved very useful to our research.

II

Scorpion's February 1968 deployment to the Mediterranean as a replacement for the USS *Seawolf* is public record. The authors learned *Scorpion* was originally scheduled for a mission to the Med later that year from interviews with several former *Scorpion* crewmen who either rotated off the boat or retired from active duty shortly before its final departure from Norfolk.

A comprehensive account of the K-129's secret mission and sinking off the coast of Hawaii is presented in Ken Sewell's previous book, with Clint Richmond, *Red Star Rogue: The Untold Story of a Soviet Submarine's Nuclear Strike Attempt on the U.S.* (New York: Simon & Schuster, 2005). *Red Star Rogue* discusses at length the USS *Swordfish*'s mission in the Sea of Japan, about two thousand miles from the K-129's position at the time of her destruction, citing multiple sources that disprove the Russian government's continued belief that the loss of K-129 resulted from a collision with *Swordfish*.

The vivid recollections of Gary Cox, Quartermaster (Ret.), who was assistant navigator aboard *Swordfish* from 1967 to 1970, gave the authors of this book new information about *Swordfish*'s actual location and mission at the time K-129 went down.

The arrival of *Swordfish* in Japan's Yokosuka Harbor for repairs is a matter of record, but our description of her sail's condition at the time comes from Doug Chisolm, a former weapons officer aboard the USS *Redfish* (AGSS-395) who witnessed *Swordfish*'s entry into port.

III

Former Soviet submarine Captain Third Rank Igor Kolosov shared many remarkable insights into Admiral of the Fleet Gorshkov's thoughts, habits, and reactions to the K-19 incident and sinking of K-129 in a 2004 interview with Ken Sewell in Los Angeles, California.

A March 2005 interview in Russia with Soviet Rear Admiral ** (Ret.), who spoke to us at risk of imprisonment or death under the regime of Vladimir Putin, was invaluable to our account of Gorshkov's call for vengeance for K-129, and other information critical to this narrative.

Published sources of information about Gorshkov that aided in our understanding of his military and geopolitical views included Gorshkov's books, *The Sea Power of the State* (London: Pergamon, 1979) and *Red Star Rising at Sea* (Annapolis: Naval Institute Press, 1974). Peter Huchthausen's *K-19 Widowmaker* (Washington, DC: National Geographic Society, 2002) and *October Fury* (New Jersey: Wiley, 2003) were also revelatory.

CHAPTER 2: OFF TO POKE THE BEAR

I–III

Commander Francis A. Slattery's official naval biography lists his hometown as West Minot, Maine. While it is possible that was his birthplace, Slattery grew up in the neighboring village of West Paris.

Our information on Slattery's life prior to his naval service comes primarily from interviews conducted in West Paris during the spring and summer of 2006. On a rainswept night in April 2006, a roomful of Francis's surviving friends and family members were kind enough to share their time and memories of him at a meeting of the West Paris Historical Society. Slattery's cousin and confidant Joe Perham provided invaluable recollections and written notes.

Eleanore P. Inman and Vance Bacon, both of West Paris, were also very gracious sharing their memories and contacts.

Patricia Makley, the wonderful librarian at the Arthur E. Mann Public Library in West Paris, opened the doors to Slattery's youthful background for us with her research and introductions. The information from his high school yearbook was taken directly from archival copies at the library and digitally scanned by Patricia's son, William Makley.

The teenage Slattery's eerily prescient story "Undersea Drama" is reprinted in our book as it originally appeared.

In researching Slattery's early years in the Navy, we relied heavily on a February 2006 telephone interview with John "Mac" Maclaren, Slattery's friend, shipmate, and fellow officer aboard the USS *Tunny* (SSG-282).

Additional background on the *Tunny*'s exploits comes from Norman Polmar and K. J. Moore's *Cold War Submarines* and *Cold War Clashes*, Richard K. Kolb, ed. (Kansas City: Veterans of Foreign Wars Publications, 2004).

Our information on Commander Slattery's later military career came from various public sources, including his naval records. A copy of the Navy's official USS *Scorpion* memorial book provided by former *Scorpion* crewman Gregg Pennington was also useful to us in this regard.

IV

While researching John Walker Jr.'s personal and military background from 1966 to 1968, we benefited greatly from recollections shared with us by Dennis Solheim, Walker's shipmate and close acquaintance aboard both the USS *Andrew Jackson* (SSBN-619) and USS *Simon Bolivar* (SSBN-641). Solheim was subpoenaed as a government witness in the successful federal prosecution of the Walker spy ring.

The insights of former naval intelligence officer Will Longman were likewise invaluable in our exploration of the Walker case.

Also of tremendous help was Paul Grandinetti, Commander USN (Ret.), Naval Intelligence.

****, a prison employee assigned to John Walker, met with Walker three to four times a week, for several hours at a time, while Walker was incarcerated at the Allenwood Federal Correctional Complex. **** provided us with a tremendous amount of information based on his conversations with Walker, including Walker's two unpublished autobiographical manuscripts.

John Walker insists to this day that his first contact with the Soviets came as a walk-in at their Washington embassy, as Pete Earley writes in *Family of Spies: Inside the John Walker Spy Ring* (New York: Bantam, 1988). However, Walker initially admitted to FBI interrogators that he was recruited in the fashion we describe. Most members of the U.S. intelligence community, including the federal agents involved in Walker's apprehension and debriefing, are convinced his version of events is a fabrication of Oleg Kalugin and Boris Solomatin, the Soviet intelligence officers who directed and oversaw his espionage activities.

The thesis by Laura J. Heath Major, U.S. Army Command and General Staff College, cited earlier, provides an excellent overview of the U.S. intelligence community's view of the facts behind Walker's recruitment as a Soviet spy, as well as the damage to U.S. national security and loss of American lives that resulted from his treason.

For this segment, we used several published books in addition to those cited earlier. The most valuable were:

Christopher Andrew and Vasili Mitrokhin's *The Sword and the Shield: The Mitrokhin Archive and the Secret History of the KGB* (New York: Basic Books, 1999).

Oleg Kalugin's *The First Directorate: My 32 Years in Intelligence and Espionage Against the West* (New York: Thomas Dunne, 1994).

Robert Hunter's *Spy Hunter: Inside the FBI Investigation of the Walker Espionage Case* (Annapolis: Naval Institute Press, 1999).

V–X

Most of our information about *Scorpion* Interior Communications Electrician Third Class Vernon Foli was derived from two lengthy interviews with his widow, Barbara Foli Lake. These interviews formed the basis of a great many subsequent e-mail correspondences with Barbara, and would in turn lead some of Vernon's other surviving relatives to contact us with their recollections, insights, and clarifications of certain biographical details.

The Navy Court of Inquiry's findings of fact and Stephen Johnson's *Silent Steel: The Mysterious Death of the Nuclear Attack Sub USS* Scorpion (Hoboken, N.J.: John Wiley, 2006) helped us place their accounts within a firm context and chronology with regard to *Scorpion*'s maneuvers and operations.

The Navy Court of Inquiry's findings of fact describes the incident involving a hot-running REXTORP training torpedo during *Scorpion*'s December 1967 exercises.

For decades, the theory that *Scorpion* was destroyed by its own hot-running torpedo has been proffered as likely by many official Navy sources. But every one of the numerous torpedomen interviewed for our book dismissed the notion.

USS *Sculpin* Fire Control Technician and qualified Chief of the Watch Joe Verse's comments are from a February 2006 interview.

Former *Scorpion* Torpedoman Chief Robert McClain's comments and assessments about hot-run fail safes and emergency procedures are from a lengthy June 2006 interview with the authors. Chief McClain last sailed aboard *Scorpion* a year before her final mission. His extensive technical knowledge of torpedoes, training, and specific torpedo room procedures aboard *Scorpion* was invaluable to us.

Wes Jones, an auxiliary mechanic aboard the Skipjack-class USS *Snook* and several Los Angeles–class 688 SSBNs, detailed his extensive hands-on experience with torpedo-firing and other equipment with us in his February 2006 interview.

It is worth noting that in 1960, a low-order detonation occurred in the aft torpedo room of the submarine USS *Sargo* (SSN-583). While changing oxygen tanks, a line failed and ignited a high-intensity oxygen fire that killed one sailor. The fire was so intense that the submarine was submerged alongside the pier with the aft hatch open, flooding the torpedo compartment with seawater. Based on an inspection of the torpedoes contained in the compartment, the Navy's Court of Inquiry concluded that two of the sub's Mk 37 warheads had undergone low-order detonations. The energy release from these torpedoes was so low that when *Sargo*'s commanding officer later inspected the compartment, he failed to identify any damage caused by the explosions.

Johnson's *Silent Steel* and Sontag and Drew's *Blind Man's Bluff* were excellent published sources of additional information.

In a December 27, 1993, article for the *Houston Chronicle* by Stephen Johnson, retired Navy Captain Zeb Alford, who commanded the Skipjack-class USS *Shark* (SSN-591), said, "If you did have a 'hot-run,' what you would do would be to let the torpedo's battery power run down and to then remove it from the torpedo tube and disarm it."

Our information about Chiefs Bishop and Mazzuchi and Lieutenant Commander Robert R. Fountain is culled from interviews and e-mails with former *Scorpion* sailors, shipmates aboard other boats, and family members too numerous to list, beyond those already cited in the narrative. The official naval biographies of these three men were also very useful.

Captain Mary Etta Bishop Nolan, NC, USN (RC), was kind enough to review some of the information about her father, COB Bishop, for us.

Additional biographical information may be found in Johnson's *Silent Steel*.

XI

Electronics Technician Jerry Shire, former friend and shipmate of Bob Davis aboard the USS *Orion*, shared his extensive recollections of Davis with us.

Some of our information about Davis comes from Johnson's *Silent Steel*.

XII

The details of *Scorpion*'s covert Holystone missions from 1965 to 1967 are culled from the firsthand recollections of several former *Scorpion* sailors speaking, for the most part, under strict condition of anonymity. Many recalled that *Scorpion* outraced a Soviet torpedo that was fired at her during one such operation, but we decided to exclude this incident from our narrative because it was not, in our opinion, completely verifiable. There is, however, a strong likelihood that this event occurred.

In a January 2006 interview with us, Jerry Pratt, interior communications electrician (FWD) aboard *Scorpion* from May 1964 to July 1967, shared as much information as he could about *Scorpion*'s Holystone missions during his tour of duty without violating his military oath of secrecy.

Douglas Kariker, a former interior communications electrician aboard *Scorpion*, added extensively to our knowledge of *Scorpion*'s missions during this period, remaining within the bounds of his oath of service.

We learned of Doc Saville's extraordinary ears from a sonarman and several former shipmates aboard the *Seadragon*. Additional information on Saville comes from several of his former shipmates and Johnson's *Silent Steel*.

XIII–XVI

In August 2006, we received a package of *Scorpion* Electrician's Mate Third Class Gerald Stanley Pospisil's letters home to his family from the Mediterranean. These were provided by his son, Tim Pospisil. Gerald's thoughts, musings, and some of our information about the mood and activities of *Scorpion*'s crew in her final months, weeks, and days, are culled from those letters.

In his letters, Pospisil wrote extensively of the activities he shared with his fellow crewmen while *Scorpion* was harbored in Naples. Our description of Naples during the Cold War years draws heavily upon his experiences, as well as those of Ken Sewell and dozens of other sailors and submariners who shared verbal and written recollections with us.

Torpedoman's Mate Third Class Robert Violetti's account of *Scorpion*'s harassment by a Soviet destroyer comes from a letter home quoted in a June 1, 1968, *Time* magazine article.

We have drawn upon many sources, including author Ken Sewell's experiences as a Cold War submariner, for our discussion of the presence of intelligence personnel, or "spook riders," aboard U.S. subs.

Our primary information about the SOSUS expert Tony Marquez was obtained in a February 2006 interview from a confidential source who was familiar with *Scorpion*'s activities and had personal contact with Marquez.

Additional information about Marquez subsequently came in confidence from a crewman aboard the submarine tender USS *Canopus* (AS-34), which received Marquez and two members of *Scorpion*'s regular crew, Bill Elrod and Joseph Underwood, at Naval Station Rota, Spain, days before *Scorpion*'s disappearance.

Canopus Engineman Second Class Tom Carlough clearly recalled three men coming aboard from *Scorpion*—not two, as public Navy records indicate.

Bill Ramey, a former sonar expert who served aboard the USS *Parche* (SSN-683), helped in our understanding of the SOSUS-related operation in which *Scorpion* was likely involved in the period between its departure from Crete on May 10, 1968, and its passage through the Strait of Gibraltar on May 16.

In our narrative, we include the possibility that *Scorpion* was trailing a Soviet ballistic submarine, or on a practice maneuver to refine trailing such a vessel, because these possibilities were suggested to us by a high-level intelligence officer. But that is speculative, and would seem unlikely unless Marquez's activities aboard the sub during its transit from the Mediterranean to Gibraltar were linked to this operation.

Published sources that help us to establish a timeline for *Scorpion*'s activities from May 1–16, 1968, are Sontag and Drew's *Blind Man's Bluff* and Johnson's *Silent Steel*. Polmar's *Cold War Submarines* is informative regarding the ability of U.S. subs to track Soviet SSBNs during the Cold War.

CHAPTER 3: BAITED

I

We relied on numerous sources for our information about the Soviet naval flotilla that *Scorpion* was detoured to investigate near the Canary Islands. Published works include, but are not limited to, U.S. Navy Court of Inquiry's findings of fact; Earley's *Family of Spies*; Sontag and Drew's *Blind Man's Bluff*; Johnson's *Silent Steel*; as well as Walter Craig Reed and William Reed's *Crazy Ivan* (Lincoln, Neb.: Writer's Showcase Press, 2003), and Ed Offley's 1998 series of articles for the *Seattle Post-Intelligencer.*

James Brantley Bryant, Captain, USN (Ret.), enhanced our knowledge of the Soviet Echo II submarine and U.S. interest in it during the Cold War. From 1991 to 1994, Captain Bryant served as a political-military officer at the Pentagon whose responsibilities included oversight of policy and public affairs for port visits of nuclear-powered warships, the law of the sea, and radioactive material dumped at sea. He was involved in negotiating the U.S-Soviet Agreement for the Prevention of Incidents at Sea (INCSEA). Captain Bryant, who was involved in the declassification of certain information regarding *Scorpion*, contributed greatly to our understanding of the Navy's official perspective on the sub's sinking.

II

Ours is the first published historical work to document *Scorpion*'s encounter with the USS *Bigelow* (DD-942) en route to Rota, Spain, on May 14, 1968.

Former *Bigelow* crewmen Terry R. McCue, Lawrence Brooks, Ed Washburn, and Phil Pagnoni all have clear recollections of this event as detailed in our narrative. While Washburn and Pagnoni were friends during their time as shipmates, their accounts are from interviews conducted separately in late 2006. McCue and Brooks did not recall being acquainted with each other, or with Washburn and Pagnoni, yet both men shared many similar and complementary memories of the encounter in e-mails to the authors.

Brooks and Washburn independently recalled *Bigelow*'s refueling problems as a reason it was not called out on the search for *Scorpion*.

Washburn's thoughts about the highline transfer of movies being a possible cover for the exchange of intelligence materials were echoed to the authors of this book by a retired Cold War submarine squadron commander, who verified that a high-risk maneuver of that sort would not be conducted unless such classified materials were delivered with the films.

The Bigelow crewmen's knowledge of *Scorpion*'s disappearance slightly over a week after their encounter with the sub (they learned of its sinking either on May 23 or 24) will become critically significant in later sections of our book.

III–IV

Elrod's and Underwood's discharge at Rota is from the Navy Court of Inquiry's findings of fact.

Dr. Andrew Urbanc passed away in 2001. Information about his medical treatment of Joseph Underwood aboard the *Canopus* comes from a memorial testament to Urbanc posted on www.ussgrant.com.

V

In his book *The First Directorate*, Oleg Kalugin reveals that John Walker had given the Soviets access to virtually every document and naval communication passing through SUBLANT's communications center at Norfolk, including the KW-7 key lists used to crack the U.S. Navy's cipher codes, and other classified materials used to inform Moscow about American ship and troop movements around the globe. Kalugin also describes the system he and Boris Solomatin would use to sort through and transmit the information to Moscow.

About Walker, KGB officer Vitaly Yurchenko said, "Walker was the greatest case in KGB history. We deciphered millions of your messages. If there had been a war, we would have won it."

Solomatin has called Walker the "most important spy ever recruited by Russia." His providing the USSR with the KW-7 codes and modifications was, Solomatin says, the equivalent of giving the USSR "a seat inside your Pentagon where we could read your most vital secrets."

This and other information about the Walker case may be examined at the Federal Bureau of Investigation's Web site, www.fbi.gov, and Court TV's Web site, www.crimelibrary.com.

VI

The Navy Court of Inquiry's findings of fact contains information about Soviet ship movements in the vicinity of *Scorpion* on or about May 18, 1968.

Paul Grandinetti, Commander USN (Ret.), Naval Intelligence, disclosed the presence of a Soviet Kanin warship unreported in the findings of fact and the February 1968 Defense Intelligence Agency supplemental report.

VII

In February 2006 e-mail exchanges with the authors, Bill Hyler, a former nuclear engineer aboard the USS *John C. Calhoun* (SSBN-630), informed us of *Scorpion* running escort for the ballistic submarine as it departed Rota.

Hyler would also recall that "Scorpion went down a few days after covering us."

His information was supported by two of his shipmates on condition of strict anonymity.

VIII–IX

As a former submariner with high-level intelligence clearances, Ken Sewell is familiar with the route *Scorpion* would have taken around the Azores based on standard operating procedures.

Information used in calculating *Scorpion*'s specific course and position as it approached the Soviet flotilla included the date and time *Scorpion* left Rota, *Scorpion*'s location on the sea bottom based on classified *Trieste* logs we obtained, and the estimated four-hour time period needed to clear the track for the SSBN *John C. Calhoun* (SSBN-630) (about four hours).

We also knew *Scorpion*'s average speed and depth, based on testimony given to the Navy Court of Inquiry by the two *Scorpion* sailors who disembarked before she sank. This allowed for a series of relatively simple navigational plots based on estimated time and confirmed distance.

Supplementing these sources were nautical charts and a pilot chart issued by the U.S. government's National Imagery and Mapping Agency for the area. These charts show prevailing currents, winds, and sea states for each month of the year.

National Oceanic and Atmospheric Administration (NOAA) charts for May 21, 1968, enabled us to calculate the Beaufort scale readings and other weather conditions for the area in which *Scorpion* vanished.

Scorpion's course from Rota to the Soviet flotilla was plotted against a "quick time" and "slow time"—i.e., inside and outside estimates—of the submarine's speed based on the above conditions and information. The alternate sets of plots were very close, falling within hours of each other. The most logical set of calculations was selected.

The precise times of *Scorpion*'s final sequence of transmissions to SUBLANT via Naval Communications Station Nea Makri, Greece, are on public record. Along with a wealth of additional information about *Scorpion*'s final weeks and days, the times are taken from the "Findings of Fact from the Record of Proceedings of a Court of Inquiry Convened by Commander in Chief U.S. Atlantic Fleet to Inquire into the Loss of USS *Scorpion* (SSN-589)," much of which was declassified in 1993.

Further information about the transmissions to Nea Makri comes from Darryl Cady, a former U.S. Navy radioman on duty at the Greek communications station when the *Scorpion* messages were received and relayed.

Our citing of *Scorpion*'s position at the commencement of her final transmissions contradicts official U.S. Navy assertions. It is calculated from confidential information from a high-placed naval intelligence source and other information developed in later sections of the book.

U.S. Navy Lieutenant John Rogers's contention that *Scorpion*'s final situation report included the message that it was on its way to conduct its surveillance of the Soviet grouping in the Canary Islands is hotly disputed by U.S. Navy officials, who claim the surveillance had already been completed when the situation report was received. However, Lieutenant Rogers, the senior duty officer at SUBLANT Norfolk when the Nea Makri communications were relayed, insisted on the accuracy of his account until his death in 1995.

Rogers gave his version of events when interviewed by journalist and author Pete Earley for his book *Family of Spies*.

After Rogers's death, journalist Ed Offley quoted his widow, Bernice Rogers, as confirming his account of an unfinished surveillance in a May 21, 1998, article written for the *Seattle Post-Intelligencer.* As Offley reports, she said: "My husband was at the message center as communications officer the night that message came in. He would have known what was going on. We had talked about it since then."

Notes

53

The information about John Walker in these segments is drawn in part from Earley's *Family of Spies* and from Jack M. Kneece's *Family Treason* (New York: Stein and Day, 1986), but additional sources were developed for later sections of the book.

Our understanding of Cold War submarine communications was vastly aided by dozens of interviews with U.S. Navy and intelligence personnel—from enlisted men to ranking officers—conducted on and off the record.

In August 2005, Wes Jones, a former crewman aboard *Scorpion*'s sister ship the Skipjack-class USS *Snook* (SSN-592), generously shared as much firsthand knowledge as his military oaths allowed about communications during reconnaissance and surveillance operations.

Also in August 2005 we obtained information on this subject from Joe Verse, who served as fire control technician and qualified chief of the watch aboard the Skipjack-class USS *Sculpin* (SSN-590).

A fascinating November 28, 2006, breakfast with a retired submarine squadron commander enlightened us about certain procedures involved in submarine communications—and in looking for subs—during *Scorpion*'s lifetime.

The information about the acoustical probe *Scorpion* detected will be developed in notes on later sections of our narrative.

CHAPTER 4: PIER 22

The remarkably detailed recollections of Gregg Pennington, a former nuclear engineer aboard *Scorpion*, took us back to Naval Station Norfolk and especially Destroyer and Submarine Pier 22 as existing in 1968.

Additional background on the pier and the submarine tender USS *Orion* (AS-18) may be found at www.oldgoat.com, www.navysite.de, and www.navsource.org.

Jerry Pospisil's letters were among our principal sources for the information in these segments. Barbara Foli Lake's memories were also instrumental in allowing us to reconstruct the events of May 27, 1968.

Ruthann Crowley, widow of *Scorpion*'s Electronics Technician First Class Richard Curtis Hogeland, was also kind enough to share her painful memories of that date.

Tim Pospisil told us of his mother, Judy's, experiences waiting for *Scorpion* to arrive at Pier 22.

Peter A. Smith, who served on a boat in the same squadron as *Scorpion*, shared his recollections of manning a phone bank aboard *Orion* from which every next-of-kin with access to a telephone was called prior to public announcements of what was known about *Scorpion*.

Additional information came from Ed Offley's 1998 series of articles on the *Scorpion* in the *Seattle Post-Intelligencer*, Stephen Johnson's articles in the *Houston Chronicle* in 1993 and 1995, and the 2000 article "Remembering the Scorpion" by Navy journalist Michaela Kekedy that may be read online at www.submarinesailor.com.

Books consulted for these segments included Johnson's *Silent Steel* and Sontag and Drew's *Blind Man's Bluff*.

CHAPTER 5: BRANDYWINE

I–IV

The hound-and-hare incident described in this segment was relayed to us by several former *Scorpion* crewmen at a USS *Scorpion* memorial gathering and dinner at Little Rock, Arkansas, in the summer of 2006.

Admiral Thomas H. Moorer was outspoken about his views on the USS *Liberty* incident until his death in 2004. His personal statements may be read at www.ussliberty.org.

The Soviet radio traffic that coincided with *Scorpion*'s final transmissions was disclosed to us by a high-placed intelligence source, speaking on strict condition of anonymity.

Our information about the three coded May 23, 24, and 25 orders to *Scorpion* requesting that she contact SUBLANT is from the Navy Court of Inquiry's findings of fact.

Darryl Cady, who served as a radioman at Nea Makri, was on duty at the Nea Makri ship-to-shore communications station when contact was lost with *Scorpion*. "We dug received messages out of the burn bag to decode," he wrote, referring to later orders from SUBLANT received at the message center. Per standard operating procedures, classified materials placed in burn bags are destroyed within twenty-four hours, indicating SUBLANT became highly concerned about *Scorpion* by May 23, well before the official SUBMISS, Sub Missing, alert.

In our November 2006 interview with a Cold War submarine squadron commander speaking on condition of anonymity, the Navy's insistence that *Scorpion*'s failure to respond would have been standard procedure was called "ludicrous."

"When you're told to reply, you make every effort to do it. Even if Scorpion tried and had trouble with atmospherics, if she was really on her way home as they claim, she would have been in pretty safe waters and had ample opportunity to respond at least once over the course of three days," he told us.

Stationed at Naval Submarine Base New London, Groton, Connecticut, at the time, the commander characterized his contemporaneous thoughts on the Navy's delay in informing the *Scorpion* families of the sub's disappearance as "the absolute nadir of human relations."

Captain Edward M. Brittingham, U.S. Navy (Ret.), a former Orion P-3 training officer and commanding officer of Orion P-3B Patrol Squadron 11 (VP-11), told us of the Lajes Orion patrol flight's detection of the *Scorpion*'s underwater death spasms on May 22, while on patrol seeking a Soviet Yankee submarine.

Captain Brittingham, who participated in the hunt for *Scorpion,* also contributed to our knowledge of the search patterns flown by Orion aircraft looking for the sub after its disappearance was made official.

Orion P-3C pilot Marty Diller helped with our understanding of how information is gathered and processed by Orion crewmen and submarine detection technologies.

Admiral Schade's departure aboard the *Pargo* (SSN-650) is from the Navy Court of Inquiry findings of fact.

Admiral Beshany's statement about "communications analysis" suggesting the Soviets had tracked and struck at *Scorpion* is from Ed Offley's May 21, 1998, article in the *Seattle Post-Intelligencer.*

Our interviews with *Bigelow* crewmen who were aware of *Scorpion*'s sinking just over a week after their encounter with her confirm that the Navy's top secret search for the submarine was underway from May 23 to 27, 1968.

In his *Seattle Post-Intelligencer* articles, Offley writes that the secret search for *Scorpion* that commenced on May 23, 1968, was conducted by "a dozen ships and submarines aided by land-based patrol planes."

In *Blind Man's Bluff,* Sontag and Drew are less specific than Offley, but suggest that a smaller number of aircraft and naval vessels were involved in the search.

While we have personally spoken with submarine sailors involved in the secret hunt for *Scorpion*, there is no available documentation to reveal precisely how many ships and aircraft took part because their participation has been stricken from official ship and flight logs.

John and Barbara Walker's reactions to the *Scorpion* sinking are from Earley's *Family of Spies*. Earley also describes the Soviets' satisfaction with the voluminous information Walker gave them about the search for the sub, and the financial benefit Walker reaped from continuing the flow of information about *Scorpion* to his Russian handlers.

V–VI

The information in these sections, including our account of the *Pargo*'s speedy trip to the Virginia Capes with the submarine rescue ship *Sunbird* (ASR-15), comes from various sources, including the Navy Court of Inquiry's findings of fact.

Of immense help to our research was a photocopied archive of newspaper articles about the search for *Scorpion* provided by former *Scorpion* sailor Gregg Pennington. Dated between May 27 and June 6, 1968, and credited to the Associated Press and United Press International, the articles were clipped from various newspapers by Pennington's sister, who kept them in a personal scrapbook for nearly four decades.

Additional information about *Pargo*'s and *Sunbird*'s role in the search for *Scorpion* may be found at www.angelfire.com.

Our account of the *Petrel*'s role is taken from the Navy Court of Inquiry's findings of fact and the Pennington articles. Johnson's *Silent Steel* was a useful supplementary reference.

The information about Admiral Moorer's May 27 news conference is drawn primarily from the Pennington archive of newspaper articles.

VII–XV

Our account of what transpired at the Bishop household after the May 27 SUBMISS alert is culled from Michaela Kekedy's article at www .submarinesailor.com, Offley's *Seattle Post-Intelligencer* articles, and Johnson's *Silent Steel*.

Barbara Foli Lake recalled her painful experiences during this period in our many interviews and correspondences.

Our information on Bob Davis's rude awakening in the brig comes from Johnson's *Silent Steel*, and was further informed by our correspondence with his former crewmate Jerry Shire.

Bill Elrod's experiences and reactions to learning of *Scorpion*'s disappearance on May 27 are culled from the Navy Court of Inquiry's findings of fact, Offley's articles, and interviews with friends of Elrod who spoke on condition of anonymity.

Jerry Pratt told us of his long trip from Norfolk to Pascagoula in an interview conducted in January 2006.

Our account of the *Standley*'s role in the search for *Scorpion* owes principally to our correspondences with former Radarman Third Class Richard Shafer. The account was supplemented and given context by various public sources and information in Johnson's *Silent Steel*.

Machinist's Mate Third Class Bob McDaniel gave us his account of the *Skate*'s participation in the search in a series of correspondences throughout 2006. Our account was supplemented by various publicly available sources.

The LBJ presidential memo was provided by Clint Richmond, co-author (with Kenneth Sewell) of *Red Star Rogue*.

Our account of Admiral Schade's May 29 return to shore comes from the Navy Court of Inquiry's findings of fact. It is further informed by Gregg Pennington's newspaper article archive and Johnson's *Silent Steel*.

CHAPTER 6: LOST

I

In 2004, Dr. John Piña Craven spoke to Ken Sewell about the K-129 and *Scorpion* investigations. These conversations were limited by Craven's oath of secrecy.

He has written of his role in the investigation at some length in his book, *The Silent War: The Cold War Battle Beneath the Sea* (New York: Simon & Schuster, 2002).

Additional information about what occurred in the Pentagon's war room on the evening of May 27, 1968, was provided by a high-level intelligence source familiar with discussions at the meeting, speaking on condition of anonymity.

Johnson's *Silent Steel* was a useful supplementary source.

II

Our information about the false *Scorpion* distress calls comes from Gregg Pennington's newspaper article archive and Johnson's *Silent Steel.*

The Norfolk naval community's reaction to the false alarm was described to us by Barbara Foli Lake.

III

Our account of the Lamont Geological Laboratory's role in gathering hydrophonic data about *Scorpion*'s final moments was provided by a top-level official in the Navy's intelligence community, speaking under condition of anonymity.

Although it is our informed opinion that Stephen Johnson minimizes Craven's role in the investigation, Johnson's book *Silent Steel* contains information about Gordon Hamilton and Lamont that we regard as essentially accurate.

Sontag and Drew's *Blind Man's Bluff* was useful to our research for this segment.

Additional information about the laboratory may be found at www.ldeo.columbia.edu/ldeo/alum/assoc/pgi.html.

IV

The information in this segment is from Gregg Pennington's archive of newspaper articles.

V

A federal prison employee familiar with the John Walker case informed our understanding of Walker's perspectives for this segment, as did our reading of Walker's unpublished manuscripts.

We also relied heavily on Earley's *Family of Spies* and Kneece's *Family Treason.*

We present the likeliest account of Walker's actions in the weeks following *Scorpion*'s disappearance based on established facts, the opinions of law enforcement personnel, information gleaned from those who have had contact with him before and since his imprisonment, and simple logic.

VI

Our information on the USNS research ship *Mizar*'s role in the search for *Scorpion*'s wreckage is culled from the Navy Court of Inquiry's findings of fact and other sources. Craven discusses it in *The Silent War,* as does Johnson in *Silent Steel.*

See Sewell and Richmond's *Red Star Rogue* for more data on the *Mizar.*

The Web sites www.history.navy.mil and www.patriot.net/~eastlnd2/ Mizar.htm contain additional information about the vessel.

VII–VIII

These segments greatly relied on our interviews with Barbara Foli Lake and a number of correspondences with Vernon's younger sister, Carol Foli.

Carol contacted us in the spring of 2006 and would subsequently share her recollections of Vernon and the night his family was informed of his death.

Our quotes from Rear Admiral James Kelly's eulogy at the June 6, 1968, *Scorpion* memorial service at the David Adams Memorial Chapel at Naval Station Norfolk are taken from official Navy transcripts.

IX

On condition of anonymity, a retired naval intelligence officer provided important insights on Kalugin and Solomatin's activities.

Kalugin's *The First Directorate* and Andrew and Mitrokhin's *The Sword and the Shield* were also useful sources of information.

X

This portion of the narrative is derived largely from our interviews and correspondences with former *Scorpion* crewman Doug Kariker.

Admiral Moorer's statements to the press are taken from June 6, 1968, AP and UPI newswire reports.

XI

Our narrative account of Barbara and Holli Foli's farewell to Norfolk comes from interviews and correspondences with Barbara Foli Lake.

XII

Our Vietnam war casualty numbers were calculated using statistics from
www.members.aol.com/warlibrary/vwc24.htm.

Our information about the *Mizar's* discovery of *Scorpion* is from the
Navy Court of Inquiry's findings of fact. Dr. John Craven's words and
writings were also very instructive.

Johnson's *Silent Steel* gives an accurate account of Buchanan's and
Craven's machinations to keep the *Mizar* at sea, and breaks down the details of its seventy-five sled runs.

XIII

In order to present a clear narrative, the body of our text does not delve
into two major theories for *Scorpion's* loss advanced by participants in the
Court of Inquiry. One is the failed propeller shaft, the other the failed
trash disposal unit theory.

The former is believed to have had its origins in 1961 when the USS
Scamp (SSN-588), a Skipjack-class submarine, reportedly experienced a
serious mishap while conducting a jammed-down aft-plane-failure drill
at depth off San Francisco.

Recovery from a jammed aft-plane was to order an emergency back
bell. As the backward motion of the propeller started to pull the submarine upward toward the surface, however, the shaft severed on the sea-
ward side of the shaft seal.

The propeller spun away from the submarine. Had the shaft failed on
the inside of the pressure hull, it would have left a sixteen-inch hole
through which water could have come rushing into the boat.

Since the engine room is one of two compartments where massive
flooding would add enough negative buoyancy to sink the boat (the
other is the operations compartment, at the bow), a submarine suffering
such a failure would be lost.

As a result of this accident, the Navy ordered an inspection of all submarine shafts to ensure the mishap would not be repeated.

Scorpion's shaft was produced by a different manufacturer than the
one that failed on *Scamp*. It was also relatively new, having been installed
only in 1965.

As *Scorpion* crashed into the ocean floor, her main engine room tele-
scoped forward about fifty feet into the auxiliary machinery compart-

ment. As the equipment in the two compartments came together, the propeller shaft was ejected from the submarine, landing about sixty yards away.

The shaft was clearly visible in photos taken by the *Trieste II*, which failed to show any fractures or damage. Its propeller had passed four separate inspections in a six-month period prior to its February 1968 departure to the Mediterranean. For these reasons, we believe that the propeller was not the cause of *Scorpion*'s sinking.

The failure of the trash disposal unit, or TDU, as the cause has been almost universally dismissed by the Navy.

In 1968, trash generated aboard a submarine was compacted into weighted cylinders. A full trash cylinder would be loaded through a breech hatch. The hatch would then be sealed with a valve and a lower ball valve opened, allowing the cylinder to be ejected.

Standard operating procedure called for the disposal of trash only when the submarine was near the surface. As a safety precaution, mechanical interlocks prevented the two valves from being opened at the same time, so any flooding from a failed TDU would have been limited and quickly minimized. The TDU almost certainly did not cause *Scorpion*'s sinking.

During our interview with James Brantley Bryant, Captain, USN (Ret.), he stated his opinion that a torpedo had struck the submarine in the aft portion of the sail, basing his evaluation on the photographic evidence of *Scorpion*'s remains.

When we pointed out the high improbability of the hot-run theory, Captain Bryant agreed with our assessment, yet insisted a hostile torpedo did not strike *Scorpion*.

But if it was not *Scorpion*'s own torpedo that struck it, then where else could the torpedo have come from?

XIV

The quote from the intelligence source in this segment comes from an interview with Ken Sewell in 2005.

CHAPTER 7: TRAPPED AND KILLED

In early 2005, Ken Sewell's Russian research assistant and translator, Svetlana Stepanova [pseud.], interviewed a Soviet rear admiral, who had been a major source of information for *Red Star Rogue*. The subject of this interview was the sinking of the USS *Scorpion*.

Only one interview was scheduled. The admiral initially denied Soviet responsibility for *Scorpion*'s destruction, but became visibly shaken when confronted with some of Sewell's research. The session, however, ended with little new information gained.

To her surprise, Svetlana received a call from the admiral shortly afterward. He had regained his composure and questioned Svetlana in detail about the items of evidence on Sewell's list. The next day, he called a third time to arrange a second meeting.

Agreeing to speak off the record, the admiral informed Svetlana that the Soviet Union did, in fact, attack and sink the *Scorpion* in retaliation for the sinking of the K-129. We had heard this before from three former Soviet submarine captains. This was the first time we heard it from a rear admiral.

The admiral then told Svetlana something that was new to Sewell: the attack had been carried out *not* by another submarine or surface ship, as some U.S. intelligence sources believed, but by a Ka-25 (NATO designation Hormone) antisubmarine warfare helicopter. He went on to describe how the attack was staged, specifying that the helicopter had taken off from one ship and landed on another.

The admiral's revelations about the antisub unit were important. In spite of what Sewell had learned about Soviet complicity in *Scorpion*'s destruction, there had always been two items that bothered him about the attack.

His first concern was that if a Soviet sub was dispatched to sink the *Scorpion*, then its entire crew would have known about it. Over time, a secret shared by so many men would be difficult to hide unless they were killed.

His second concern was how a Soviet submarine got the drop on a swift American fast-attack boat. From personal experience, he knew U.S. submariners were able to detect a silent-running Soviet diesel or nuclear sub long before the Russians could hear their American counterparts.

When U.S. submarines encountered Soviet subs on their missions, they would simply change course, steer around them, and continue their business.

(Every one of the dozens of *Scorpion* and Skipjack-class crewmen we interviewed would share nearly identical experiences. In separate conversations, Jerry Pratt and Douglas Kariker told us *Scorpion*'s crewmen could audibly detect a Russian sub through their hull with a sound Pratt compared to a "train" and Kariker to a "garbage truck" going past.)

The Soviet use of a helicopter in their strike on *Scorpion* answered both of Sewell's questions. A Ka-25 required only two or three men to operate it. With the helicopter leaving on one ship and landing on another, there would be no one to know that a torpedo was missing.

Prior to being attacked, *Scorpion* had reported to SUBLANT headquarters, giving her exact location and ETA to target (the Russian flotilla near the Canaries). Using that information, even an inexperienced Soviet navigator would have been able to plot *Scorpion*'s course and pinpoint the location of the sub.

While the Soviets may or may not have known this from their intercepts, *Scorpion* was unfortunately limited to a depth of three hundred feet, making her a perfect target. She couldn't dive beneath one of the deeper thermal barriers. As the admiral would reveal, the helicopter only had to fly out beyond visual range of the flotilla to a point along the submarine's projected track, dip its sonobuoys, and wait. When *Scorpion* came along, the helicopter went active, acquired its target, and attacked. It was the perfect plan.

What *Scorpion*'s final moments must have been like for those aboard is something we deduced from Sewell's research into the forensic evidence left by *Scorpion*'s destruction, his firsthand experience with standard operating procedures aboard a nuclear submarine, and our numerous interviews with experts and Skipjack officers and sailors.

On hearing the active ping of the Ka-25's sonobuoy, *Scorpion*'s commander would have had her turn, accelerate, and attempt to leave the area. But despite the sub's speed, the helicopter would have quickly closed and dropped the torpedo at close range—so close that the sub did not have time to evade.

In formulating our reenactment of *Scorpion*'s destruction, we utilized two important technical reference works:

Roy Burcher and Louis J. Rydill's *Concepts in Submarine Design* from the Cambridge Ocean Technology Series 2 (Cambridge, UK: Cambridge University Press, 1994) and Polmar's *Cold War Submarines*.

Following an interview in the autumn of 2006, Gene Lee, a former interior communications electrician second class aboard *Scorpion*'s sister ship the USS *Skipjack* (SSN-585), aided our research by providing us with his remarkably detailed original sketches of a Skipjack-class submarine's interior configuration. These proved invaluable to our reconstruction of the tragic events surrounding *Scorpion*'s demise.

Lee's former *Skipjack* shipmate Torpedoman Third Class Todd "Pit" Slater contributed additional information and sketches that were also of tremendous help to us.

Because duty shifts change regularly aboard a submarine on patrol, attempting to place any individual *Scorpion* sailor besides Commander Slattery at a specific location or watch station on the boat when she was attacked would have been speculative.

Also critical to our account of *Scorpion*'s destruction was the hydrographic data in the Navy Court of Inquiry's findings of fact, our inspection of *Trieste* and *Alvin* photos of her wreckage, and consultations with a high-level intelligence source close to the search for and eventual discovery of *Scorpion*'s wreckage in 1968.

CHAPTER 8: BOAT'S WAKE

I

The information here comes from interviews and correspondence with the surviving friends and family of Commander Francis A. Slattery in West Paris, Maine.

II

Our information here comes from public sources, interviews, and correspondences.

The former chief petty officer who provided us with Bucher's "The chiefs don't judge me" comment did so on condition of anonymity.

III

Earley's *Family of Spies* and Kneece's *Family Treason* provided detailed accounts of John Walker's arrest.

A trip to the Allenwood Federal Correctional Complex in Pennsylvania yielded our information about Walker's post-incarceration years, as well as information about his health and legal status as of this writing.

IV

Our information about Bob Davis in this segment comes from our correspondence with his former shipmate Jerry Shire.

V

We thank Barbara Foli Lake for assisting us with this segment.

INDEX

["